Teaching
Beyond the Test

Differentiated Project-Based Learning in a Standards-Based Age

For Grades 6 & Up

By Phil Schlemmer, M.Ed., and Dori Schlemmer

Edited by Meg Bratsch

free spirit
PUBLiSHiNG®

Meeting kids'
social & emotional
needs since 1983

Library of Congress Cataloging-in-Publication Data
Schlemmer, Phil.
  Teaching beyond the test : differentiated project-based learning in a standards-based age for grades 6 & up / by Phil Schlemmer and Dori Schlemmer ; edited by Meg Bratsch.
     p. cm.
  Includes bibliographical references and index.
  ISBN-13: 978-1-57542-259-6
  ISBN-10: 1-57542-259-X
  1. Individualized instruction. 2. Project method in teaching. 3. Curriculum planning. I. Schlemmer, Dori.
II. Bratsch, Meg. III. Title.
  LB1031.S27 2007
  371.39'4—dc22

2007023065

At the time of this book's publication, all facts and figures cited are the most current available. All telephone numbers, addresses, and Web site URLs are accurate and active; all publications, organizations, Web sites, and other resources exist as described in this book; and all have been verified as of June 2007. The authors and Free Spirit Publishing make no warranty or guarantee concerning the information and materials given out by organizations or content found at Web sites, and we are not responsible for any changes that occur after this book's publication. If you find an error or believe that resource listed here is not as described, please contact Free Spirit Publishing. Parents, teachers, and other adults: We strongly urge you to monitor children's use of the Internet.

Excerpts from *Principles and Standards for School Mathematics* are reprinted with the permission of the National Council of Teachers of Mathematics. Copyright © 2000 by the National Council of Teachers of Mathematics. All rights reserved.

10 9 8 7 6 5 4 3 2 1
Printed in the United States of America

Cover design by Marieka Heinlen
Interior design by Percolator

Free Spirit Publishing Inc.
217 Fifth Avenue North, Suite 200
Minneapolis, MN 55401-1299
(612) 338-2068
help4kids@freespirit.com
www.freespirit.com

Dedication

To the millions of kids across America who are
trusting the adults in their lives to prepare them
for a demanding, unpredictable world, and to
the teachers who work to fulfill that trust.

Acknowledgments

We wish to thank the many students and educators
who have provided valuable input over the years
as these materials were developed. Their insights,
discoveries, and affirmations were helpful in designing
differentiated projects that work on many levels.

Contents

Part 1: The Differentiation Strategies

Part 2: The Model Projects

List of Reproducible Pages

Message in a Capsule

Moments in Time

One World

Bonus Project Materials Included on CD-ROM Only

Time Traveler

Introduction

Assignment Sheet

Assessment Sheet

You Gotta Have an Angle

Task Sheet 1 Answer Guide

Task Sheet 2 Answer Guide

Task Sheet 3 Answer Guide

Task Sheet 5 Answer Guide

Task Sheet 6 Answer Guide

Task Sheet 7 Answer Guide

Task Sheet 8 Answer Guide

Task Sheet 9 Answer Guide

Introduction

Trail Map to the Cave of Treasure Mountain

Treasure Mountain Expedition Training Level 1:
Trigonometry Basics (Task Sheet 1)

Express Yourself

Hear Ye! Hear Ye!

List of Figures

Bonus Project Figures Included on CD-ROM Only

Preface

Every school system in the United States is dedicated to graduating skillful, knowledgeable, motivated learners who are ready to fend for themselves in a demanding, unpredictable world. The focus in most schools is on academic achievement, which makes sense: Of *course* we must have students who can read, write, and compute; of *course* we should base our expectations on rigorous content standards and graduation requirements; of *course* we want our students to be competitive with students from other countries. But we also need to seriously reflect on what has historically made the United States great. Ours is an entrepreneurial society. Our greatest achievements come from innovation, invention, and risk taking. If our aspiration is to become the greatest nation of test takers the world has ever seen, we could easily reach the goal but lose the global battle for economic leadership. Tests by themselves cannot predict which children sitting in classrooms today may have the insights, inspiration, persistence, or just plain guts that will be needed to keep us at the forefront of global competition as we move through the 21st century. In addition to standardized tests, we must implement other strategies to help students thrive in their uncertain future.

Most people accept that children today need to prepare for a rapidly changing world, and that they will continue learning and adjusting for their entire lives. But how do students transform into confident, self-directed, lifelong learners? How do they become problem solvers and learn to authentically apply the knowledge and skills that teachers try to pass on? The answers to these questions, in our experience, have been differentiated instruction and project-based learning. These two approaches to education are combined in a concept we refer to as "structured freedom."

In a structured freedom environment, students are all held accountable to well-defined learning guidelines and expectations (structure), but their final products and demonstrations are unique because they are given responsibility and allowed to make informed choices and decisions about their learning (freedom). As educators, our biggest challenge is to help students recognize their individual capabilities by requiring them to take significant responsibility for their own growth as learners. Because people continue learning throughout their lives, they must have opportunities all along the way to study areas that fit their goals and interests, and to discover and develop their personal strengths. Students need to gain confidence in their ability to find relevant information, think critically, make decisions, and transform knowledge into something they can use for specific purposes. This book offers ways to provide students both the structure and the freedom they need to become actively engaged in their own learning.

Feel free to contact us with your questions and comments. Email us at help4kids@freespirit.com or send a letter to us in care of:

Free Spirit Publishing
217 First Avenue N, Suite 200
Minneapolis, MN 55401-1299

Phil & Dori Schlemmer

Introduction

This book began with a simple desire to share ideas with teachers who, like you, are resolutely facing the difficulties and challenges of today's education environment. Our goal in writing it was to help kindred spirits effectively integrate content standards, differentiated instruction, and project-based learning into their teaching repertoires. We feel that we know you quite well, and we have written this book especially for you. This is who we think you are:

- You are a dedicated professional who has devoted your career to making a difference in kids' lives.

- You willingly shoulder responsibility for the education of many unique individuals every year.

- You communicate morning, afternoon, and evening with parents who offer suggestions and make demands, some reasonable and some not.

- You have a substantial set of content standards that must all be addressed in less time than seems humanly possible.

- You teach a curriculum that has become a constantly moving target, with tests to prove that you've covered it.

- You are expected to consistently increase rigor, improve achievement, and meet the needs of all students.

- You go home at night exhausted and somehow come to work the next morning with renewed enthusiasm for the task at hand.

We know from our own classroom experiences what you are going through, and we think we know what you want. You are looking for balance, trying to find the equilibrium point between meaningful, student-centered education and the realities of modern U.S. schools. This is not an easy task.

The demands on today's teachers are far different and more intense than in years past. Ethnic, cultural, and socioeconomic diversity add both richness and challenge to nearly every classroom. The range in students' readiness to learn is wide, and the gap seems to be increasing. The federal No Child Left Behind legislation has caused a seismic shift in how schools do business. We have entered a standards-based age in which curriculum, instruction, and assessment are all focused on state and federal mandates. Testing is a permanent part of the landscape, and the stakes are high: AYP (adequate yearly progress) is determined by how kids do on tests. As a result, school districts have established goals to ensure the highest possible success rate on state assessments. No wonder curriculums are being modified and teachers are under pressure to "teach to the test."

This is where the concept of differentiation comes in. Differentiated instruction was not devised as a way to improve test scores. However, school boards, school administrators, parents, and many teachers are beginning to place great emphasis on the idea of providing instruction that "differentiates" among students, based on their readiness to learn, their interests, and their learning strengths and preferences. You may have read books or articles by the guru of differentiated learning, Carol Ann Tomlinson, or other experts in the field. The case they make is compelling and difficult to refute. Who can deny that instruction should be tailored to the needs of individuals; that students should be challenged just beyond their comfort level; that pre-assessment and flexible grouping are keys to accommodating the needs of all learners; that content, process, and product may be differentiated in various combinations to produce optimal results? The idea of differentiated instruction is logical, and a well-balanced 21st century classroom will certainly be a differentiated one. Yet mastering the concept requires new learning and ongoing skill development.

"Projects are a key to student engagement and motivation."

Together with content standards and differentiated instruction, a final component to the well-balanced classroom is project-based learning. This is an idea that is in danger of being abandoned as schools and teachers try to consolidate instruction, maximize time efficiency, and focus on test preparation. However, projects are a key to student engagement and motivation. They allow students to examine topics in depth from a variety of perspectives and take greater ownership in the results of their efforts. Projects reward innovative thinking, allow hands-on learning, require teamwork, emphasize employability skills, and offer a context for learning that cannot be achieved in any other way. It is impractical to have the entire curriculum be project-based, but it is important to ensure that, at some point each year, students have an opportunity to apply what they have learned to something beyond recalled facts and completed tests.

A critical key to implementing project-based learning is for teachers to have fully developed project models. Useful models are carefully constructed and provide everything needed to make the projects work. Teachers may implement a project as it is designed, or follow the model to create a new project based on personal preferences, student needs, or curriculum demands.

This book includes all three of the critical elements just discussed:

- Standards-based content
- Differentiated instruction
- Project-based learning

The first section contains teacher-tested, researched differentiation strategies that lend themselves to classroom projects. These are brief, clearly described instructional concepts that can be quickly read, easily understood, and immediately put to use. The second section is composed of fully developed classroom projects in all core content areas that will engage your students in focused, meaningful learning experiences. The projects in English/language arts, math, science, and social studies are based on standards created by the following national organizations: the National Council of Teachers of English, the National Council of Teachers of Math, the National Research Council, and the National Council for the Social Studies. Most of the standards correspond to middle school learning objectives, but may be readily substituted with higher-level standards to fit a high school curriculum.

Now that you have the book in your hands, try browsing through it to find ideas that will work for you and your kids. Don't focus exclusively on what you already know or the content you teach. Just put yourself into a reflective mood and flip the pages. In your mind's eye you will see certain things working in your classroom. You will recognize that an idea may be just the thing for Felicia, or that an activity might really engage Jorge, or that a differentiation strategy might finally motivate Esther, raise the achievement of James, or challenge Erin. Try this: Write down the names of three students whom you work with and know well—one struggling, one on-target, and one advanced. Think about those three individuals as you browse, and ask yourself whether you are seeing ideas that would benefit all three. If so, you have the right book and you are ready to make good use of it.

About This Book

Part 1: The Differentiation Strategies

The first part of the book focuses on differentiation. The transition to differentiated instruction happens incrementally, and awareness is the first critical step. In this section we introduce you to a variety of terms, concepts, and practical ideas that will help you understand what it means to differentiate and how that might be accomplished through the use of classroom projects.

Each differentiation strategy in this section stands on its own in addition to being implemented in one or more of the projects in the next section. You will find descriptions of strategies that primarily differentiate instruction in three areas: content (what is taught), process (how students make sense of what is taught), or product (how students express their understanding of what is taught). You probably already know about some of the ideas presented here, and others you may have never heard of. All of the strategies are based on respected research and have been successfully employed in thousands of classrooms, including our own.

A Differentiation Strategy Matrix is provided on pages 13–16 to help you see at a glance what strategies are included and how each is aligned with one or more projects in this book.

Part 2: The Model Projects

The second part of the book provides fully developed, ready-to-use projects that focus on clearly identified content standards and one or more differentiation strategies. Although each project is unique, a common format has been used to organize the project materials. A description of the format follows. As you familiarize yourself with the projects, it is important to understand that they represent models: You may use them exactly as they are presented, but they can also be modified or serve as blueprints for entirely new projects that you create yourself.

Some of the projects are quite extensive, and the quantity of material may seem a bit overwhelming at first glance. Please consider what "fully developed" means, and remember that the purpose of each model project is to demonstrate how a diverse group of students can achieve similar results while following separate paths. Each path requires a different assignment, and thus there are multiple assignments provided for each project. In the end, students receive only the materials you (or they) decide they need to complete their individual project requirements.

Important note: Four additional bonus projects appear on the accompanying CD-ROM only, and not in the book. These four bonus projects follow the same format as the projects in the book.

Here is a description of the project materials:

PROJECT PLANNER

The Project Planner provides you with an overview of the project. It is divided into twelve sections:

Content Focus—Identifies the content area the project is built around.

Class Periods—Tells how many hour-long class periods the project is likely to require.

Project Scenario—Describes a role that students assume as they work on the project. The scenario is like a story that provides a learning context within which students are expected to complete specified tasks.

Project Synopsis—Briefly describes the project's key features and how it may be conducted.

Differentiation Strategies—Lists each differentiation strategy that is incorporated into the project. Detailed information is provided in the "Methods of Differentiation" section of the Project Planner.

Student Forms—Lists each student handout that is included with the project.

Content Standards—Lists nationally aligned content standards as the targeted learning expectations for the project.

How to Use This Project—Provides recommendations for step-by-step implementation of the project, as well as additional teaching ideas and tips.

Methods of Differentiation—Explains how the differentiation strategies embedded in the project are implemented and why they are effective.

Ideas for Extending or Modifying the Project—Suggests alternate ways of implementing or differentiating the project.

Suggested Content Modifications—Lists numerous ways the project might be tailored for use in other core content areas.

STUDENT MATERIALS

Introduction—This is a one- or two-page handout that all students receive before they begin their differentiated work, as a way of initiating the project. Its purpose is to briefly describe the project, present guidelines, and communicate to students that everyone is participating in the same project and will be doing the same kinds of things. The introduction includes these sections:

● Explanation Paragraph—The first paragraph tells students what the basic assignment is and what tasks are required of them.

● Project Scenario—The scenario is an imaginary situation that provides a context for the learning that will take place. The scenario:

✔ Assigns students a role to play.

✔ Describes the tasks that students will complete as they assume this role.

✔ Identifies the products that students will create or develop.

✔ Specifies how students will demonstrate or present their work.

The effectiveness of the scenario is greatly enhanced by your willingness as the teacher to endorse it. If you choose not to promote the scenario, neither will students place much stock in it. If you enthusiastically endorse the scenario and encourage students to embrace the role they have been assigned, then it becomes a key to the success of the project. Two important points:

1. The scenario allows you to assume a role also, if you choose. For example, you may become editor-in-chief, or campaign manager, or lead scientist. You can use your role to justify an increased emphasis on quality by holding students accountable for each task the scenario prescribes. If you

use the scenario in this way, you will find it becomes an ally in your attempt to motivate students to strive for higher achievement.

2. The scenario provides a basis for emphasizing workplace readiness skills. You can establish expectations that students perform their tasks as if they were involved in a real situation. In other words, you can use the project scenario to talk with students about the skills that employers look for in their workers, and you can require that those skills be demonstrated in your students' work.

● Assignment—The final section of the introduction is the assignment, which is a concise explanation of the tasks students will undertake as they complete the project requirements. An important point to be made here is that, even though students will ultimately work from differentiated assignment sheets, the basic project format is the same for all students. Struggling students, on-target students, and advanced students will all do essentially the same things, but at different levels of complexity or with varying levels of teacher and peer support.

Assignment Sheets and Handouts—Each project includes a number of assignment sheets and handouts that support the project scenario. These materials are differentiated in a wide variety of ways, depending on the project. You provide students with the appropriate project materials, based on their readiness to learn, their interests, or their learning profile.

Assessment Sheet—Assessment checklists are provided for each project, usually as a separate sheet. In some cases, where a project has many assignment sheets for different levels of readiness or challenge, the assessment checklist for each level is included on the corresponding assignment sheet. It is a good idea to hand out and discuss the assessment checklist with students at the beginning of the project so they know what is expected. At the end of the project, you can allot time for students to complete the checklist, and you can complete a checklist for each student as well, if you choose.

However, the assessments are checklists, not actual rubrics. They cover applied skills, content knowledge, key concepts, and important elements of the project process. An intentional effort has been made to keep them simple and user friendly. You may decide to develop criteria for the items on a checklist to create a rubric. See the "Creating Assessment Rubrics" section on pages 48–51 for more detailed instructions and to see a sample rubric for one of the projects.

A Model Projects Matrix is provided on pages 52–53 to help you see at a glance what projects are included and how each is aligned with one or more differentiation strategies in this book. Also, the Content Standards Matrix on pages 54–63 is intended as a quick reference of all standards covered by the projects.

Teacher Forms

DIFFERENTIATION PLANNER

In addition to being used in the projects in this book, the differentiation strategies outlined in Part 1 can be integrated into various points of your curriculum during the school year. Use the Differentiation Planner on page 225 to begin this process.

PROJECT ORGANIZER

The Project Organizer on pages 226–227 can help you analyze individual projects and determine how each might be used or modified to fit your specific needs.

TECHNOLOGY PLANNER

A Technology Planner form is provided on page 228 to help you think of ideas for integrating technology into any project. *Teaching Beyond the Test* provides many opportunities to implement technology. If you or your school places a premium on technology-based student activities and demonstrations, then you will immediately recognize the potential for any of these projects to be supported or expanded with technology.

Recommended Resources

The "Recommended Resources" section on pages 229–231 provides brief descriptions of helpful books and Web sites pertaining to select strategies, projects, and other topics discussed in this book.

CD-ROM

The CD-ROM that accompanies this book includes all of the reproducible project forms and teacher forms listed on pages ix–x. All forms appear as view-only PDF documents. Some forms also appear as customizable Word documents, where appropriate. In addition, the CD-ROM contains four bonus projects: "Time Traveler" (English/Language Arts), "You Gotta Have an Angle" (Math), "Express Yourself" (Science), and "Hear Ye! Hear Ye!" (Social Studies). Everything that is needed to implement these projects is available on the CD-ROM, either as PDF documents or customizable Word documents. See the Model Projects Matrix for a brief description of each of these four bonus projects.

Getting Started with This Book

Teaching Beyond the Test is organized into two main parts: descriptions of eighteen useful differentiation strategies, and a section of model projects that details how these strategies would look in the classroom. The eight projects (along with the four bonus projects on the CD-ROM only) are complete with a teacher's Project Planner and Student Materials, most of them are reproducible and included on the CD-ROM.

The book can be used in a variety of ways, depending on your interests:

Part 1: The Differentiation Strategies

- Read over all of the strategies as a type of "quick course" on differentiated instruction.

- Turn to a strategy of interest to find out what it is, how it works, and how you could use it.

- Look up the project(s) that models the strategy you just read about.

- Find references to other resources cited for a particular strategy, in a footnote or in the Recommended Resources section.

Part 2: Model Projects

- Read through one project in its entirety—all of the projects have the same format.

- Look up projects by the content area that you teach.

- Look up projects by a differentiation strategy of interest.

- Peruse the "Suggested Content Modifications" section of each Project Planner to see how the project can be used with other core content areas.

- Check out the reproducibles in the "Student Forms" section—you may be able to use some of the materials even if you don't use the entire project.

- Browse the "Recommended Resources" section for suggested sources to use for each project.

PART 1

The Differentiation Strategies

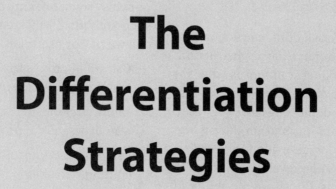

Introduction to Differentiated Instruction

What Is Differentiated Instruction?

Differentiated instruction means allowing students to learn and demonstrate understanding in ways that take advantage of their strengths and support their weaknesses. It's about bringing out each student's unique intelligence and spark. One approach to this is through project-based learning. By carefully developing projects that focus on key learning expectations, and taking into account the range of learning needs in your classes, you make it possible for all students to become actively and successfully engaged in their learning. An important key to effectively infusing differentiated projects into your instruction is a clear understanding of *what* to differentiate and *how* to differentiate.

Differentiate What?

There are three areas of classroom instruction that constitute the *what* of differentiated instruction: content, process, and product. Content is what we want students to know and be able to do; process means the activities students engage in as they make meaning of the content; and product is the way in which students provide evidence of understanding. Teachers have some level of control over these areas. In other words, they have the ability to decide how each will be addressed within the curriculum, and to make modifications when necessary. The differentiation strategies described in this section of the book have been organized around these three areas to help clarify which aspect of classroom instruction they are most likely to support (although they naturally interconnect and overlap in places). Carol Ann Tomlinson discusses content, process, and product in depth in her book *How to Differentiate Instruction in Mixed-Ability Classrooms*.

DIFFERENTIATING CONTENT

We live in a standards-driven age where content is mandated by federal and state governments. Even with government mandates, though, it is possible to differentiate much of the content students are expected to master. Here are some suggestions:

- Give students a choice of specific topics about which to learn. Choice is a powerful strategy for differentiating content.

- Focus on concepts, principles, essential questions, and big ideas related to the required content. These things may be differentiated by adjusting the level of complexity, based on the needs of individual learners.

- Use varied resources. Resources may be differentiated by reading level, depth, and complexity.

- Provide varied support systems (scaffolding). Help all students master the same content by giving more or less support to students, depending on their needs.

DIFFERENTIATING PROCESS

Tomlinson suggests calling the processes students go through as they learn new ideas, information, or skills "sense-making activities." There are many such activities, which can be differentiated in various ways. For example:

- Use small groups to allow more flexibility in matching activities to the needs of students.

- Allow students to use graphic organizers as a way of visually representing information.

- Establish learning centers that focus on specific content and skills.

- Develop tiered assignments (assignments designed for struggling learners, on-target learners, and advanced learners).

- Provide as many ways as possible for students to compare and contrast information.

DIFFERENTIATING PRODUCT

Products are a motivating factor in the learning process. Students take ownership in the products they create, and thus the product is a personal statement: tangible evidence of creativity, understanding, and effort. Products may take many forms, but they have some traits in common. Products should make students think, demonstrate real learning, be based on standards, incorporate skills that the content expectations demand, and place a high premium on quality. Products may be differentiated by allowing students to choose from a menu of product options, or by letting them design their own product option that reflects standard-level work. You may also establish completion criteria that allow students to add their own complexity or incorporate areas of personal interest beyond the product requirements.

Differentiate How?

There are three fundamental student characteristics that can be used to determine how to differentiate instruction: readiness to learn, interest areas, and learning profile. Teachers have no control over these things. Students walk into the classroom as they are, and therefore it is necessary to know your learners if instruction is going to be differentiated appropriately. Readiness to learn refers to what students currently know and are able to do. Interest areas are the things students enjoy doing or learning about. Learning profile is related to intelligence preference, learning style, gender, and culture. Each of these three characteristics can be used to differentiate content, process, and product. Again, Carol Ann Tomlinson's work is an excellent reference for anyone looking for additional information about how to do this.

DIFFERENTIATE BY READINESS

Differentiating by readiness means that pre-assessment is necessary. In some reliable way you must determine what students know and can do, and plan to accommodate the continuum of needs that you identify. Since it is impractical to create an individual learning plan for every student, differentiating by readiness is often done by developing three tiered levels of instruction or student activity: for struggling learners, on-target learners, and advanced learners. Ways of differentiating by readiness include varied texts by reading level, tiered assignments, scaffolding based on need, small group instruction, curriculum compacting, varied homework options, and learning contracts.

DIFFERENTIATE BY INTEREST

The primary reason for differentiating by interest is to tap into student motivation. Students who are learning about something of interest naturally bring increased enthusiasm to the task. That's how the brain works. There are two ways of approaching the idea of student interest. One is to determine what students are currently interested in, and allowing them to pursue those interests. The other is to create new interests in students by getting them excited about various aspects of the content being studied. Ways of differentiating by interest include interest groups, student choice, learning contracts, resident experts, Web Quests, literature circles, independent study, jigsaw grouping, and optional applications of technology.

DIFFERENTIATE BY LEARNING PROFILE

While students can be smart in all ways, they do have natural strengths. And if we want their best work, we try to align with those strengths. Students also have individual preferences about their learning environment and personal approach to learning. If these factors can be determined for individuals, for example, by using Howard Gardner's theory of multiple intelligences (see page 43), their learning will be more effective and efficient. They will do better in class and they will understand themselves better as they become lifelong learners. Ways of differentiating by learning profile involve offering varied methods of gathering information, organizing information, analyzing information, synthesizing information, and presenting information. Giving students choices will lead to a natural self-selection of learning preferences.

On the following page is a simple chart to summarize the *what* and *how* of differentiated instruction.

You can differentiate instruction by focusing on any combination of the nine empty cells. The items in the "Differentiate What?" column on the left are the things you control (content, process, product). The items in the "Differentiate How?" row at the top are the unique attributes that students bring with them into the classroom that are not under your control and must be determined through assessment, survey, or other means.

"DIFFERENTIATE HOW? DIFFERENTIATE WHAT?" CHART

Differentiate What?	Differentiate How?		
	By Learner Readiness	By Learner Interest	By Learner Profile
Differentiate Content			
Differentiate Process			
Differentiate Product			

Why Differentiate Through Project-Based Learning?

"Projects" are a natural human enterprise. When a person intrinsically wants to apply a skill, understand a process, grasp a concept, reach a goal, or solve a problem, a project often materializes. What is the best way to learn how to raise a garden? Design a Web site? Repair a car? Plan a vacation? Remodel a kitchen? Sew? Cook? Fish? Golf? For these and myriad other things that are being learned all the time, it is necessary to get your hands involved to help your brain do its job. If you want to master gardening, for example, you can't just read about it or watch videos; you have to plant a garden! The knowledge and understanding you seek comes from *doing*. Reflect for a moment on projects in your personal life. Your own experiences are proof enough that becoming engaged in active learning is a key to mastering skills and remembering information. If it works for you, it will work for your students. That's worth thinking about.

Project-based learning is the purest form of differentiated instruction. Projects incorporate the most fundamental concepts of differentiation, in ways that engage students, motivate them, and enhance their learning. They can be used to differentiate content, process, or product, and they can be used to address student readiness, interests, and learning profiles. When students work on carefully developed, curriculum-aligned projects, they:

- Make personal choices and decisions that result in individualized learning experiences.
- Participate at an appropriate readiness level.
- Take ownership in, and accept responsibility for, their own learning.
- Become active workers rather than passive observers.
- Tackle authentic tasks that represent the kinds of things done in the "real" world.
- Apply skills and knowledge within a context that makes the learning meaningful.
- Build confidence in themselves as self-directed learners.
- Develop unique final products.
- Demonstrate in personalized ways what they know and can do.
- Work independently, with a partner, or in small groups.
- Focus on topics of interest.

A well-designed project requires students to apply an array of important skills to answer essential questions. Primary among these is a set of eight skills that constitute the basis for successfully participating in project-based learning. When you use projects in your classroom, you are placing high priority on these eight skills:

1. Reading

2. Writing

3. Research

4. Planning

5. Problem solving

6. Self-discipline

7. Self-evaluation

8. Presentation

We encourage you to explicitly talk to your students about these skills, and have a dialogue about the importance of each one. Students should understand that effectively applying self-directed learning skills is not a matter of fulfilling assignment requirements to earn a grade. Mastering these critical work skills will affect their lives beyond school as they enter their chosen careers.

Tips for Differentiating Projects

A fine line separates an active, productive classroom from an active, chaotic one. The difference is effective classroom management. A differentiated classroom must be well ordered and time efficient if it is to maximize the achievement of all students. Here are some ideas and tips gleamed from a wide variety of researchers and educators whose experiences may be of use to you.

- Begin slowly—just begin! Don't overwhelm yourself at first. Develop a three- to five-year plan and work steadily toward your goals. Start your journey toward differentiated instruction with a simple, achievable objective and commit to doing it. (Use the Differentiation Planner on page 225.)

- Establish clearly articulated rules and procedures for using particular differentiation strategies; let your students help develop them. Post them prominently on a wall and refer to them often.

- Provide clearly developed project criteria and expectations (guidelines, checklists, and rubrics). (See "Creating Assessment Rubrics" on pages 48–51.)

- Be ready! It is critical to preempt problems by carefully thinking through the process you are putting in place. Don't try to figure out on the fly what you are doing.

- Prepare students for the project (prerequisite skills and knowledge); students must believe they can accomplish the task without hand-holding.

- Emphasize quality and define it so that students understand the target. Work with students to develop their own sense of quality and commitment to striving for it.

- Emphasize employable skills when introducing a new project. In a differentiated classroom, students are constantly using skills that are highly valued in the workplace. They should know that and understand that they are accomplishing more than just academic achievement.

- Create a contract for positive behavior and hold students accountable to it.

- Establish a specific process for students to receive assignments, pick up materials, and turn in work.

- Have anchor (or "sponge") activities ready when starting a new project (see "Anchor Activities" on page 38). It is critical to have meaningful work for students who finish early.

- Establish a "home base" for students—this is where students begin and end each class period. Institute a system for telling students when it's time to move, such as ringing a bell or chimes.

- Teach students to rearrange furniture. Have coded plans for room configurations that students understand; for example, if you say, "Red arrangement today," students should know what that means and move furniture accordingly.

- Designate a "question courier" for each small group. This is the only person permitted to leave the group to ask the teacher questions.

- Develop "assistance signals" for students to use to silently ask for help. For example, laminate a piece of red paper and a piece of green paper back to back. If an individual or group displays green, everything is okay; if red is displayed, help is needed.

- Assign "skill assistants" who are available to help others. Don't overuse this, and don't burden gifted students with the job of tutoring. But if you have students who know how to do something on the computer, for example, designate them as skill assistants who can show others how to do it.

- Develop a record-keeping system that helps you keep track of each student's progress.

- Keep a personal journal and write in it ten minutes every day. This is an extremely valuable way for you to keep track of what you have done—what works and what doesn't work. Your journal takes the place of long-term memory. You may think you will remember important details about how things should be modified for next time, but you won't. Write it down!

Differentiation Strategy Matrix

Strategies can be used with any content area. Projects model how a strategy can be used with specific content. The assignment of each strategy to a specific curricular element (content, process, or product) is necessarily ambiguous, as the three elements naturally overlap. The alignment here is based primarily on the way a strategy is used in the projects in this book.

Differentiation Strategy	See Pages	Differen-tiated By	Descriptor	Model Project(s)	Content Area(s)	See Pages
All-Most-Some	17–19	Content	A course and unit planning strategy where critical content that all students must learn to understand the discipline is identified. Beyond this level is content that most students will master and content that only some students will master.	Life on Planet X	Life Science	126–152
Curriculum Compacting	19–20	Content	Compacting allows students to move beyond mate-rial they already know, through the use of contracts that spell out what they will do instead of the regular curriculum. Compacting can be used to eliminate repetition of mastered content or skills, increase the challenge level, or provide time for further study of concepts taught in the regular curriculum.	Math Investment Plan	Math	96–115
Flexible Grouping	20–22	Content	Flexible grouping means that students are grouped and regrouped as appropriate for particular activities. It does not create permanent groups or label students in any way. Grouping may be based on interest, choice, multiple intelligences, readiness, and so forth.	Continental Cubing Competition	English/Language Arts	84–95
Scaffolding	22–24	Content	Everyone is given the same assignment, but scaffold-ing (more support) is provided for struggling learners.	Express Yourself	Science	CD-ROM
1-2-4 Present!	24–25	Process	A grouping strategy that allows students to study individually, collaborate as partners, and finally join in a group of four to prepare and present their work.	Moments in Time	Social Studies	169–197

continues 👉

DIFFERENTIATION STRATEGY MATRIX *continued*

Differentiation Strategy	See Pages	Differentiated By	Descriptor	Model Project(s)	Content Area(s)	See Pages
Bloom's Taxonomy	25–27	Process	The six levels of thinking Bloom identified provide a tool for adding rigor and relevance to the lessons we teach. Bloom's wording has been revised to more accurately reflect the nature of thinking.	One World	Social Studies	198–224
Bring-Something-to-the-Group	27–28	Process	Students complete basic assignments individually before being placed in groups for a project or activity. They must show through this first assignment that they are willing to work and contribute before they are allowed to join a group.	The Mathematute	Math	116–125
Clock Partners	28–30	Process	Partners are chosen or assigned and kept on record for an extended period of time, allowing you to group students quickly and smoothly (e.g., "Meet with your 3 o'clock partner for this activity").	Message in a Capsule	Earth/Space Science	153–168
Cubing	30–31	Process	A novel way to offer different perspectives of the same topic. Students roll a numbered die to determine which one of six assignments they will work on.	Continental Cubing Competition	English/ Language Arts	84–95
Jigsaw Grouping	31–33	Process	A cooperative learning strategy where students meet in small groups to become experts on a topic before rejoining their home base groups to share information and complete the assignment.	Hear Ye! Hear Ye!	Social Studies/ History	CD-ROM
Kids-Teaching-Kids	33–35	Process	Students present what they've learned to each other, which helps them retain essential information at a higher rate than most other instructional methods. This strategy shows trust in a student's ability to learn, and helps students realize they can learn from each other and aren't dependent on a teacher for learning to occur.	Hear Ye! Hear Ye! The Candidates' Debate	Social Studies/ History English/ Language Arts	CD-ROM 64–83

continues ☛

DIFFERENTIATION STRATEGY MATRIX *continued*

Differentiation Strategy	See Pages	Differen- tiated By	Descriptor	Model Project(s)	Content Area(s)	See Pages
Task Sheets	35–37	Process	Task sheets provide specific guidelines that clearly explain or show what students are expected to do as they work independently. These sheets allow you to answer questions, monitor progress, or handle problems rather than having to repeatedly explain the assignment.	You Gotta Have an Angle	Math	CD-ROM
Tiered Assignments	36–39	Process	Three difficulty levels of the same assignment are developed to ensure that struggling, on-target, and advanced students master the lesson's benchmarks.	Continental Cub- ing Competition	English/ Language Arts	84–95
				Hear Ye! Hear Ye!	Social Studies/ History	CD-ROM
				The Mathematute	Math	116–125
				Moments in Time	Social Studies	169–197
Anchor Activities	38–41	Product	Anchor activities are meaningful, engaging opportuni- ties available to students who complete required work before the rest of the class. Students work independently on anchor activities according to rules and guidelines that you establish before the required lesson begins.	Life on Planet X	Life Science	126–152
				Math Investment Plan	Math	96–115
Choice Boards	41–42	Product	When students complete required assignments at different rates, they can go to a choice board and choose options for additional activities that build on the project's basic requirements. Choice boards can also be designed to provide options for students on a designated "activity" day, or to offer assignments based on demonstrated proficiency. There are many variations for implementing choice boards.	Life on Planet X	Life Science	126–152

continues ☛

DIFFERENTIATION STRATEGY MATRIX *continued*

Differentiation Strategy	See Pages	Differen- tiated By	Descriptor	Model Project(s)	Content Area(s)	See Pages
Choice-as-Motivator	42–43	Product	Choice allows students to take ownership of their work and gain a sense of independence. You can offer choice of content, process, or product in a wide variety of ways to motivate students.	Time Traveler	English/ Language Arts	CD-ROM
				The Candidates' Debate	English/ Language Arts	64–83
				Message in a Capsule	Earth/Space Science	153–168
Multiple Intelligences	43–45	Product	Multiple intelligences influence how students approach learning. Addressing all multiple intel- ligences by varying the way you deliver curriculum, and by offering options for student expression, can profoundly improve student achievement.	One World	Social Studies	198–224
				Mathematute	Math	116–125
				The Candidates' Debate	English/ Language Arts	64–83
Tic-Tac-Toe	45–46	Product	Nine assignments are developed for the nine squares of a tic-tac-toe board. Students choose any three assignments that line up vertically, horizontally, or diagonally. The position of each assignment on the tic-tac-toe board can be carefully crafted so that any line choice includes the things you want students to learn.	One World	Social Studies	198–224

Differentiating Content

All-Most-Some

"All-most-some" is a course and unit planning strategy developed by Keith Lenz, senior research scientist at the University of Kansas Center for Research on Learning. His idea, in turn, is based largely on the concept of "enduring understandings," promoted by curriculum experts Grant Wiggins and Jay McTighe. In a nutshell, this strategy says that every unit of study includes certain core ideas that all students must know and demonstrate in order to better understand the discipline. It is not acceptable for students to complete the unit without mastering these critical concepts because a learning deficiency at this point means almost certain failure in the future. Beyond this key level of learning, the unit includes content that most students should master, and it also includes content that only some students will master.

In terms of differentiated instruction, the important point is that an all-most-some unit should be designed to ensure that *all* students master the portion of the content that is deemed essential for fundamental understanding and continued learning. Every student who can demonstrate understanding of these concepts is guaranteed a grade of C, even if it takes the entire time allotted for the unit to do so. Meanwhile, *most* students will be able to go beyond the essential learning to gain additional knowledge and understanding of the unit content. These students will earn a B for the unit. Finally, *some* students will exceed this level and go even further, or deeper, into the content and receive an A.

Dr. Lenz asks us to visualize a course as a pie cut into slices. A small circle at the center of the pie represents the essential course content. The outer ring of the pie is content that is not essential but is still important to the discipline. Each slice of pie is a unit. If we remove a slice, its narrow end contains the unit's essential content that all students must learn. The rest of the slice contains material that most or some of the students will learn. Every discipline has considerably more content than can possibly be covered in a single course. Thus the critical content in the narrowest part of the slice is the key to understanding the larger body of knowledge at the broader end of the slice. Here is a graphic to help explain this strategy:

PRIORITIZING CONTENT FOR INSTRUCTION IN SECONDARY CORE CURRICULUM COURSES

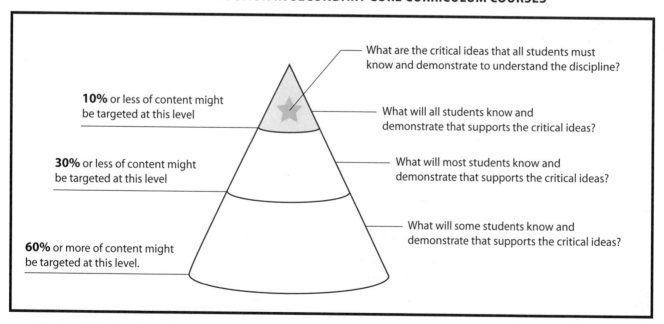

From Lenz, B. Keith, Donald D. Deshler, with Brenda R. Kissam. *Teaching Content to All: Evidence-Based Inclusive Practices in Middle and Secondary Schools,* 1/e. Published by Allyn and Bacon, Boston, MA. Copyright © 2004 Pearson Education. Reprinted by permission of the publisher.

An All-Most-Some Scenario

A simple example of how this strategy might be implemented in your class is based on the table below. It represents a ten-item assessment. You (or your department) have identified four items as being absolutely essential to the content of the course and future learning about the subject. *All* students should demonstrate mastery of these four key concepts; they represent content at the narrow end of the pie slice. Another four items have been identified as important content that *most* students should master. The final two items are considered to be beyond the curriculum and likely to be mastered by only *some* students. The table indicates how several students might do on this assessment, and the grades that they would receive for the unit based on the traditional grading system and on the all-most-some (A-M-S) strategy.

Let's take a quick look at each of the students in the table to see the differences between a traditional grading system and an all-most-some grading system.

- Student 1 got all four of the essential content questions correct, but missed almost all of the other questions. In a traditional grading system, this student gets an F (50% correct) even though the evidence shows mastery of the essential parts of the curriculum. In an A-M-S grading system, the same student gets a C.

- Student 2 got all four of the essential content questions correct, and also all of the next level questions correct, thus earning a B in the A-M-S

SAMPLE ALL-MOST-SOME ASSESSMENT TABLE

	Assessment Item	Student I	II	III	IV	V	VI
All students are expected to get items 1–4 correct	1	C	C	W	C	C	C
	2	C	C	W	C	C	W
	3	C	C	W	W	C	W
	4	C	C	W	C	C	C
Most students are expected to get items 5–8 correct	5	W	C	C	C	C	C
	6	W	C	C	W	C	C
	7	C	C	C	C	C	W
	8	W	C	C	C	C	W
Some students are expected to get items 9–10 correct	9	W	W	C	C	C	W
	10	W	W	C	C	C	C
	Items 1–4: % correct	100	100	0	75	100	50
	Items 5–8: % correct	25	100	100	75	100	50
	Items 1–10: % correct	50	80	60	80	100	50
	Traditional Grade	F	B	D	B	A	F
	A-M-S Grade	C	B	I	I	A	I

Key: C = Correct   W = Wrong   I = Incomplete

system. The resulting 80% total score earns a B in the traditional system as well.

- Student 3 missed all four essential content questions, but correctly answered the other six. In a traditional grading system, this student passes with a D and probably moves on without ever revisiting the essential content that has not been mastered. In an A-M-S system, the student gets an Incomplete and is required to go through a re-teach, review, and retest cycle.

- Student 4 missed one essential content item and got a total score of 80%. In a traditional system this student gets a B. In an A-M-S system he or she gets an Incomplete: A student cannot receive a grade of C or better until all four essential content questions are correctly answered.

- Student 5 got all ten items correct. This meets the criteria for an A in both the traditional and the A-M-S systems.

- Student 6 got 50% correct overall, just like Student I, which translates into an F in the traditional system. However, because Student VI missed two essential content items, he or she gets an Incomplete (rather than a C like Student I) in the A-M-S system.

See model project **Life on Planet X** on pages 126–152 for another example of all-most-some implementation.

Curriculum Compacting

Curriculum compacting is a strategy in which students are allowed to advance past lessons they have previously mastered. Virtually every book written about differentiated instruction has a section devoted to curriculum compacting. Researchers Joseph Renzulli and Linda Smith developed the idea in the 1970s, and it remains just as relevant and logical today. It makes sense to let students move beyond material they already know.

All school districts use curriculum compacting, although it is often called something different. If a student is allowed to skip a grade, that is curriculum compacting. Students who jump past the eighth-grade math book to take Algebra 1 have

benefited from curriculum compacting, just like students who move right into Spanish 2 because they don't need Spanish 1. Students who test out of classes, and students who take advanced placement classes, have had the curriculum compacted for them. Dr. Renzulli provided a simple economic metaphor: Compacting allows students to "buy" back class time by demonstrating proficiency, thus "earning" the right to "spend" their time more "profitably."

For classroom teachers, curriculum compacting begins by determining what students already know, and then using learning contracts to specify what the students may do instead of following the regular curriculum. The concept is usually applied to gifted students whose level of content knowledge or skill development exceeds that of their classmates. As educator Diane Heacox writes in *Differentiating Instruction in the Regular Classroom*, "When you compact curriculum, you examine a particular subject area and identify content or skills that could be accelerated, eliminated, or pre-assessed." She goes on to say that compacting may be used for one or more of the following purposes:

1. To eliminate repetition of mastered content and/or skills

2. To increase the challenge level of the regular curriculum

3. To provide time for the investigation of a curricular topic that is beyond the scope of the regular curriculum[1]

It is important to recognize that gifted students potentially have gaps in their understanding. They may have mastered most of the material in an upcoming unit, for example, but still may not grasp every aspect of the subject. A compacting contract should take this into account and specify certain learning activities to cover gaps, if necessary.

National educational consultant Bertie Kingore states a compacting contract should have three distinct sections:

1. Documented mastery of standards, concepts, and skills (These are things that may be

---

[1] *Differentiating Instruction in the Regular Classroom* by Diane Heacox (Free Spirit Publishing, 2002), p.137.

"compacted out" of the student's learning regimen, as determined by pre-assessment data.)

2. Needs for further instruction (These are areas where the student should meet with the whole class, do targeted homework assignments, or participate in other learning activities.)

3. Recommended replacement tasks (These are extended or accelerated tasks the student will complete as alternatives to the regular curriculum.)[2]

A Curriculum Compacting Scenario

Ryan and Simone are students in the same math class. At the beginning of a new unit, the teacher spends a day going over fundamental concepts and skills that apply to the content that will be covered. She then informs the class that the following day they will take a pre-assessment to determine where everyone is in terms of understanding and skill

---

[2] *Differentiation: Simplified, Realistic, and Effective: How to Challenge Advanced Potentials in Mixed-Ability Classrooms* by Bertie Kingore (Professional Associates Publishing, 2004), p. 16.

mastery. Simone, who is quite advanced in her understanding of math, scores a 92% on the assessment. Ryan, who often struggles in math, scores a 58%. These scores indicate that Ryan should follow the regular curriculum, but Simone should have this unit compacted for her because she understands most of it (though not all—a 92% means there are a few things that she still may not fully understand). Working with the teacher, Simone completes the compacting contract shown below. During the next few weeks, she will work from the contract rather than follow the class through its daily instructional sequence.

See model project **Math Investment Plan** on pages 96–115 for another example of curriculum compacting implementation.

Flexible Grouping

The wide range of learning needs found in every classroom is a dilemma faced by all teachers. Each child is different, and this fact alone can be overwhelming to teachers who recognize that student differences require a variety of strategies. One

SAMPLE CURRICULUM COMPACTING CONTRACT

Unit 5—Fractions, Decimals, and Percents	Pre-Assessment Date: 12/4
Name: Simone	Pre-Assessment Score: 92%
Unit Sections Mastered	5-1 through 5-6 5-8 5-10 through 5-12
Required Curriculum Work	Attend class discussions and do all class assignments for Section 5-7. Work with the teacher to identify problems from Section 5-9 to do independently.
Replacement Tasks	Complete the challenge problem on textbook page 97. Select a project from the choice board and present finished work to the class. Develop solutions to story problems on pages 24–25 in *Can You Solve This?* Explore at least two Web sites from the list provided by the teacher, and write a summary of what they offer and what was learned.
Student Signature:	Teacher Signature:

solution to this dilemma is flexible grouping. When you group flexibly, you create instructional groups and prescribe specific activities that respond to students' individual learning needs. Flexible grouping is often used to differentiate content, by varying the type or level of instruction and resources of each group, but can also be used to differentiate process, by varying the nature or complexity of each group's task.

It is important to understand that flexible grouping does not create permanent groups or label students in any way. "Flexible" means that students are grouped and regrouped as appropriate for particular activities. For example, students may sometimes be grouped heterogeneously and at other times homogeneously; for one activity students may be grouped by interest and for another by intelligence type. One day students may be grouped randomly and the next by student choice. In other words, student groups are routinely rearranged as the situation demands.

The key to using flexible grouping effectively is to start slow and build a repertoire of grouping ideas that you can replicate and modify to meet your needs and those of your students. Don't go overboard; if you can find two or three ideas that allow you to group and regroup students, start with those and build in more over time. Bertie Kingore has identified ten flexible grouping implementation choices, which are great starting places:

- Learning centers or stations
- Cooperative learning groups
- Guided research studies
- Independent research studies
- Interest groups
- Literature circles (fiction or nonfiction)
- Peer-tutor pairs
- Problem-based learning groups
- Project-centered learning groups
- Skill groups[3]

Finally, think about the basic needs of any small group, and be sure to build those things into your flexible grouping plan. Educators Gayle Gregory and Carolyn Chapman list six things that groups need to be successful:

1. Ample space to work
2. Clear directions
3. Established guidelines
4. Individual roles assigned for group responsibilities
5. A time frame assigned for on-task work
6. An opportunity to tap into all members' strengths[4]

A Flexible Grouping Scenario

Tania, Jose, Charles, and Sun are all in Mr. Medellin's social studies class. Mr. Medellin has made flexible grouping something of an art form in his classes. His students know that almost every day, in one way or another, they will work with a partner or in a small group to have discussions, complete assignments, and perform learning tasks. On any given day, however, the students have no idea with whom they may be grouped.

One day Mr. Medellin greeted students at the door and randomly handed each person a playing card (at least it *seemed* to be random). Tania got the three of diamonds, Jose got the seven of clubs, Charles got the ace of spades, and Sun got the two of hearts. The four friends looked at each other; they had not seen this approach to grouping before.

Mr. Medellin said to the group, "Today you will be working in cooperative learning groups as we begin our study of the Declaration of Independence, the Constitution, and the Bill of Rights. You each received a playing card as you came in. Since there are twenty-eight students in this class, I used cards from ace through seven in each of the four suits. I have designated seven areas in the room as group meeting areas. If you got an ace, you will be a member of Group 1 and will meet in Area 1. If you got a two, your group will move your desks into

---

[3] *Differentiation: Simplified, Realistic, and Effective: How to Challenge Advanced Potentials in Mixed-Ability Classrooms* by Bertie Kingore (Professional Associates Publishing, 2004), pp. 58–64.

[4] *Differentiated Instruction Strategies: One Size Doesn't Fit All* by Gayle Gregory and Carolyn Chapman (Corwin Press, 2002), p. 70.

Area 2, and so on. Each group of four will follow assignment guidelines as you prepare a presentation for the class. Part of the assignment requires you to work with a partner within your group. Partners are determined by the color of your card. Red cards will be partners and black cards will be partners. As you work in your group, each person will have a specific job title and responsibilities, which are described on your assignment sheet. Your job is determined by your card's suit. Clubs are group leaders. Diamonds are research experts. Hearts are in charge of graphic design. Spades are presenters. Okay, let's get to work!"

Tania, Jose, Charles, and Sun headed to their respective group meeting areas to receive their assignments. Tania is the research expert for Group 3; Jose is the leader for Group 7; Charles is the presenter for Group 1; and Sun is the graphic designer for Group 2. The chart below shows how the grouping system for this project was organized.

See model project **Continental Cubing Competition** on pages 84–95 for another example of flexible grouping implementation.

Scaffolding

"Scaffolding" means to provide the support that is necessary for students to reach their learning goals. The most common use of scaffolding is to help struggling learners complete assigned tasks and demonstrate understanding. "Scaffolding" and "tiering" are sometimes used interchangeably, but there is a fundamental difference. Tiering provides multiple assignments, typically for three types of learner: struggling, on-target, and advanced. The teacher determines which level best fits each student's readiness and gives that student the appropriate assignment (see "Tiered Assignments" on pages 36–39 for more detail). By contrast, scaffolding often begins with the same assignment for

SAMPLE FLEXIBLE GROUPING CHART

Group	Black Partners		Red Partners	
	Clubs (Group Leaders)	**Spades** (Presenters)	**Diamonds** (Research Experts)	**Hearts** (Graphic Designers)
1		Charles		
2				Sun
3			Tania	
4				
5				
6				
7	Jose			

everyone. The teacher differentiates by determining how much support each student needs in order to complete the assignment.

The most direct and obvious way to scaffold an assignment is to provide resource materials written at varied reading levels. Reading is a key factor in many students' struggle to learn, and simply making information available in an easy-to-read format can have a dramatic effect on final results. Educator Sheryn Spencer Northey advocates the use of a wide variety of content literacy strategies to help students process the information in their textbooks. Northey breaks these into three categories of scaffolding activities:

1. "Pre-reading" activities teach students to access prior knowledge, using strategies such as KWL charts, Frayer models, or concept mapping.

2. "During Reading" activities teach students to identify vocabulary words and main ideas as they read, using strategies such as two-column note taking, study guides, or graphic organizers.

3. "After Reading" activities teach students to ask and answer questions about what they have just read.[5]

Here are other ideas for scaffolding learning activities:

● Give students "study buddies" with whom to collaborate while working on assignments.

● Narrow the choices students are allowed to make, based on the availability of resources. In other words, don't let struggling students choose a topic unless there is an abundance of information available on it.

● Build in assignment checkpoints that require students to show you their work before it is due. This allows you to intervene, offer feedback, or provide support while the work is in progress.

● Develop support materials in the form of "how to" study guides or step-by-step procedures that students can employ as needed.

Finally, it is not just the struggling learner who benefits from scaffolding. Carol Ann Tomlinson makes the point that all students should be challenged just beyond their comfort level. Thus, if all students are being stretched through tiering or other forms of differentiated instruction, then all students need scaffolding. Here's what she says: "Scaffolding is whatever kind of assistance is needed for any student to move from prior knowledge and skill to the next level of knowledge and skill. In a good differentiated classroom, the teacher is constantly raising the stakes for success for any individual, then doing whatever is necessary to help the students succeed in taking the next step. Remember that everyone's next step will not be identical, and that every student needs scaffolding in order to stretch."[6]

A Scaffolding Scenario

Following is an example of a scaffolded social studies project. The assignment is the same for every student in the class:

1. Choose an event from a timeline.

2. Conduct research to learn about the event.

3. Write a newspaper editorial in the voice of a journalist living at the time of the event, explaining what happened and why it happened, and expressing an opinion about its impact on people.

The teacher has decided to scaffold this assignment for three levels of learners: struggling, on-target, and advanced. Everybody is expected to complete the same final product—a newspaper editorial. The assignment is differentiated based upon readiness to complete the assigned task. The table on the following page summarizes how the assignment might be scaffolded.

---

[5] *Handbook on Differentiated Instruction for Middle and High Schools* by Sheryn Spencer Northey (Eye on Education, 2005), pp. 40–61.

[6] *How to Differentiate Instruction in Mixed-Ability Classrooms,* 2nd ed. by Carol Ann Tomlinson (ASCD, 2001), pp. 22–23.

SAMPLE SCAFFOLDING TABLE

	Struggling Learners	On-Target Learners	Advanced Learners
Event Choice (color-coded red, white, and blue)	Choice of any red event. These events have been explicitly covered in class and there are plenty of resources available.	Choice of any white event. These events have been discussed in class but require more background information to fully understand.	Choice of any blue event. These events have been indirectly mentioned in class, if at all. They require that connections be made to other events in order to make sense of them.
Resources	There are plenty of carefully identified and highly reliable resources available in the room for each red event.	Some resources are available in the room, but some additional searching will be required. Plenty of information is available on the Internet and in the library.	Resources may or may not be available in the room, and significant searching and synthesizing will be required to find sufficient information.
Reading Level	Resources are written at a reading level that allows students to learn.	Resources are written at grade-appropriate reading levels.	Resources may be more advanced than grade-appropriate reading levels.
Writing Support	Students are given specific guidelines and a structured template for completing the assignment.	Students are given guidelines for completing the assignment, but no template.	Students are given general expectations, and they develop their own approach to the assignment.

See model project **Express Yourself** on the CD-ROM for another example of scaffolding implementation.

Differentiating Process

1–2–4 Present!

1–2–4 Present! (also sometimes called think-pair-share) is a grouping strategy that lets students collaborate on ideas, opinions, research topics, problem-solving procedures, debate resolutions, textual analyses, and small group activities. It is usually used to differentiate process, or how students make sense of the assigned curriculum. The box to the right shows how the strategy works.

1-2-4 PRESENT! GROUPING

1: Students think about or research the assigned problem, issue, or topic on their own.

2: Students share their ideas and discoveries with a partner. Their task is to combine their best information and ideas as a pair.

4: Pairs of students combine to form groups of four. They work on the assigned small group activity, project, or group presentation, using their combined ideas and information as a starting point. (Note: If you have an odd number of students, some "pairs" can have three students, and "groups of four" can have five students.)

PRESENT: Groups of four present their work to the class.

You can be very intentional in the way you group students with this strategy. For example, prepare a set of index cards numbered 1 through 28 (e.g., if there are twenty-eight students in the class). Assign one of four colors (such as blue, yellow, red, and green) to each card either by using colored cards or putting a colored sticker on each card. For example:

Card 1: blue
Card 2: yellow
Card 3: red
Card 4: green

Repeat the colors for cards 5–8, 9–12, and so forth.

Hand a card to each student at the beginning of the activity. When it's time to pair, have Student 1 join Student 2, Student 3 join Student 4, and so forth. When it's time to form groups of four, put Students 1–4 together, Students 5–8 together, and so forth.

Assign tasks to the colors. For example:

Blue: leader
Yellow: writer
Red: graphic artist
Green: presenter

Using this system predetermines who partners will be and who will be in groups of four. This can be a totally random process (just hand the cards out), or it can appear to be random when in fact you have put some thought into how you are going to distribute the cards. For example, you may want to identify ahead of time which students will be group leaders. Simply be sure to give those students blue cards. Or, you may know that certain students should not be in the same group. Just give them cards that are not in the same set of four.

A 1–2–4 Present! Scenario

Students are told to develop a list of pros and cons for this statement: *The United States should land human beings on Mars within the next ten years.* They work individually on this task, using available resources. When they form pairs, each partner comes to the meeting with a list of pros and cons. Time is spent discussing, combining, and expanding ideas. Pairs then combine to create groups of four, and each group is assigned to either support or oppose the statement in a presentation. This assignment is made randomly so that half of the groups of four support the statement and half of the groups oppose it. Each group of four now begins the task of developing solid arguments for one side of the issue or the other, based on the ideas that each pair has contributed. Finally, each group of four presents its arguments and a class debate ensues.

See model project **Moments in Time** on pages 169–197 for another example of 1–2–4 Present! implementation.

Bloom's Taxonomy

Student assignments may be differentiated by adjusting the thinking levels required for various learning activities. The most common way to do this is with Bloom's Taxonomy of Educational Objectives, which was developed by Benjamin Bloom in the 1950s and is familiar to most educators. Bloom's taxonomy is typically used in conjunction with such strategies as tiered assignments, cubing activities, tic-tac-toe, and choice boards. (For more detail on each of these strategies, see individual sections.)

Recent revisions have been made to Bloom's taxonomy. During the 1990s, Lorin Anderson (a former student of Benjamin Bloom) worked with a group of cognitive psychologists to revise the taxonomy, making it more appropriate to the current emphasis on rigor and assessment. Differentiating by thinking levels requires familiarity with the new taxonomy and its vocabulary. See the chart on the following page.

The revised categories have been changed to more accurately reflect the active nature of thinking. *Knowledge* has been changed to *Remembering; Comprehension* has been changed to *Understanding;* and *Synthesis* has been changed to *Creating.* Anderson's team determined that creative thinking is a more complex form of thinking than evaluative thinking, so the highest level in the new taxonomy is *Creating.*

BLOOM'S TAXONOMY COMPARISON CHART

Bloom's Original Taxonomy	Anderson's Revised Taxonomy
Knowledge	Remembering
Comprehension	Understanding
Application	Applying
Analysis	Analyzing
Synthesis	Evaluating
Evaluation	Creating

Here is a brief description of Andersons' revised taxonomy:

Remembering: Can the student recall information?
Tasks involved: define, describe, duplicate, identify, list, name, recognize, repeat, reproduce, retrieve, state

Understanding: Can the student explain ideas or concepts?
Tasks involved: classify, describe, discuss, explain, identify, infer, interpret, locate, paraphrase, recognize, report, select, summarize, translate

Applying: Can the student use information in another familiar situation?
Tasks involved: carry out, choose, demonstrate, dramatize, employ, illustrate, implement, interpret, operate, schedule, sketch, solve, use, write

Analyzing: Can the student distinguish between constituent parts?
Tasks involved: appraise, attribute, compare, contrast, criticize, deconstruct, differentiate, discriminate, distinguish, examine, experiment, organize, question, test

Evaluating: Can the student justify a stand, decision, or course of action?
Tasks involved: argue, check, critique, defend, evaluate, hypothesize, judge, select, support, value

Creating: Can the student generate new products, ideas, or ways of viewing things?

Tasks involved: assemble, construct, create, design, develop, formulate, plan, produce, write

Two Bloom's Taxonomy Scenarios

Here are two ways in which the revised Bloom's taxonomy might be utilized in a differentiated classroom:

SCENARIO ONE

Give students options for their final assessment:

- Take a 100-item multiple-choice test, based primarily on remembering and understanding important content from the course. (Remembering, Understanding)

- Answer 50 multiple-choice items, plus respond to an essay question that requires thinking at the analysis level by comparing and contrasting two issues related to the core content of the course. (Remembering, Understanding, Applying, Analyzing)

- Answer 20 multiple-choice items, plus develop an evaluative response to a debate-like statement (for example: Resolved that the U.S. government should eliminate illegal immigration by increasing border barriers and protection) by producing a "Taking a Stand" essay or oral presentation that offers arguments and counterarguments to an issue that is central to the content of the course. (Remembering, Understanding, Applying, Analyzing, Evaluating, Creating)

SCENARIO TWO

Tiered assignments are a common differentiation strategy (see pages 36–39 for more detail). An important rule for tiering is that the assignments designed for more-advanced or high-achieving students should not be simply more of what is being asked of struggling students. Instead, each successive tier should be focused on higher levels of the taxonomy.

- Tier 1 assignment: Struggling students must successfully demonstrate that they remember and understand core content information. (Remembering, Understanding)

- Tier 2 assignment: On-target students should be expected to go beyond remembering and understanding information. Tier 2 assignments ask these students to apply information to specific situations, and to analyze issues, concepts, ideas, conditions, and so forth. (Remembering, Understanding, Applying, Analyzing)

- Tier 3 assignment: Advanced students need the challenge of evaluating information and creating new ways of looking at things. Tier 3 assignments are designed to push these students slightly out of their comfort zone by requiring them to think at a higher level. For example, students might be asked to make judgments (supported with evidence) about open-ended statements, or develop ways of representing divergent or conflicting ideas or points of view, or demonstrate more than one way of solving problems. (Remembering, Understanding, Applying, Analyzing, Evaluating, Creating)

See model project **One World** on pages 198–224 for another example of Bloom's taxonomy implementation.

Bring-Something-to-the-Group

Much of differentiated instruction depends on the concept of flexible grouping (see "Flexible Grouping" on pages 20–22). One of the most difficult obstacles to collaborative group work is the student who makes little or no contribution to the group, relying instead on other group members who are willing to do whatever is necessary to complete required tasks. Teachers frequently express concern about the value of small groups that contain students who choose to be passive observers rather than active participants.

The bring-something-to-the-group strategy addresses this concern about small group work. Simply stated, the strategy says that only students who can contribute something useful will be allowed to join the group. This, of course, implies that it must be possible for every student to make a positive contribution, and that this contribution must be evident before the group is organized. How is this to be accomplished? The key is in the assignment itself. It must include a way for students to demonstrate that they have something to bring to the group.

This strategy requires that, prior to the beginning of group work, every student complete a task that is directly related to the group assignment. Students who do this task with sufficient quality are placed in a group with their peers and bring with them the completed assignment. Students who do not complete the individual assignment receive a separate assignment, or are placed in a group led by the teacher. The result is that every student who is placed in a peer-only group has already made a contribution by (1) demonstrating a willingness to work on the assignment and (2) developing a useful product.

When you create an assignment using this strategy, be sure to provide clear guidelines, and focus it specifically on tasks that will be useful to the group once it is formed. Here are some ideas for assignments that all students can be expected to prepare before group work begins.

- Data retrieval chart
- Map
- Lab sheet
- Experimental procedure
- Graphic organizer
- Background research paper
- Biographical sketch
- Idea list
- Concept map
- Venn diagram
- Problem solution

- Explanation/Description
- Story explication
- Creative writing sample
- Introductory paragraph
- Presentation plan
- Outline

A Bring-Something-to-the-Group Scenario

A social studies class is starting a project called "The Geography of Human Movement." Its focus is on historical movements of people. Students will work in small groups of three or four to trace the movements of specific people, and analyze the social, economic, and environmental forces or conditions that precipitated their migration. Before being placed in a group, each student is given the assignment to complete a graphic organizer. The graphic organizer provides spaces for answers regarding the who, what, when, where, why, and how of an assigned group of migrants.

Ella and Luis are members of the class. They have both been given as a topic the movement of Cherokee Indians from Georgia and North Carolina to Oklahoma. This means they will be partners in a small group studying this historical migration, upon demonstrating that they each have something to bring to the group. Ella gets right to work and completes the task. On the due date she turns in a correctly completed graphic organizer that contains a substantial amount of accurate information. Luis, on the other hand, does not complete the task. On the due date he hastily fills in some inadequate information and turns in the graphic organizer. After assessing the graphic organizers, the teacher returns them to the students along with their group placements. Ella is grouped with two other students to study the Trail of Tears. All three students in the group have demonstrated their readiness for this study and will bring their graphic organizers with them to their first meeting.

Luis, too, has been assigned to a group, in this case led by the teacher. The group will focus on a new, highly structured assignment. This system ensures that Luis, who has provided little evidence that he is ready and willing to participate in a group project, will not be a negative factor in a small group. At the same time, Luis is still actively involved in learning and is gaining more than if he had been a nonparticipating member of a small group.

See model project **The Mathematute** on pages 116–125 for another example of bring-something-to-the-group implementation.

Clock Partners

One method of quickly pairing students in a variety of ways for learning activities is to use clock partners. This is a very simple concept that can save time in the classroom and allow every student to have up to twelve predetermined partners, each presenting a unique challenge and potential for process, and often content, differentiation.

To implement the clock partners strategy, give each student a clock face template like the one shown on the following page.

You will assign a different partner for each hour on the clock face (following are some suggestions for how to do this). Some teachers like to assign twelve partners; some prefer to limit the number of partners to four, using only the 12 o'clock, 3 o'clock, 6 o'clock, and 9 o'clock slots. Once you have identified the partner pairings, have students record their partners' names on the template, one for each hour. Be sure that partners have coordinated their clocks (e.g., 12 o'clock partners each have the other's name recorded in the correct time slot).

When it is time for student pairs to work together on a learning activity, you can designate who the partners will be by saying something like this: "Please meet with your 3 o'clock partner and work on a solution to the problem." Students know who their 3 o'clock partners are and can smoothly form pairs to begin work.

Keep clock partners for an extended period of time so that transitions can become automatic. However, it is important to change them occasionally, just as you would periodically change the seating arrangement in your classroom.

Following are some suggestions for identifying clock partners. Using different criteria for each partner assignment allows you to more effectively use

SAMPLE CLOCK PARTNERS TEMPLATE

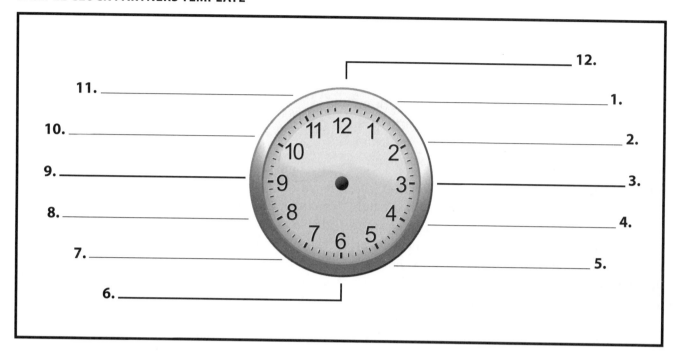

clock partners for a variety of tasks. Look at these pairing ideas and think about how each might be useful for certain kinds of collaborative activities.

1. Similar reading or math level: allows pairs to work from appropriately challenging resources

2. Different reading or math level: allows struggling students to work with more-advanced students

3. Interest: allows students who share certain interests to work together

4. Learning profile: uses intelligence type and/or preferred learning style as a basis for pairing

5. Teacher choice: uses knowledge of student compatibility to make pairings

6. Student choice: allows students to work with friends

7. Random: pairs students by chance

8. Technology skills: pairs technologically proficient students with less-skilled students

A Clock Partners Scenario

Alysha is in a math class where the teacher uses a clock partners system. At least once a week students work in pairs for part of the class to collaborate on problem solving, crosscheck each other's homework, work on math challenges, or participate in discovery or hands-on activities. Alysha has four clock partners: 12 o'clock, 3 o'clock, 6 o'clock, and 9 o'clock. Her partners were determined in the following way:

12 o'clock: Liam—This partner was assigned by the teacher. Liam and Alysha have similar levels of math skill development. On days when 12 o'clock partners work together, the tasks are different for each pair, depending on their readiness. Since Alysha and Liam are both exceptional math students, on 12 o'clock days they are asked to work together on challenging problems that require all of their collective skills and knowledge.

3 o'clock: Hazel—This partner was also assigned by the teacher. Unlike Alysha, Hazel struggles with math. The 3 o'clock partners often work on hands-on and discovery activities that require them to measure, construct, gather, and organize data; analyze solutions; work on puzzles; and so forth.

6 o'clock: Isabel—This partner was self-selected. Alysha chose her friend Isabel. On 6 o'clock days, partners typically crosscheck homework, work on problems of the day, participate in warm-up exercises, and so forth.

9 o'clock: Devan—This partner was randomly chosen. All of the students' names were placed in a bowl and then drawn out two at a time to determine partners. The 9 o'clock partners usually work on sample problems from the current unit, participate in 1–2–4 Present! activities (see pages 24–25 for more detail), and participate in class discussions.

When Alysha walks in the classroom at the beginning of a class period, she glances at the bulletin board. If a sign saying "Work with a partner today" is displayed, she knows that she will be working with one of her clock partners. Beneath the sign is a large clock face. A hand on the clock tells her which partner to join. Because the students have been trained to do this, the class begins with everyone finding the appropriate partner and sitting with him or her at the start of class. Without saying a word or wasting a minute, the teacher has initiated a "partner day" and begins instruction smoothly and on time.

See model project **Message in a Capsule** on pages 153–168 for another example of clock partners implementation.

Cubing

Cubing is a way of differentiating and adding novelty to the learning process. It allows students to approach material from various angles. Credit for developing the concept of cubing is generally given to Elizabeth and Gregory Cowan, who originally developed the cubing strategy as an approach to reading and writing. The beauty of the idea is its adaptability.

Just as a cube has six sides, a cubing activity offers an opportunity for students to explore a topic from six different perspectives. Each perspective is represented by a verb:

1. Describe
2. Compare
3. Associate
4. Analyze
5. Apply
6. Argue for or against

Begin thinking about cubing as a small group activity for reading and writing. After reading, divide the class into six small groups and assign each group one of the perspectives just listed. Each group's task is to compose a paragraph that looks at the reading from the assigned perspective. The groups share their paragraphs with the class, and the other students provide feedback and ideas. The small groups then reconvene and make needed revisions. Finally, the paragraphs are turned in and each one is mounted on one side of a large cardboard cube that is then displayed in the room. The display cube demonstrates how the reading can be viewed from each of the six perspectives.

You can modify this basic idea in a wide variety of ways, most notably by introducing an element of chance that is engaging for most students. Instead of assigning students to groups, have each student roll a numbered die to determine which perspective he or she will be assigned. Offer a second chance to roll so that a decision has to be made: Do I accept the results of my first roll, or do I try for one of the other perspectives?

You may also decide to group differently. For example, after rolling the die, students may be asked to work independently. Or, you might group two or three students together and have each roll the die, and then collaborate to combine their work. Another possibility is to group students by their readiness to learn, and differentiate the cubing tasks for each group.

In addition, different sets of verbs may be chosen for cubing activities, depending on the learning goals and content being covered. For example: demonstrate, compose, construct, illustrate, predict, classify.

A Cubing Scenario

In his English class, Nate has just finished reading the novel *Hatchet* by Gary Paulsen. Now he and his classmates will complete a writing assignment determined by a cubing activity. Each student will roll a die. The numbers on the die represent different writing assignments based on the story that the teacher pre-determined. When Nate rolls the die, the number that comes up becomes his assignment. He may choose to roll again, but if he does,

SAMPLE CUBING CHART

Number	Assignment
1	Describe how Brian used the hatchet and what it meant to him.
2	Compare Brian's first few days in the wilderness with his last few.
3	Associate Brian's thinking about food with how most people think about it.
4	Analyze "The Secret." What was it and why did Brian think about it a lot?
5	Apply the phrase "There were these things to do" to something in your life.
6	Argue for or against this statement: "What happened to Brian was good for him."

he must take whatever comes up the second time. See the cubing assignments in the above chart.

Nate rolls a 4 in his turn. Since "The Secret" is not his favorite topic, he decides to roll again and gets a 1 on his second try. His assignment is to describe how Brian used the hatchet and what it meant to him. Nate now joins a group of six, with each member having rolled a different number. The six group members' final essays, along with those of the rest of the students, are affixed to the six faces of a large cube and displayed in the classroom.

See model project **Continental Cubing Competition** on pages 84–95 for another example of cubing implementation.

Jigsaw Grouping

Jigsaw grouping is a strategy in which students are grouped, assigned roles, and regrouped in various ways, with a goal of maximizing interaction and cooperation. Elliot Aronson and his associates invented the jigsaw grouping strategy in 1971, in Austin, Texas. The city schools had just been desegregated and there was a serious problem of division among the various racial and ethnic groups in the public schools. Aronson discovered that the typical classroom was organized around individual competition for grades, which pitted student against student. The jigsaw strategy was developed to create a cooperative learning environment in which students depended on each other to supply necessary information as they prepared for tests.

Aronson's research showed that the jigsaw strategy had a significant positive effect on both social and academic growth.

Jigsaw grouping is accomplished by following these steps:

1. Put students into small "home base" groups of four or five.

2. Give the home base groups an overall assignment, such as preparing for a test, developing a presentation, or creating a display.

3. Develop the assignment so that it has the same number of unique components as there are students in each group. For example, if the content focus is body systems and there are four students in each group, then the four components of the assignment could be the respiratory system, circulatory system, nervous system, and digestive system.

4. Designate an area of expertise for each student in the home base group. For instance, in the assignment just described, one student will become a respiratory system expert; another will become a circulatory system expert, and so forth.

5. Reorganize students into "expert" groups. For example, all of the respiratory system experts will meet together to visit Web sites, read articles, study texts, examine models, analyze diagrams, and compile information on that topic.

6. Have students return to their home base groups. Each student's job is to share the knowledge he or she has gained in the expert group with the other home base group members.

7. Conduct the final assessment, demonstration, or performance.

You may group students in many ways, depending on your purposes. Aronson's goal was to intentionally mix students of diverse racial or ethnic backgrounds to promote cooperation and harmony. This may be your goal as well. Following is another way of grouping, also using the body systems example.

A Jigsaw Grouping Scenario

Amanda, Vinh, Estella, and Isaac are in a science class that is beginning a project on body systems. The class has been divided into home base groups of four. Amanda, Vinh, Estella, and Isaac make up Group A. Each student has been given a number. Amanda is 1, Vinh is 2, Estella is 3, and Isaac is 4. Their group can be represented like this:

SAMPLE JIGSAW HOME BASE GROUP

Amanda 1	Vinh 2
Estella 3	Isaac 4

There are twenty-eight students in the class, so there are seven home base groups. Each home base group is expected to develop a final product to explain the function of four different body systems (respiratory, circulatory, nervous, and digestive), and to describe how the four systems work together. The home base is a heterogeneous group. Amanda is an advanced science student, Vinh is an on-target student, Estella is a below-target student, and Isaac is a struggling student.

The project begins with home base groups discussing the assignment and completing preliminary tasks. They are given an assignment sheet and a detailed rubric to help guide them as they examine project expectations and determine what needs to be done.

The next step of the project is to jigsaw into expert groups. All of the students assigned the number 1 join together to study the nervous system. Students assigned number 2 meet to study the circulatory system, and so forth. The expert groups are homogeneous. In other words, the students Amanda works with in her expert group have all been assigned number 1 and are the most advanced learners in the class. They will study the nervous system. The students Isaac works with are all struggling to some extent. They will study the respiratory system. The other two expert groups will study the circulatory and digestive systems. Because the expert groups are homogeneous, the teacher can provide resources and materials differentiated by reading level and complexity of the content.

The expert groups work together for three to four class periods, studying their assigned topics, gathering and organizing information, completing data retrieval charts, and preparing to take the results of their work back to their home base groups. When Home Base Group A meets again, each person brings new expertise to the group. Amanda has learned a great deal about the nervous system. Vinh brings information about the circulatory system. Estella has become the group's expert on the digestive system, and Isaac shares information about the respiratory system with the group. The remainder of the project time is devoted to the home base groups completing a product that explains the function of each of the body systems and how they work together.

The chart on the following page shows how the jigsaw process just described works.

See model project **Hear Ye! Hear Ye!** on the CD-ROM for another example of jigsaw grouping implementation.

SAMPLE JIGSAW GROUPING CHART

Home Base Group A	Topic	Expert Groups in Horizontal Rows							Home Base Group A
1 Amanda	Nervous System *Advanced*	1A (Amanda)	1B	1C	1D	1E	1F	1G	1 Amanda
2 Vinh	Circulatory System *On-Target*	2A (Vinh)	2B	2C	2D	2E	2F	2G	2 Vinh
3 Estella	Digestive System *Below Target*	3A (Estella)	3B	3C	3D	3E	3F	3G	3 Estella
4 Isaac	Respiratory System *Struggling*	4A (Isaac)	4B	4C	4D	4E	4F	4G	4 Isaac
1 period	4 periods								3 periods

Kids-Teaching-Kids

One of the most powerful strategies for process differentiation that you can build into your instructional repertoire is the concept of kids teaching kids. In his book *How the Brain Learns,* educational consultant David Sousa presents a learning pyramid (see below) developed from studies of how well students retain information learned via different teaching methods.

THE LEARNING PYRAMID

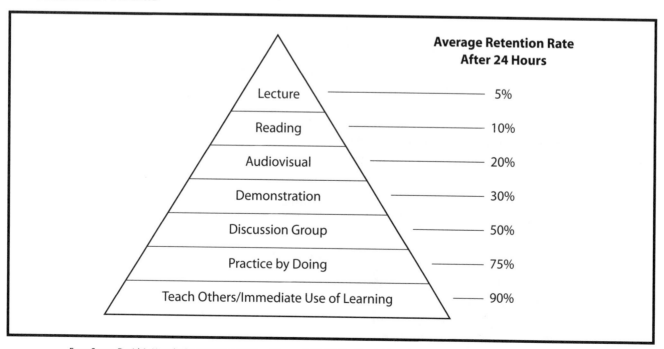

	Average Retention Rate After 24 Hours
Lecture	5%
Reading	10%
Audiovisual	20%
Demonstration	30%
Discussion Group	50%
Practice by Doing	75%
Teach Others/Immediate Use of Learning	90%

From Sousa, David A. *How the Brain Learns,* 3rd ed., p. 95, copyright 2006 by Corwin Press. Reprinted by Permission of Sage Publications, Inc.

The pyramid shows the average percentage of new learning that students recall twenty-four hours after being taught. (Retention after twenty-four hours indicates the memory is in long-term storage.)

Given these research findings, what should you do to ensure that your students retain essential information? You should have them teach it! It happens naturally all the time when children interact with each other. They routinely teach one another on their own, and when they do, you can observe the bottom two levels of the pyramid in action: "Practice by Doing" and "Teach Others/Immediate Use of Learning." Your goal is to harness the power of that process and incorporate it into the classroom.

You can accomplish the kids-teaching-kids strategy in many ways, ranging from simple to complex. Here are four examples of ways you can promote the strategy in your classroom:

1. Introduce "teachable moment" breaks into class instruction. Have students turn to a neighbor and explain in thirty seconds what has just been discussed. Then have the neighbor explain it back, using different terms or examples if possible. Randomly choose two or three pairs to share their explanations with the class. Before moving on, take time to add critical information if necessary and to correct any misconceptions that may have been mentioned.

2. Have students teach each other in small groups. For example, ask each student to study an assigned topic from the curriculum, join a partner assigned the same topic, and together prepare a one- to two-minute mini-lesson. This pair then joins another pair assigned a different topic, and the pairs teach one another.

3. Conduct small group projects requiring a final presentation that teaches the rest of the class about some aspect of the curriculum. It is critical that each student in the small group be an equal contributor to the lesson development and presentation. Also, small groups should focus on different topics to avoid boredom during presentations, and to ensure that each

presentation is based on original ideas and not copied from what previous groups did.

4. Designate a period of time when individual students are responsible for teaching the class. This could be one five-minute lesson presented each day by a different student. The requirements could include an oral presentation, a written report, a visual display, and a question-answer session with the audience. Topics should be directly related to the curriculum.

A Kids-Teaching-Kids Scenario

Darnell and Marissa are in a social studies class together. Their teacher, Mrs. Huff, has recently introduced an individualized presentation project that requires students to teach the class. Each student's task is to open a class period with a five-minute lesson about a self-selected topic that is connected to the curriculum and supports the content currently being covered. Mrs. Huff refers to the students doing this project as "resident experts," and she calls the presentations "openings." There are twenty-five students in the class, so the project will require five weeks to complete. Each day, one student will present an opening and share his or her expertise with an audience of peers. An opening consists of an oral presentation, a written report, a visual display, and a question-answer session.

Mrs. Huff introduced the project two weeks before the first opening was to be presented. After describing the requirements and expectations for student presentations, she conducted an "explore the text" activity with the class. Students joined partners to analyze the portion of the textbook the class planned to cover over the next seven to eight weeks. Darnell and Marissa worked together to examine the main text, along with pictures, charts, graphs, maps, sidebars, bold words, "What Do You Think?" questions, and so forth, to brainstorm ideas for interesting presentation topics. Following this activity, each pair contributed to a full group discussion that resulted in an extensive list of potential topics. Mrs. Huff made it clear that all topics were to be chosen from this list, and that every student must choose a unique topic—no duplications were allowed.

Obviously, when only one student presents each day, some students have less time to prepare than others. To help compensate for this disparity in preparation time, Mrs. Huff had three perks to offer students who volunteered to go first:

1. She offered "motivated learner" credit to the first five presenters. In other words, while extra credit is usually awarded for doing additional work, these students would earn extra credit for giving their presentations early, because they not only would have less time to prepare, but they would also serve as models for others.

2. She announced that students would choose their topics in the same order as they were presenting, meaning that the first person to present would also get first choice of topic, and the last person to present would be the last one to choose.

3. She pointed out that procrastination is alive and well in most students, and therefore those who go later are likely to just wait longer before starting to work on their presentations. Volunteering to go early provides the relief of getting the project over with and then not having to worry about it.

Mrs. Huff asked everyone who wished to volunteer to be an early presenter to write his or her name on a slip of paper and put it in a bowl. There were eleven volunteers, including Darnell. She then drew names out of the bowl, one at a time, to determine the order of presentation for the volunteers and also to identify the five students who would receive "motivated learner" credit. Darnell was the third name drawn, which meant he would get third choice of topic and the extra credit he wanted. At this point, Mrs. Huff asked the remaining students to put their names in the bowl along with the six volunteers' names not drawn initially. Then she drew to determine the presentation (and topic selection) order for the rest of the class.

See model projects **The Candidates' Debate** on pages 64–83 and **Hear Ye! Hear Ye!** on the CD-ROM for more examples of kids-teaching-kids implementation.

Task Sheets

A valuable strategy for differentiating process and ensuring student engagement is the use of task sheets (also called task cards, work cards, or task assignments). Students are more likely to be engaged and focused if they clearly understand what they are supposed to do and have the freedom to work at their own pace. Task sheets provide specific guidelines that students can follow independently. Using well-designed task sheets allows students to start work on an assignment immediately and frees the teacher up to answer questions, deal with problems, and monitor progress rather than spending valuable time explaining the assignment.

Task sheets are often combined with other differentiation strategies, such as choice boards. For example, students enter the classroom and find their names on a list that indicates which choices are available to them (e.g., "William Smith, you may choose any task from row A"). Next, they go to the choice board to see what the choices are, then choose a task and pick up a task sheet from a folder. The task sheets may be graphic organizers or activity guidelines.

Here are some ideas for developing task sheets. Be sure to include clear directions, as the sheets lose their value if you still have to explain to students what they are expected to do.

KWL Chart: This is a three-column chart that students fill out before and after they read or participate in a learning activity. The "K" column is what the student knows (or thinks she knows); the "W" column is what the student wants to know (or what he wonders about); the "L" column is what the student has learned.

Venn Diagram: This is the familiar diagram of overlapping circles that students use to compare and contrast two concepts, theories, opinions, characters, events, and so forth.

Data Retrieval Chart: This is a matrix in which students record information discovered through research. For example, across the top row could be five pre-Columbus Native American groups. Along the left side could be five categories such as dwellings, food, weapons/tools, clothing, and beliefs.

Students enter data into each of the twenty-five cells to complete the chart.

Two-Column Note Taking: Two-column notes help students organize their thinking and are great analysis tools. Sheryn Spencer Northey advocates the use of two-column notes in *Handbook on Differentiated Instruction for Middle and High Schools*. Here are five left-right column types that she mentions:

1. Main Idea—Supporting Details
2. Compare—Contrast
3. Opinion—Proof (or Fact)
4. Vocabulary—Definition
5. Problem—Solution[7]

Assignment Checklist: This is a list of required tasks that students check off as they are completed. For example:

☐ Begin a KWL chart.

☐ Read Chapter 7.

☐ Choose a topic from the list provided by your teacher.

☐ Find two additional sources of information.

☐ Compose an imaginary journal entry in the voice of a person from the chapter.

☐ Use the journal entry to explain why an event took place.

☐ Complete the KWL chart.

A Task Sheets Scenario

Ms. Johnson's English class has just finished reading novels. Several novels were offered as options and each student chose one to read. Ms. Johnson differentiated the class by reading level, so each student chose from a reading list that was tailored to his or her readiness. Now that the reading is complete, the students will begin work on projects based on what they have read. The projects, too, are differentiated. Students know that on the day the project begins, they will receive task sheets that specify what they are to do. They are expected to

follow directions independently to complete their assigned tasks.

Jonathan and Kenya are in Ms. Johnson's class. They are both advanced readers. Jonathan read the novel *Hatchet* by Gary Paulsen. Kenya read *Island of the Blue Dolphin* by Scott O'Dell. When they come to class on the day projects begin, they immediately go to the task board to see what their assignments are. Jonathan finds this instruction next to his name on the task board: "Work with Kenya on Task #6." And, of course, Kenya finds this: "Work with Jonathan on Task #6." Each of them pulls a copy of Task Sheet #6 from the task sheets folder to find out what they will be doing together. While other students tackle a variety of different tasks, Kenya and Jonathan begin working on their assigned task, outlined on the following page.

See model project **You Gotta Have an Angle** on the CD-ROM for another example of task sheets implementation.

Tiered Assignments

Tiered assignments are intentional efforts to accommodate the range of learning needs found in any classroom. The most common reason for creating tiered assignments is to differentiate by readiness, as a way to provide for struggling, on-target, and advanced learners. All students are expected to focus on essential content and skills, but the assignments are differentiated so that each student is faced with tasks that meet his or her individual needs. This means that there is more than one way for students to reach the same basic learning goals. Each assignment is a tier (think of stairway steps); the higher the tier, the more complex or challenging the assignment.

In a typical classroom, there might be three tiered assignments developed for a given unit. Using pre-assessment information to determine readiness, the teacher gives each student whichever assignment is most appropriate. There is no rule for how many students should be at each tier. There may be only a few assigned to the top tier while the majority work at the middle tier.

It is critical that each tier provide respectful work that reflects the learning goals of the unit. It should never be the case that lower tier students are

[7] *Handbook on Differentiated Instruction for Middle and High Schools* by Sheryn Spencer Northey (Eye on Education, 2005), p. 56.

SAMPLE TASK SHEET

Task #6

Participants:

For this task, one of you has read *Hatchet* and the other has read *Island of the Blue Dolphin*. Your task is to analyze the two novels by completing the chart below. For each question, describe what is unique to the story of *Hatchet*, what is unique to the story of *Island of the Blue Dolphin*, and what is the same for both stories.

Question	Hatchet	Island of the Blue Dolphin	Same for Both Stories
What is the setting for the story?			
What is the plot of the story?			
What are some traits of the main character?			
What key challenges does the main character face?			
What general theme or universal truth can be found in the story?			

completing worksheets while higher tier students are doing something active and exciting. Assignments should be similar, and everybody in the class should be equally engaged in their work.

Diane Heacox identifies six ways to structure tiered assignments:

1. Challenge: Each tier focuses on a different level of Bloom's taxonomy (see pages 25–27 for more detail).

2. Complexity: Each tier focuses on a different level of abstraction, analysis, in-depth investigation, or advanced concepts.

3. Resources: Each tier utilizes different resources at appropriate reading levels or depth of coverage.

4. Outcome: Each tier utilizes the same resources, but requires a different application of learning (outcome).

5. Process: Each tier has the same outcome, but utilizes a different process to get there.

6. Product: Each tier has a different product expectation, often based on intelligence type.[8]

A Tiered Assignments Scenario

A simple example of a tiered assignment in social studies might be:

Tier 1 (struggling learners): Study an assigned event from a timeline. Use available resources to find out what happened during this event—who, what, and when. Write a report or make a poster that describes the event.

Tier 2 (on-target learners): Choose an event from a timeline. Use available resources, along with resources that you find on your own, to help you discover why the event happened. Write a report or make a poster that explains what caused this event to take place.

Tier 3 (advanced learners): Choose an event from the timeline. Find resources to help you discover why this event happened and what the results of the event were. Write a report or make a poster that explains the significance of the event in history.

On the following page is a planning tool, based on Heacox's six methods of tiering, which may be used for developing such an assignment. This particular planner is based on a project found later in this book titled "Moments in Time" in which students study an event from a timeline.

See model projects **Continental Cubing Competition** on pages 84–95, **The Mathematute** on pages 116–125, **Moments in Time** on pages 169–197, and **Hear Ye! Hear Ye!** on the CD-ROM for more examples of tiered assignments implementation.

[8] *Differentiating Instruction in the Regular Classroom* by Diane Heacox (Free Spirit Publishing, 2002), pp. 91–94.

Differentiating Product

Anchor Activities

When students work independently or in small groups, it is inevitable that some will complete the basic requirements before others. The answer to the age-old question "What do I do now?" lies in providing meaningful, engaging tasks to which students may turn their attention once they have completed an assignment. These tasks are not merely time-fillers, but are intended to ensure that all kids are focused on the curriculum at all times, so as to extend learning. Such tasks are called anchor (or "sponge") activities, and they are an important key to successfully implementing differentiated instruction.

Anchor activities may be short, straightforward activities that can be completed in one class period or less, such as solving challenge math problems or developing entries for a "Did You Know?" bulletin board. Or, they may be more complex projects that students can be involved with whenever opportunities arise, such as composing a short story or tracking and analyzing over time the performance of certain stocks on the stock market. In either case, students must be able to smoothly transition from class assignment to anchor activity without disrupting the classroom or demanding any of the teacher's time.

Here is a set of guidelines that will be helpful as you utilize anchor activities with your students:

1. Establish clear quality expectations for class assignments to ensure that students don't move on to an anchor activity after turning in hastily completed or incorrect assignment work. A rubric is useful in this regard.

2. Put a class list next to the tray, folder, or other assignment repository, and have students check off their names when they turn in a class assignment. At the top of the sheet, include a statement such as "By checking my name in the list below, I verify that I have completed and turned in a high-quality assignment that represents my best work."

3. Make anchor activities readily available in the classroom. For example, put a sign on a wall

SAMPLE TIERED ASSIGNMENT PLANNER FOR "MOMENTS IN TIME"

Tier 1 (Red Assignment Sheet)—Struggling Learners

Tier 2 (Blue Assignment Sheet)—On-Target Learners

Tier 3 (Green Assignment Sheet)—Advanced Learners

Standards: (apply to all learners)	**1)** Students use key concepts such as causality, change, conflict, and complexity to explain, analyze, and show connections among patterns of historical change and continuity. **2)** Students describe selected historical periods and patterns of change within and across cultures, such as the rise in civilization, the development of transportation systems, the growth and breakdown of colonial systems, and others. **3)** Students identify and use processes important to reconstructing and reinterpreting the past, such as using a variety of resources; providing, validating, and weighing evidence for claims; checking credibility of sources; and searching for causality. **4)** Students analyze group and institutional influences on people, events, and elements of culture.

Tier	Challenge	Complexity	Resources	Outcome	Process	Product
1	Students study an assigned topic, or choose from a limited set of topics	Assignment is straightforward with little ambiguity and plenty of support	Plenty of quality resources are readily available at appropriate reading levels	Outcome is based on content standards; the same for all students	Highly structured, with templates for students to follow	The same basic product is required of all students
2	Students choose any topic other than those deemed by the teacher to be too challenging	Assignment has some ambiguity, meaning there is no single right answer, response, or solution	Some resources are available, but students have responsibility to locate their own	Outcome is based on content standards; the same for all students	General guidelines are provided to help students complete required tasks	The same basic product is required of all students
3	Students choose any topic other than those reserved for Tier 1	Assignment is open-ended, with multiple possible answers, responses, or solutions	Students are entirely responsible for finding their own resources	Outcome is based on content standards; the same for all students	Suggestions are provided, but students develop their own approach	The same basic product is required of all students

that says, "This Week's Anchor Activities," and in trays beneath it place instructions for each activity.

4. Provide a detailed instruction sheet or task-completion checklist that will allow students to confidently work on the anchor activity independently.

5. Institute an efficient procedure for turning in completed work. Students should have a specific place to deposit both their finished class assignments and anchor activities, rather than tracking you down and handing them to you or just laying them on your desk.

Start slowly with anchor activities, to help both you and your students grow accustomed to their use. Carol Ann Tomlinson advises teachers to begin by introducing an anchor activity and having half of the class work on it while the other half engages in a regular content-related assignment. Then, flip the groups so all students begin to see how the anchor activity process works. As she says, "Do whatever feels best to phase you and your students into an environment where multiple avenues to learning are the norm. Ultimately, your aim is to have all students understand that when they complete a given assignment, they must automatically move to an anchor activity and work with that activity with care and concentration."[9]

An Anchor Activities Scenario

Joshua and Grace are part of a science class that is engaged in an individualized classroom project. The project is designed to last three days, and students have been given an assignment sheet, task checklist, and rubric to help guide their work. The project has several parts. Briefly, it requires students to develop a macro and a micro water cycle description, explanation, and representation. The macro level looks at the water cycle as a big-picture, weather-related process. The micro level looks at the water cycle at a molecular level. Students work independently to complete the project requirements.

Joshua is a fast worker and loves science. He tackles the project with gusto and even takes some of it home the first night. Grace is more methodical and less motivated to learn about science. Her goal is to get the project done on time, but she is not interested in speeding up the process or going further with the science. Ultimately, both Joshua and Grace complete projects of equal quality, but Joshua is done midway through the second day while Grace finishes at the end of the third day.

When Joshua turns in his completed project on day two, he does not approach the teacher and ask, "I'm done—now what do I do?" Instead, he goes to a designated place in the room to turn in his project. There he finds a class list and checks off his name to indicate he has turned in a quality project. He then proceeds to an area of the room marked with a sign that says, "Anchor Area: Please choose one of the four anchor activities in the trays on the table. Follow directions to complete the task." Joshua peruses the anchor activities and chooses one that appeals to him. Here are the options available:

- Discover how the water cycle is involved in changing Earth's surface.

- Write an adventure story in which the main character is a drop of water.

- Examine the structure and characteristics of the water molecule.

- Create an entry for the classroom's "Did You Know?" bulletin board that focuses on violent weather.

Joshua understands that he can use the remainder of the class time designated for the original project to complete his chosen anchor activity. He may or may not get extra credit for the activity (this is up to the teacher), but he is expected to make his time meaningful and worthwhile. He may be asked to present his completed anchor activity to the class. In the end, both Joshua and Grace have been actively engaged for the entire project period of three days because anchor activities have been employed to accommodate the natural tendency of students to complete their work at different rates.

See model projects **Life on Planet X** on pages 126–152 and **Math Investment Plan** on pages

---

[9] *How to Differentiate Instruction in Mixed-Ability Classrooms,* 2nd ed. by Carol Ann Tomlinson (ASCD, 2001), p. 35.

96–115 for more examples of anchor activities implementation.

Choice Boards

Choice boards offer a way for students to self-select appropriate assignments. They can be used in many ways; three different implementation ideas are presented here as examples. Create your own choice board plan to fit your unique classroom needs.

Choice Boards: Version One

A teacher offers full class instruction the first three days of the week. On the other two days, students participate in differentiated activities. When they walk into the classroom on Thursday, each student goes to the choice board to see what his or her options are. The choice board has three rows labeled A, B, and C. There are at least two activity options in each row. The teacher tells each student which row he or she may choose from, based on demonstrated proficiency with the curriculum covered in the previous three days. The options in Row A are designed for students who need help with basic concepts. Row B offers applications of the material covered in the curriculum. Row C provides tasks that require students to analyze and synthesize information. Students choose tasks from their assigned rows, and go to designated areas of the room to work.

Choice Boards: Version Two

A teacher has developed a project that students must complete individually. It covers basic content and skills required by the curriculum, and everyone has two weeks to complete the project. Because students work at different rates and there is a range of readiness in the class, the teacher expects that students will finish the project in a staggered manner. To accommodate the varying amounts of time needed by students, the teacher has created a choice board that offers activities requiring anywhere from one to four class periods to complete. There are several one-period activities, fewer two- and three-period activities, and only one four-period activity. Students who finish the class project early may choose any combination of activities

to equal the number of days remaining in the two-week project window. For example, a student who finishes the project at the end of the first week has five class periods available. He or she may choose any of these combinations of activities from the choice board:

- 1 four-period activity and 1 one-period activity
- 1 three-period activity and 1 two-period activity
- 1 three-period activity and 2 one-period activities
- 2 two-period activities and 1 one-period activity
- 1 two-period activity and 3 one-period activities
- 5 one-period activities

Choice Boards: Version Three

A teacher provides a two-week window (ten class periods) for students to work on individualized activities all related to course content. Students choose activities from a choice board that has three rows: A, B, and C. Every row contains several activity options, each with a designated amount of completion time, from one to four class periods. Students must choose at least one activity from each row, and all activities must add up to ten class periods. Each row represents a part of the content area (for example, if it were social studies, row A might focus on history, row B on geography, and row C on economics; there could also be a row D that focuses on civics). The rows could also be differentiated by challenge or complexity, or they could represent three intelligence types, such as visual/spatial, verbal/linguistic, and mathematical/logical.

A Choice Boards Scenario

On the following page is an example of a choice board that could be used for either Version Two or Version Three of the strategy. The content area is social studies; each row comprises a strand. Each column represents an amount of completion time.

See model project **Life on Planet X** on pages 126–152 for another example of choice boards implementation.

SAMPLE CHOICE BOARD

	1 Class Period	2 Class Periods	3 Class Periods	4 Class Periods
A History	Complete a data retrieval chart for a person chosen from a "historical figures" list provided by your teacher.	Construct a timeline that includes at least 10 events from the period being studied. Identify what you think is the most important event and why.	Write an article about the impact of a major decision made in U.S. history during the period being studied. Use the voice of a journalist from that time.	Create a visual display that describes the impact of an important person, event, institution, or invention from the time period being studied.
B Geography	Locate a city or populated area on a map and explain why humans chose to live there.	Construct a timeline that tracks the movement of a specific group of people from one geographic area to another, and explain why this movement occurred.	Write an article about the consequences of human interactions with the environment, and cite a specific event from the time period and/or region being studied. Use the voice of a journalist from that time.	Create a visual display that identifies and describes how and why people, goods, services, and information moved within and between regions in the U.S. during the period being studied.
C Economics	Complete a graphic organizer that shows and explains select economic indicators and forms of economic measurement.	Construct a timeline that shows the history of a commodity, such as oil, and graphically illustrates the concept of supply and demand.	Write an article about a specific event in U.S. history that shows how supply and demand, prices, incentives, and profits determine what is produced and distributed in the American economy.	Create a visual display that shows the life and accomplishments of a successful entrepreneur and illustrates the importance of concepts like business practices, profits, and the willingness to take risks.

Choice-as-Motivator

Probably the simplest way to differentiate instruction is to give students opportunities to make choices. When students are allowed to make choices, they take more ownership in their work. They gain a sense of independence and feel that they are trusted to make decisions. Most books on differentiated instruction do not explicitly list choice as a differentiation strategy, but nearly all emphasize the importance of choice in one way or another. Choice actually is a specific strategy that can be implemented without dramatically changing what is currently being taught.

When offering students choice, the key to success is to start small. Offering some choice is far better than permitting no choice at all. If you tell your students they have two options and the choice is theirs, you are differentiating your class infinitely more than if you say, "This is what you will do." Two is the magic number. Once you have managed two choices for students, three and beyond will come in time. Remember: Two is infinitely greater than zero, but three is just one more than two.

The projects in this book primarily use choice to differentiate product, however you can build choice into any of the three curricular elements: content (input), process (activity), and product (output).

A Choice-as-Motivator Scenario

A social studies teacher offers the choices below to differentiate instruction within a particular unit.

CONTENT

Choice 1: Describe the impact of George Washington's presidency on U.S. history.

Choice 2: Describe the impact of Thomas Jefferson's presidency on U.S. history.

PROCESS

Choice 1: Work on your own to complete a data retrieval chart about an assigned topic.

Choice 2: Work with a partner to compare and contrast two assigned topics.

PRODUCT

Choice 1: Produce a diary or journal and present it in the voice of someone living at the time.

Choice 2: Produce a multimedia final presentation.

See model projects **The Candidates' Debate** on pages 64–83, **Message in a Capsule** on pages 153–168, and **Time Traveler** on the CD-ROM, for more examples of choice-as-motivator implementation.

Multiple Intelligences

Teachers who differentiate instructional activities or products by learning profile tend to focus on multiple intelligences, which were originally described by Howard Gardner in his seminal 1983 work *Frames of Mind: The Theory of the Multiple Intelligences* and expanded on later in *Intelligence Reframed: Multiple Intelligences for the 21st Century.* Although there are additional factors that influence a student's learning profile (such as learning style, gender, and culture) and there are other theories of intelligence, Gardner's multiple intelligence theory still receives by far the most attention.

Eight intelligences have been identified thus far by Gardner.[10] It is important to understand that everyone possesses some measure of all eight intelligences, and that each student is almost always strong in more than one. Traditional classroom instruction has placed an extreme emphasis on verbal/linguistic and logical/mathematical intelligences while virtually ignoring the others. This approach forces a surprising number of students to operate outside their comfort zone nearly all of the time. Imagine never being asked to put your best foot forward to demonstrate what you know and can do!

It is not necessary to differentiate everything you teach eight ways. By occasionally offering instruction that has been differentiated by multiple intelligence, you are sending a strong message to students that you understand how they think and learn best, and that you value them as individuals. Even if you choose just two of the intelligences to focus on each time you differentiate in this way, over time you will cover them all in various combinations and will have greatly helped your students discover their strengths as learners.

Here is a quick review of the eight intelligences identified by Gardner:

Verbal/Linguistic ("Word Smart"): Students prefer to learn by listening, talking, and following written or verbal directions. They like to read and write. A textbook- or lecture-based class is perfectly suited to them.

Logical/Mathematical ("Number Smart"): Students prefer to learn by applying number, computing, and logic skills. They like to look for patterns and relationships through classifying and sequencing activities.

---

[10] More intelligences have been suggested and explored but do not, as of yet, meet all the required criteria.

Visual/Spatial ("Picture Smart"): Students prefer to learn by working with pictures, models, and graphic organizers. They like to create and manipulate images to represent ideas, and perform other spatial tasks.

Bodily/Kinesthetic ("Body Smart"): Students prefer to learn through physical activities, such as building models or using manipulatives to solve problems. They like to be active and move while they learn.

SAMPLE MULTIPLE INTELLIGENCES CHART

Multiple Intelligence	Option A	Option B
Verbal/ Linguistic	Write a story that could be made into a skit.	Prepare a report that could be presented orally as a lecture.
Logical/ Mathematical	Create a graph, table, or chart that could be used to help a presenter explain the topic.	Create a graphic organizer that shows how facts or concepts are related, using lines, symbols, matrices, numbers, or some other system that you develop.
Visual/Spatial	Create a picture or drawing that could help a presenter explain the topic.	Create a concept map that uses shapes, patterns, colors, or drawings to show how facts and concepts are linked or connected.
Musical/ Rhythmic	Create a song that explains the topic by writing lyrics that go with a familiar tune.	Create a rap that explains the topic; write lyrics in a rap format that clearly present information about the topic.
Interpersonal	Coordinate a small group presentation by recruiting at least two other students to join you in making a presentation to the class. You will plan, organize, and produce the presentation, and create materials to make it complete.	Coordinate a small group display by recruiting at least three other students to let you combine their products to create an attractive, informative display. You will plan the display and explain how it would be used on TV.
Intrapersonal	Compose a reflection journal in the voice of someone who has firsthand knowledge of the topic.	Think of a "why" question that applies to the topic being studied, then develop an answer that can be used as part of a "Did You Ever Wonder Why…?" TV program segment.
Naturalist	Develop a method of organizing information about the topic into a classification system.	Produce a collection of artifacts and organize them into an exhibit.
Bodily/ Kinesthetic	Create a one-person skit that explains the topic. You will perform the skit, with your class as the audience.	Develop a demonstration of some aspect of the topic. For example, you might show how (1) an experiment is conducted, (2) a process works, (3) a concept map is organized, (4) a timeline is constructed, (5) a cycle is represented, (6) an event took place, or (7) a graph is built.

Musical/Rhythmic ("Music Smart"): Students prefer to learn by listening to, or engaging in, musical and rhythmic activities. They like to dance and compose, play, or conduct music.

Interpersonal ("People Smart"): Students prefer to learn and work collaboratively. They like to participate in cooperative games, group projects, discussions, dramatic activities, and role-playing activities.

Intrapersonal ("Self Smart"): Students prefer to learn independently, through reflective thinking. They like to explore their inner world of emotions and thoughts via independent projects and journal writing.

Naturalist ("Nature Smart"): Students prefer to learn by observing, categorizing, and classifying. They like to explore nature, understand the world of plants and animals, and collect, study, and group objects.

A Multiple Intelligences Scenario

The table on the previous page indicates how a project might be organized around the multiple intelligences. It is based on a science project that asks students to develop a presentation for a television show about a science topic. Each student is allowed to choose a product to contribute to the show, and the product choices are differentiated by multiple intelligence.

See model projects **One World** on pages 198–224, **The Mathematute** on pages 116–125, and **The Candidates' Debate** on pages 64–83 for more examples of multiple intelligences implementation.

Tic-Tac-Toe

Educator Susan Winebrenner is generally given credit for developing the concept of tic-tac-toe menus. The idea is simple: Create nine learning or performance tasks related to the content and skills being taught, and put each in a square of a tic-tac-toe board. Allow students to choose any three tasks that line up vertically, horizontally, or diagonally. There are eight possible combinations of tasks and thus eight different ways for students to complete

the assignment. The tasks may be arranged so that some are simple and some are more complex.

Begin each task with an active verb. For example, here are nine tasks that could be included on a tic-tac-toe menu for a study of animals and ecosystems, based on middle school content standards:

1. Compare and contrast the classification characteristics of a bird with those of an insect.

2. Demonstrate how changes in one population of an ecosystem may affect other populations.

3. Explain how two body systems or processes function together in an animal of your choice.

4. Construct an authentic food web that contains at least 12 life forms.

5. Describe a body system or process for an animal of your choice: what it does and how it works.

6. Diagram the flow of energy in an ecosystem from its source to a top predator.

7. Define these terms: natural balance, population, dependence, and biodiversity.

8. Compare and contrast the classification characteristics of a fish with those of a mammal.

9. Describe three survival adaptations for an animal of your choice.

One way to effectively differentiate using a tic-tac-toe menu is to put the two most challenging or complex tasks in the upper left and upper right corners. Thus, the most challenging three-in-a-row will be the top row. You can require your most able learners to include at least one of those corners in their selections (this allows five possible assignment combinations), while your struggling learners may choose the middle vertical column or the middle or bottom horizontal row, which include the less challenging tasks.

The Winebrenner model for using tic-tac-toe menus includes putting the menu on a handout along with a mini-learning contract that requires a student signature and date. The contract asks students to commit to three specific tasks, and also provides an option for them to suggest an alternate task that would take the place of one of the tasks on the menu.

A Tic-Tac-Toe Menus Scenario

Below is a sample tic-tac-toe menu based on the standards just listed. The menu is arranged so that the upper left and upper right tasks are the most challenging, making the top row more difficult than the others. Your advanced learners must include at least one of those corners in their selections, while your struggling learners may choose the middle vertical column or the middle or bottom horizontal row. The bottom row is the least challenging set of tasks.

See model project **One World** on pages 198–224 for another example of tic-tac-toe implementation.

SAMPLE TIC-TAC-TOE MENU

Choose any combination of three tasks that make a straight tic-tac-toe line (up and down, across, or diagonal) and record the task numbers in the spaces below the chart. There are eight possible task combinations.

1. Demonstrate how changes in one population of an ecosystem may affect other populations.	**2.** Compare and contrast the classification characteristics of a bird with those of an insect.	**3.** Explain how two body systems or processes function together in an animal of your choice.
4. Describe a body system or process for an animal of your choice: what it does and how it works.	**5.** Define these terms: natural balance, population, dependence, and biodiversity.	**6.** Diagram the flow of energy in an ecosystem from its source to a top predator.
7. Construct an authentic food web that contains at least 12 life forms.	**8.** Describe three survival adaptations for an animal of your choice.	**9.** Compare and contrast the classification characteristics of a fish with those of a mammal.

I have decided to complete these three tasks to make a tic-tac-toe:

You may propose an alternate task to replace one of the tasks in your tic-tac-toe if you have something in mind that goes along with the animal unit. Describe your idea in the space below and then talk with your teacher to get approval.

Alternate Task proposal, to replace Task #_____:

Student Signature:

Date:

Teacher Signature:

Date:

PART 2

The Model Projects

Introduction to the Model Projects

The material in this book is based on the premise that the most effective projects are ones that engage students' imagination with learning that is interesting and relevant. Simply put, we want students to be internally motivated to direct their own learning. The projects in this book have been developed for that purpose. They are ready to use as-is, while also infused with flexibility, to accommodate your individual needs. With modifications, each project format could be used to reach your specific classroom goals and to teach a variety of content to students within a broad age range. This is important to keep in mind as you contemplate using the projects that follow.

We strongly encourage you to take a few minutes to browse through the projects and examine them without regard to their content designation. Look at how the projects are designed, what students are asked to do, and what they produce. Ask yourself whether the project *scenario (content), process,* and/ or *product* would engage and motivate your students. Regardless of the subject you teach, or the age of your students, consider how any given project could be modified to work in your classroom. For example, the English/language arts project titled "Continental Cubing Competition" is based on a trivia contest concept and provides reproducible handouts that are differentiated using tiering. Although the project materials are currently tied to English/language arts standards, with some modification in content and task requirements, these same materials could be used in any discipline across the curriculum. For example, in a math class students might compete to solve a given problem using one of six different problem-solving methods. Likewise, the science project "Life on Planet X" now involves documenting life forms on a newly discovered planet. However, with some rethinking, the project could instead focus on the geography and natural resources of the planet (social studies), on the surveying of landforms using graphs (math), or on media stories reporting on the discovery (English/language arts).

Suggested content modifications like this are included at the end of every Project Planner.

Use the Project Organizer on pages 226–227 to analyze individual projects for your own use. It may help you realize, for example, that as a social studies teacher, you could make great use of "The Candidates' Debate" English/language arts project, or that your English/language arts students would love the "Message in a Capsule" science project.

Project-based activities provide a context for learning and teaching. Structure the projects in this book around the standards that you teach to and the processes that you believe will resonate with your students. May these materials serve as a catalyst to enliven the minds and personalities that live and breathe in your classroom every day.

Creating Assessment Rubrics

A rubric is a clear description of the criteria and standards by which a product, performance, demonstration, or other outcome will be assessed or developed. The criteria and standards specify what a student will know, produce, or be able to do in a given situation.

The assessment checklists included with the projects in this book provide a quick and efficient way to communicate project expectations and give direct feedback to students; they can be developed into more-detailed rubrics, should you choose to do so. Instead of providing multiple rubrics for each project to cover all the ways a project could be taught, we offer here some background information and tips for you to create your own.

A rubric consists of three basic components:

1. Specific assessment items based on key requirements of the assignment (down the left side)

2. Numbered levels (across the top) that represent a continuum of quality expectations for each assessment item

3. Specific descriptors for each cell in the rubric matrix

A sample rubric is provided on the following page.

SAMPLE ASSESSMENT RUBRIC FOR "CONTINENTAL CUBING COMPETITION"

Name of Project: Continental Cubing Competition, Assignment Sheet 3, Task 1: Compose an Essay, pages 92–93

Content Standards:

1) Students apply a wide range of strategies to comprehend, interpret, evaluate, and appreciate texts. They draw on their prior experience, their interactions with other readers and writers, their knowledge of word meaning and of other texts, their word-identification strategies, and their understanding of textual features (e.g., sound-letter correspondence, sentence structure, context, graphics).

2) Students adjust their use of spoken, written, and visual language (e.g., conventions, style, vocabulary) to communicate effectively with a variety of audiences and for different purposes.

3) Students employ a wide range of strategies as they write and use different writing-process elements appropriately to communicate with different audiences for a variety of purposes.

4) Students apply knowledge of language structure, language conventions (e.g., spelling and punctuation), media techniques, figurative language, and genre to create, critique, and discuss print and nonprint texts.

Assessment Item	Level 4 Exceeded Expectations	Level 3 Achieved Expectations	Level 2 Needs Time to Achieve Expectations	Level 1 Provided Little or No Evidence of Achieving Expectations
Composed an essay	Wrote a piece that exceeded a Level 3 through the use of rich, varied, precise vocabulary, complex sentence structures, and ideas that were clearly connected to the topic.	Wrote a piece that was grammatically correct, was logically organized, was consistent in its development, and contained few unrelated ideas.	Wrote a piece that was grammatically correct part of the time; organization was uneven, and ideas were at times vague or unrelated.	Wrote a piece that was often grammatically incorrect; little organization was evident, and ideas were confused or not related to the topic.
Demonstrated a general understanding of how authors highlight differences among characters as a writing technique	Explained why authors strive to show differences among characters, and cited examples from the story to illustrate why this is an important aspect of storytelling.	Cited examples in the story where characters were shown to be different through traits such as gender, race, culture, age, dress, class, physical size, intelligence, social status, economic standing, religion, and so forth.	Demonstrated some understanding of how authors highlight differences among characters, but struggled to provide solid examples.	Offered little insight into the technique of highlighting differences among characters.
Described the author's use of distortion and stereotypes to highlight individual differences among characters	Compared and contrasted characters to provide clear, insightful examples of the author's use of distortion and stereotypes; explained why this technique contributes to character development in the story.	Correctly described the author's use of distortion or stereotypes to show differences between at least two characters, and cited details and examples from the story to show how this was done.	Provided a vague or general explanation of distortion and stereotypes, but without enough specific detail to make it clear how the author used the technique.	Provided little or no evidence of understanding what distortion or stereotypes are or how the author used them.
Demonstrated a commitment to quality	Demonstrated a desire to continue working on the piece until it met with personal standards of excellence; actively sought input on quality and made changes accordingly.	Demonstrated a willingness to listen to constructive criticism, recognize that things can be improved through revision, and take the time to make suggested changes.	Made changes when required to, but took little personal initiative to improve work; inclined to accept first attempt as best attempt.	Showed little evidence of wanting to produce quality work; did not make changes when asked, or made minimal changes that did not improve quality.

Basic Process for Developing and Using an Assessment Rubric

1. **Identify standards.** Base the project assignment on targeted content standards from the subject area and grade level that you teach.

2. **Identify assessment items.** These are key requirements of the assignment based on how you plan to teach it. Enter each of these in a different cell down the left-hand column of the rubric.

3. **Develop criteria for each assessment item.** Articulate how students will show that they have met the requirements of the assignment. Write detailed descriptions of what would represent a 4, 3, 2, and 1 level of quality for each assessment item. Show a continuum of quality as the levels progress within each category (see "Using a 4-3-2-1 Scoring System" that follows).

4. **Involve students.** An effective way to gain student ownership and teach the class about rubrics is to hold a class discussion and develop the rubric together.

   - Show or model examples of finished work for students to critique. (Use project examples from a previous year or examples of a similar type of student work.)

   - Ask students to point out examples of work that is well done and work that could be improved.

   - Identify wording for the different levels of quality.

   - Avoid negative language as much as possible (For example: "Identified one resource that related to the topic" instead of "Failed to find enough resources.")

5. **Establish project expectations.** Review the completed rubric with the class before the project begins, and post it in the classroom.

6. **Check progress.** Have students use the rubric part way through the project to peer-assess and/or self-assess. This gives students a chance to review their progress and modify their efforts as needed.

7. **Do a final assessment.** Use the same rubric at the end of the project to assess students' final work.

8. **Assess the rubric.** Revise the rubric when needed to reflect any changes that would improve the language or criteria.

USING A 4-3-2-1 SCORING SYSTEM

This system refers to levels of quality for each task in the project assignment. Here is an explanation of the four levels, from highest to lowest:

- **Level 4:** A "4" indicates that the standard for quality on the associated performance task has been exceeded. It is important for students to know that they can achieve beyond the expected level of quality—that it is possible to invest additional time, creativity, enthusiasm, and skills to develop a performance that fits their own concept of quality and is not restricted to the Level 3 description. The language used here is very important. To exceed expectations, a student should take the performance to an increased level of complexity or deeper understanding, not merely produce a larger quantity of the same thing.

- **Level 3:** A "3" indicates that the standard for quality on the associated performance task has been achieved. Level 3 criteria are the most critical ones; therefore, these measures should be very carefully developed so that it is perfectly clear what a student must do to accomplish this level of quality. All of the criteria in Levels 1, 2, and 4 are in reference to Level 3. Every student should understand clearly and without ambiguity what needs to be done or demonstrated to achieve a Level 3 assessment for each performance task.

- **Level 2:** A "2" indicates that work has been done, but it doesn't meet the quality standard described for Level 3. When a student receives a "2," he or she should be able to tell without a doubt why the work is below standard. The deficiencies that are cited must be evident in the language of Level 3, because that is the expected level of quality toward which students were expected to strive.

Level 1: A "1" indicates that the student has not provided sufficient evidence to make a reasonable judgment or assessment of any kind. This is not an assessment of effort; nobody can tell with certainty how much effort a student has put into a task, and it is especially difficult to determine lack of effort. There are many reasons why a student may appear to not try, but the actual assessment must be based on evidence, not opinion. If there is no evidence, then the student receives a "1" until evidence is provided.

The purpose of assessment is to give students feedback about their performances. Students who want to use assessment feedback to improve the quality of their work should be allowed to do so. This means that a student who receives 3s has an option of improving the work to 4s after consulting with the teacher. Using the rubric as a guide, a teacher can point out specifically what needs to be done to increase the quality of a performance.

Factors that Influence Your Expectations for the Project

- The amount of time you give students to complete the project
- The standards that the content expectations will be based on
- The amount and types of resources students will have available
- Your students' prior knowledge about the topic

- Your students' previous experience with project-based learning
- The level of challenge you want to build into the project
- The range of student readiness in your classroom
- How much pre-teaching you plan to do

Impact on Student Learning

A carefully crafted rubric can have a significant impact on student learning:

- It clearly defines what is expected, before the project begins.
- Students can use the rubric to make judgments about their work during the project and adjust their efforts to improve results.
- A teacher can quickly circle an item on the rubric to pinpoint an area that is being discussed with the student or a parent.
- The rubric ensures that assessment is consistent for everyone.
- It is a tool that works well with a range of learning readiness.
- It provides language for students to articulate what they have learned and how they could improve their work.
- Rubrics help students develop the insight, confidence, and maturity to establish and achieve their learning goals.

Model Projects Matrix

Ready-to-use projects model how one or more differentiation strategies can be used with specific content. All strategies can potentially be used with all projects. Model projects may be adapted to fit other content areas.

Model Project	Project Scenario	See Pages	Content Area	Differentiation Strategy
The Candidates' Debate	Students choose a role/perspective from which to create material for a presidential candidate's platform on a specific topic.	64–83	English/Language Arts	• Choice-as-Motivator • Multiple Intelligences • Kids-Teaching-Kids
Continental Cubing Competition	Students prepare to represent their school district at the annual Continental Cubing Competition in the area of literature.	84–95	English/Language Arts	• Flexible Grouping • Tiered Assignments • Cubing
Time Traveler	Time travelers go back in time from the year 2099 to learn about popular culture in the early 21st century.	CD-ROM ONLY	English/Language Arts	• Choice-as-Motivator
Math Investment Plan	Math entrepreneurs learn how to invest their class time wisely to expand their math knowledge.	96–115	Math	• Curriculum Compacting • Anchor Activities
The Mathematute	Mathematicians prepare and present the solution to a problem at a mathematics conference.	116–125	Math	• Tiered Assignments • Bring-Something-to-the-Group • Multiple Intelligences
You Gotta Have an Angle	Treasure hunters complete a basic training in trigonometry so they can solve the clues that will lead them to a buried treasure.	CD-ROM ONLY	Math	• Task Sheets
Express Yourself	Students create artwork for a Web site that expresses an aspect of the consequences resulting from human interaction with the environment.	CD-ROM ONLY	Science	• Scaffolding

continues ☞

MODEL PROJECTS MATRIX *continued*

Model Project	Project Scenario	See Pages	Content Area	Differentiation Strategy
Life on Planet X	A scientific space-exploration team is sent to explore and document life on a new planet just discovered in our solar system.	126–152	Life Science	• All-Most-Some • Choice Boards • Anchor Activities
Message in a Capsule	A scientific research team prepares documents about our solar system for a special interstellar communication capsule called the Life Finder.	153–168	Earth/Space Science	• Clock Partners • Choice-as-Motivator
Hear Ye! Hear Ye!	Documentary film teams produce a documentary about an important event in American history.	CD-ROM ONLY	Social Studies/History	• Jigsaw Grouping • Tiered Assignments • Kids-Teaching-Kids
Moments in Time	Historians research events and create informative timelines for "clickable" classroom wall webs.	169–197	Social Studies	• 1-2-4 Present! • Tiered Assignments
One World	Social science experts research cultures and make recommendations to the International Olympic Games Committee about how to host visitors from around the world.	198–224	Social Studies	• Tic-Tac-Toe • Bloom's Taxonomy • Multiple Intelligences

Content Standards Matrix

Please note that these are approximate alignments between standards and projects; they do not directly correspond in most cases.

Content Area	Strand	Standard	Project Name	See Pages
English/Language Arts	Literature	Students read a wide range of print and nonprint texts to build an understanding of texts, of themselves, and of the cultures of the United States and the world; to acquire new information; to respond to the needs and demands of society and the workplace; and for personal fulfillment. Among these texts are fiction and nonfiction, and classic and contemporary works.	Continental Cubing Competition	84–95
English/Language Arts	Literature	Students read a wide range of literature from many periods in many genres to build an understanding of the many dimensions (e.g., philosophical, ethical, aesthetic) of human experience.	Continental Cubing Competition	84–95
English/Language Arts	Reading Strategies	Students apply a wide range of strategies to comprehend, interpret, evaluate, and appreciate texts. They draw on their prior experience, their interactions with other readers and writers, their knowledge of word meaning and of other texts, their word-identification strategies, and their understanding of textual features (e.g., sound-letter correspondence, sentence structure, context, graphics).	Continental Cubing Competition	84–95
English/Language Arts	Language Use	Students adjust their use of spoken, written, and visual language (e.g., conventions, style, vocabulary) to communicate effectively with a variety of audiences and for different purposes.	The Candidates' Debate Continental Cubing Competition Time Traveler	64–83 84–95 CD-ROM

continues

CONTENT STANDARDS MATRIX *continued*

Content Area	Strand	Standard	Project Name	
English/Language Arts	Language Use	Students employ a wide range of strategies as they write and use different writing-process elements appropriately to communicate with different audiences for a variety of purposes.	The Candidates' Debate	64–83
			Continental Cubing Competition	84–95
			Time Traveler	CD-ROM
English/Language Arts	Language Use	Students apply knowledge of language structure, language conventions (e.g., spelling and punctuation), media techniques, figurative language, and genre to create, critique, and discuss print and nonprint texts.	The Candidates' Debate	64–93
			Continental Cubing Competition	84–95
			Time Traveler	CD-ROM
English/Language Arts	Research and Inquiry	Students conduct research on issues and interests by generating ideas and questions, and by posing problems. They gather, evaluate, and synthesize data from a variety of sources (e.g., print and nonprint texts, artifacts, people) to communicate their discoveries in ways that suit their purpose and audience.	The Candidates' Debate	64–83
			Time Traveler	CD-ROM
English/Language Arts	Research and Inquiry	Students use a variety of technological and informational resources (e.g., libraries, databases, computer networks, video) to gather and synthesize information to create and communicate knowledge.	The Candidates' Debate	64–83
			Time Traveler	CD-ROM
English/Language Arts	Collaborative Learning	Students participate as knowledgeable, reflective, creative, and critical members of a variety of literacy communities.	The Candidates' Debate	64–83
			Continental Cubing Competition	84–95

continues 👉

CONTENT STANDARDS MATRIX *continued*

Content Area	Strand	Standard	Project Name	See Pages
English/Language Arts	Practical Application	Students use spoken, written, and visual language to accomplish their own purposes (e.g., for learning, enjoyment, persuasion, and the exchange of information).	The Candidates' Debate	64–83
			Continental Cubing Competition	84–95
			Time Traveler	CD-ROM
Math	Number and Operations	Students understand numbers, ways of representing numbers, relationships among numbers, and number systems. Expectation: Students work flexibly with fractions, decimals, and percents to solve problems.	Math Investment Plan	96–115
			The Mathematute: A Meeting of the Minds on Fractions, Decimals, and Percents	116–125
			The Mathematute: Symposium on Rates, Ratios, and Proportions	116–125
			You Gotta Have an Angle	CD-ROM
Math	Number and Operations	Students understand numbers, ways of representing numbers, relationships among numbers, and number systems. Expectation: Students develop an understanding of large numbers and recognize and appropriately use exponential, scientific, and calculator notation.	The Mathematute: The Exponent Zone	116–125
Math	Number and Operations	Students understand meanings of operations and how they relate to one another. Expectation: Students understand the meaning and effects of arithmetic operations with fractions, decimals, and integers.	Math Investment Plan	96–115
			The Mathematute: A Meeting of the Minds on Fractions, Decimals, and Percents	116–125
			You Gotta Have an Angle	CD-ROM

continues

CONTENT STANDARDS MATRIX *continued*

Content Area	Strand	Standard	Project Name	See Pages
Math	Number and Operations	Students understand meanings of operations and how they relate to one another. Expectation: Students understand and use the inverse relationships of addition and subtraction, multiplication and division, and squaring and finding square roots to simplify computations and solve problems.	The Mathematute: The Exponent Zone	116–125
Math	Number and Operations	Students compute fluently and make reasonable estimates. Expectation: Students develop and analyze algorithms for computing with fractions, decimals, and integers, and develop fluency in their use.	Math Investment Plan The Mathematute: A Meeting of the Minds on Fractions, Decimals, and Percents You Gotta Have an Angle	96–115 116–125 CD-ROM
Math	Number and Operations	Students compute fluently and make reasonable estimates. Expectation: Students develop, analyze, and explain methods for solving problems involving proportions, such as scaling and finding equivalent ratios.	Math Investment Plan The Mathematute: Symposium on Rates, Ratios, and Proportions You Gotta Have an Angle	96–115 116–125 CD-ROM
Math	Algebra	Students represent and analyze mathematical situations and structures using algebraic symbols. Expectation: Students explore relationships between symbolic expressions and graphs of lines, paying particular attention to the meaning of intercept and slope.	The Mathematute: The X-Y Equations and Graphing Exposition	116–125
Math	Algebra	Students represent and analyze mathematical situations and structures using algebraic symbols. Expectation: Students use symbolic algebra to represent situations and to solve problems, especially those that involve linear relationships.	The Mathematute: The X-Y Equations and Graphing Exposition You Gotta Have an Angle	116–125 CD-ROM

continues ☛

CONTENT STANDARDS MATRIX *continued*

Content Area	Strand	Standard	Project Name	See Pages
Math	Algebra	Students use mathematical models to represent and understand quantitative relationships. Expectation: Students model and solve contextualized problems using various representations, such as graphs, tables, and equations.	The Mathematute: The X-Y Equations and Graphing Exposition	116–125
Math	Algebra	Students represent and analyze mathematical situations and structures using algebraic symbols. Expectation: Students understand the meaning of equivalent forms of expressions, equations, inequalities, and relations.	You Gotta Have an Angle	CD-ROM
Math	Geometry	Students analyze characteristics and properties of two- and three-dimensional geometric shapes and develop mathematical arguments about geometric relationships. Expectation: Students precisely describe, classify, and understand relationships among types of two- and three-dimensional objects using their defining properties.	The Mathematute: Plane Geometry Forum	116–125
Math	Geometry	Students analyze characteristics and properties of two- and three-dimensional geometric shapes and develop mathematical arguments about geometric relationships. Expectation: Students understand relationships among the angles, side lengths, perimeters, areas, and volumes of similar objects.	The Mathematute: Plane Geometry Forum You Gotta Have an Angle	116–125 CD-ROM
Math	Geometry	Students analyze characteristics and properties of two- and three-dimensional geometric shapes and develop mathematical arguments about geometric relationships. Expectation: Students create and critique inductive and deductive arguments concerning geometric ideas and relationships, such as congruence, similarity, and the Pythagorean relationship.	The Mathematute: Focus on Pythagorus You Gotta Have an Angle	116–125 CD-ROM

continues 👉

CONTENT STANDARDS MATRIX *continued*

Content Area	Strand	Standard	Project Name	See Pages
Math	Geometry	Students apply transformations and use symmetry to analyze mathematical situations. Expectation: Students describe sizes, positions, and orientations of shapes under informal transformations such as flips, turns, slides, and scaling.	The Mathematute: Plane Geometry Forum	116–125
Math	Geometry	Students apply transformations and use symmetry to analyze mathematical situations. Expectation: Students examine the congruence, similarity, and line or rotational symmetry of objects using transformations.	The Mathematute: Plane Geometry Forum	116–125
Math	Geometry	Students analyze characteristics and properties of two- and three-dimensional geometric shapes and develop mathematical arguments about geometric relationships. Expectation: Students use trigonometric relationships to determine lengths and angle measures.	You Gotta Have an Angle	CD-ROM
Math	Measurement	Students understand measurable attributes of objects and the units, systems, and processes of measurement. Expectation: Students understand relationships among units and convert from one unit to another within the same system.	Math Investment Plan	96–115
Math	Measurement		The Mathematute: Symposium on Rates, Ratios, and Proportions	116–125
Math	Measurement	Students apply appropriate techniques, tools, and formulas to determine measurements. Expectation: Students develop and use formulas to determine the circumference of circles and the area of triangles, parallelograms, trapezoids, and circles, and develop strategies to find the area of more-complex shapes.	The Mathematute: Perimeter, Area, and Volume	116–125
Math	Measurement	Students apply appropriate techniques, tools, and formulas to determine measurements. Expectation: Students develop strategies to determine the surface area and volume of selected prisms, pyramids, and cylinders.	The Mathematute: Perimeter, Area, and Volume	116–125

continues ☛

CONTENT STANDARDS MATRIX *continued*

Content Area	Strand	Standard	Project Name	See Pages
Math	Measurement	Students apply appropriate techniques, tools, and formulas to determine measurements. Expectation: Students solve simple problems involving rates and derived measurements for such attributes as velocity and density.	The Mathematute: Symposium on Rates, Ratios, and Proportions	116–125
Math	Data Analysis and Probability	Students formulate questions that can be addressed with data and collect, organize, and display relevant data to answer them. Expectation: Students select, create, and use appropriate graphical representations of data, including histograms, box plots, and scatter plots.	The Mathematute: Investigating Data Analysis	116–125
Math	Data Analysis and Probability	Students select and use appropriate statistical methods to analyze data. Expectation: Students find, use, and interpret measures of center and spread, including mean and interquartile range.	The Mathematute: Investigating Data Analysis	116–125
Math	Data Analysis and Probability	Students select and use appropriate statistical methods to analyze data. Expectation: Students discuss and understand the correspondence between data sets and their graphical representations, especially histograms, stem-and-leaf plots, box plots, and scatter plots.	The Mathematute: Investigating Data Analysis	116–125
Math	Data Analysis and Probability	Students develop and evaluate inferences and predictions that are based on data. Expectation: Students make conjectures about possible relationships between two characteristics of a sample on the basis of scatter plots of the data and approximate lines of fit.	The Mathematute: Investigating Data Analysis	116–125
Math	Data Analysis and Probability	Students understand and apply basic concepts of probability. Expectation: Students understand and use appropriate terminology to describe complementary and mutually exclusive events.	The Mathematute: Probing Probability	116–125
Math	Data Analysis and Probability	Students understand and apply basic concepts of probability. Expectation: Students use proportionality and a basic understanding of probability to make and test conjectures about the results of experiments and simulations.	The Mathematute: Probing Probability	116–125

continues 👉

CONTENT STANDARDS MATRIX *continued*

Content Area	Strand	Standard	Project Name	See Pages
Math	Data Analysis and Probability	Students understand and apply basic concepts of probability. Expectation: Students compute probabilities for simple compound events, using such methods as organized lists, tree diagrams, and area models.	The Mathematute: Probing Probability	116–125
Science	Earth and Space Science	Students develop an understanding of the structure of the earth system.	Message in a Capsule	153–168
Science	Earth and Space Science	Students develop an understanding of Earth in the solar system.	Message in a Capsule	153–168
Science	Life Science	Students develop an understanding of matter, energy, and organization of living things.	Life on Planet X	126–152
Science	Life Science	Students develop an understanding of the structure and function in living systems.	Life on Planet X	126–125
Science	Life Science	Students develop an understanding of the interdependence of organisms.	Life on Planet X	126–125
Science	Science in Personal and Social Perspectives	Students develop an understanding of natural and human-induced hazards.	Express Yourself	CD-ROM
Science	Science in Personal and Social Perspectives	Students develop an understanding of science and technology in local, national, and global challenges.	Express Yourself	CD-ROM
Social Studies	Culture	Students compare similarities and differences in the ways groups, societies, and cultures meet human needs and concerns.	One World: Topics 1 & 6	198–224
Social Studies	Culture	Students explain and give examples of how language, literature, the arts, architecture, other artifacts, traditions, beliefs, values, and behaviors contribute to the development and transmission of culture.	One World: Topics 1 & 6	198–224

continues

CONTENT STANDARDS MATRIX *continued*

Content Area	Strand	Standard	Project Name	See Pages
Social Studies	Time, Continuity, and Change	Students use key concepts such as causality, change, conflict, and complexity to explain, analyze, and show connections among patterns of historical change and continuity.	Moments in Time One World: Topic 7 Hear Ye! Hear Ye!	169–197 198–224 CD-ROM
Social Studies	Time, Continuity, and Change	Students describe selected historical periods and patterns of change within and across cultures, such as the rise in civilization, the development of transportation systems, the growth and breakdown of colonial systems, and others.	Moments in Time Hear Ye! Hear Ye!	169–197 CD-ROM
Social Studies	Time, Continuity, and Change	Students identify and use processes important to reconstructing and reinterpreting the past, such as using a variety of resources; providing, validating, and weighing evidence for claims; checking credibility of sources; and searching for causality.	One World: Topics 4 & 7 Moments in Time Hear Ye! Hear Ye!	198–224 169–197 CD-ROM
Social Studies	People, Places, and Environments	Students examine, interpret, and analyze physical and cultural patterns and their interactions, such as land use, settlement patterns, cultural transmission of customs and ideas, and ecosystem changes.	One World: Topic 2	198–224
Social Studies	Individuals, Groups, and Institutions	Students analyze group and institutional influences on people, events, and elements of culture.	Moments in Time Hear Ye! Hear Ye!	169–197 CD-ROM
Social Studies	Power, Authority, and Governance	Students compare different political systems (their ideologies, structure, institutions, processes, and political cultures) with that of the United States, and identify representative political leaders from selected historical and contemporary settings.	One World: Topic 9	198–224
Social Studies	Production, Distribution, and Consumption	Students differentiate among various forms of exchange and money.	One World: Topic 8	198–224

CONTENT STANDARDS MATRIX *continued*

Content Area	Strand	Standard	Project Name	See Pages
Social Studies	Production, Distribution, and Consumption	Students use economic concepts to help explain historical and current developments and issues in local, national, or global contexts.	One World: Topics 3 & 8	198–224

Standards for the English Language Arts are from the National Council of Teachers of English (NCTE).

Principles and Standards for School Mathematics are listed with the permission of the National Council of Teachers of Mathematics (NCTM). NCTM does not endorse the content or validity of these alignments.

Expectations of Excellence: Curriculum Standards for Social Studies are from the National Council for the Social Studies (NCSS).

National Science Education Standards are from the National Research Council (NRC).

The Candidates' Debate

Content Focus: English/Language Arts
Class Periods: 9

Project Scenario

Students have been hired to work on one of two presidential candidates' election campaign teams and to prepare and present a paper that will help the candidate communicate in debates his or her position on an important issue. First, the students must choose between two candidates based on their stances on a campaign issue. You will play the role of campaign manager for both candidates.

Project Synopsis

After receiving a campaign issue statement and discussing the pros and cons as a class, students choose to work for one of two presidential candidates: the one who is for the statement or the one who is against it. Students also choose which type of expert they will be as they prepare support materials for their candidate's position: statistician, screenwriter, journalist, politician, scientist, or sociologist. Class time is provided for students to do research, complete the assignment they chose, and present their work to the rest of the class.

Differentiation Strategies

- Choice-as-motivator
- Multiple intelligences
- Kids-teaching-kids

Student Forms

- Introduction
- Assignment Sheet: Statistician
- Assignment Sheet: Screenwriter
- Assignment Sheet: Journalist
- Assignment Sheet: Politician

- Assignment Sheet: Scientist
- Assignment Sheet: Sociologist
- Assessment Sheet

Content Standards*

1. Students adjust their use of spoken, written, and visual language (e.g., conventions, style, vocabulary) to communicate effectively with a variety of audiences and for different purposes.

2. Students employ a wide range of strategies as they write and use different writing-process elements appropriately to communicate with different audiences for a variety of purposes.

3. Students apply knowledge of language structure, language conventions (e.g., spelling and punctuation), media techniques, figurative language, and genre to create, critique, and discuss print and nonprint texts.

4. Students conduct research on issues and interests by generating ideas and questions, and by posing problems. They gather, evaluate, and synthesize data from a variety of sources (e.g., print and nonprint texts, artifacts, people) to communicate their discoveries in ways that suit their purpose and audience.

5. Students use a variety of technological and informational resources (e.g., libraries, databases, computer networks, video) to gather and synthesize information to create and communicate knowledge.

6. Students participate as knowledgeable, reflective, creative, and critical members of a variety of literacy communities.

Standards for the English Language Arts are from the National Council of Teachers of English (NCTE).

7. Students use spoken, written, and visual language to accomplish their own purposes (e.g., for learning, enjoyment, persuasion, and the exchange of information).

How to Use This Project

Follow these steps to implement "The Candidates' Debate":

BEFORE YOU BEGIN

1. Identify a specific current national issue on which to focus the project.

2. Compose a campaign issue statement in the style of a debate resolution. For example,

Resolved: "Legislating a mandatory cap on greenhouse gas emissions is the first step the U.S. government should take to combat global warming."

3. In the project scenario, Candidate A supports the resolution. On your own, develop a list of arguments that this candidate might make to support his or her position. You will introduce these arguments to the class only if they don't think of them on their own, but it is important for you to identify them ahead of time so that you are prepared to offer them if necessary.

4. In the scenario, Candidate B opposes the resolution. Develop a list of arguments that this candidate might make to support his or her position. Again, you will give these arguments to the class only if they don't think of them on their own.

5. This is a research project. Before beginning, consider these issues related to research:

- The project includes a specific requirement that each student use and properly cite two Internet sources. You may also want to require information from books and/or periodicals. In the case of the example resolution topic, global warming, the Web is where students will find a wealth of the most up-to-date information. Students will need Internet access to complete this part of the project.

- You may want to provide links to pre-identified Internet sites to help students get started. See suggestions in "Recommended Resources" on pages 229–230.

- If you expect students to follow specific research guidelines, be sure to clearly define your expectations and give them to students in written form at the outset of the project.

6. Decide what your expectations will be for the written position papers and for the oral presentations. The latter may include requirements for visual materials and guidelines regarding the use of notes, outlines, or other written prompts during the presentation.

7. Schedule class time for completing project requirements. The project is designed to last nine class periods:

- Period 1: Project introduction and class discussion of the campaign issue statement. (*Optional:* You may want to use two class periods here: one period to introduce the project and the campaign issue statement and have students do preliminary research about the topic, and another period to discuss the topic as a class.)

- Period 2: Students choose a presidential candidate, identify an area of expertise, and begin filling out the Position Paper Proposal.

- Period 3: Students continue working and hand in their Position Paper Proposal for approval.

- Period 4: Students receive approval to begin researching and writing their position papers.

- Period 5: Students continue writing their papers.

- Period 6: Students finish writing their papers and begin preparing for oral presentations.

- Period 7: Students make final oral presentations.

The Candidates' Debate | Project Planner *continued*

- Period 8: Students make final oral presentations.
- Period 9: Students make final oral presentations and complete the Assessment Sheet.

IMPLEMENT THE PROJECT

1. Hand out the Introduction and Assessment Sheet, and explain the project. Go over the points on the assessment so that students understand how their project will be graded.

2. Give students the campaign issue statement that you have created for the project, and have them record it on their Introduction handout. The statement should be in the form of a debate resolution.

3. Conduct a class discussion during which students think of supportive arguments for both sides of the issue. Use two flip charts or chalkboards to record the arguments, one for each candidate. For example, suppose the issue statement is this:

   Resolved: "Legislating a mandatory cap on greenhouse gas emissions is the first step the U.S. government should take to combat global warming."

   In this case the class will discuss arguments that support the idea of legislating caps on emissions and arguments that do not support this approach. Record each idea for the appropriate candidate. Encourage students to be open-minded and to think of arguments for both sides. Try to elicit as many ideas as you can from the class before offering your own suggestions. The more arguments that originate from students, the better.

4. Have each student choose a presidential candidate for whom to write a position paper. Candidate A supports the resolution and Candidate B opposes it.

5. Let students examine the assignment sheets for the six areas of expertise: statistician, screenwriter, journalist, politician, scientist, and sociologist. Students may support their candidate's position from any one of these perspectives, using the voice of an expert from the chosen field.

6. Give each student the assignment sheet for the area of expertise he or she chooses. The assignment sheet provides the necessary guidelines for composing a position paper and includes a Position Paper Proposal form that must be filled out and submitted to you for approval before writing can begin.

7. Provide time for students to complete the proposals on their assignment sheets; this will include accessing sites on the Internet.

8. At a designated time, students will turn in their completed Position Paper Proposal and Citing Internet Sources forms for you to evaluate. If you have added research requirements such as note cards, an outline, or a graphic organizer, they should be handed in at the same time. Once you approve the forms and have all the required items, sign the Position Paper Proposal.

9. After students receive approval to move on to the writing phase, they will begin researching and composing a position paper using the voice of an expert in the field they have chosen.

10. Upon completion of the position paper, students prepare to present their information orally. Again, this presentation is to be done in the voice of an expert.

11. Consider allowing students to take unconventional approaches to their oral presentations. The expert voices that they are encouraged to use also provide an opportunity for creative students to come up with unique ideas for their presentations. For example, the screenwriter area of expertise might lend itself to an actual performance. In this case, the writer may need support from friends. The scientist, on the other hand, may want to use multimedia with video to help illustrate a point. Students should be encouraged to make these kinds of choices about their presentations.

Methods of Differentiation

The primary methods of differentiation for this project are choice-as-motivator, multiple intelligences, and kids-teaching-kids. First, students choose which side of the campaign issue to support by deciding which candidate they want to work for. In addition, each of the six areas of expertise offers a different way of approaching the assignment, a different voice with which to present the same information. Students may choose the approach that interests them most. The reason one area of expertise may be more interesting to a student than others is likely related to that student's intelligence preference. For example, the student who is strong in mathematics and logic will probably prefer the voice of a statistician or a scientist. Linguistically inclined students are more likely to choose to be journalists or politicians. Students with strong interpersonal skills may prefer the role of sociologist or politician. Students who are "body smart" may choose to be screenwriters (and perform their work rather than present it). And so forth.

This project also employs the kids-teaching-kids strategy. Giving students the responsibility to gather, organize, and present information to others results in greater understanding on the part of those who teach. Audience members learn as well, but the kids-teaching-kids strategy specifically focuses on the educational value of having students assume the role of teacher.

Ideas for Extending or Modifying the Project

1. Modify the scenario to focus on a race for governor or mayor. This allows your class to study a local issue, but resources may be more difficult to locate.

2. Add other areas of expertise. For example, you might expand the list to include artist, poet, musician, doctor, lawyer, engineer, or teacher/professor.

3. For a different kind of differentiation, use a cubing activity that adds an element of chance (see "Cubing" on pages 30–31 for more detail). For example, have each student roll a die to determine which candidate he or she will support. An odd number on the die indicates Candidate A and an even number indicates Candidate B. As in a debate class, students must be ready to defend either side of the resolution. You can also have a roll of the die determine which area of expertise each student will assume. Roll a 1 and you are a statistician; roll a 2 and you are a screenwriter; and so forth. In this case, you may want to offer an optional second roll so that students are not absolutely stuck with a role they don't want.

4. Have students present both sides of the issue in their position papers. For example, describe the pros and cons of legislating caps on greenhouse gas emissions from the perspective of statisticians.

5. Create a class glossary of words and phrases related to the topic and have students contribute to it as they work on the project. Spend time during the writing process discussing with students how to strengthen their papers with more powerful or descriptive vocabulary.

6. Have each student choose one sentence from his or her position paper that could be used as a pull-quote if the paper were published in a journal or magazine. This is a sentence from the piece that the student deems exceptionally descriptive, engaging, or insightful. Instruct each student to underline the weakest word or phrase in the pull-quote and think of a way to strengthen it to make the sentence even more compelling.

7. Create campaign buttons or bumper stickers using the slogans that students used as titles for their position papers.

8. Conduct a vote on the campaign issue at the end of the project. Create a ballot and have students in the class cast votes. This idea can be taken beyond the classroom to the entire

school by giving students on each side of the issue an opportunity to present their case to the school and then have a school-wide vote.

9. Modify the project to help struggling learners complete it successfully. Here are three possibilities:

- Work directly with students to ensure that they identify relevant, useful, understandable resources that are clearly related to the topic and written at an appropriate reading level.

- Choose two of the six areas of expertise and scaffold them with suggestions, graphic organizers, resources, instructions, checklists, explanations, guiding questions, templates, examples, rubrics, and so forth. Ask struggling students to choose between these two, rather than from all six, so that you can give them carefully targeted additional support. (Of course, you may scaffold three or more areas of expertise in this way. Doing two is merely a way to make less work for you while still giving students a choice.)

- Establish a "briefing" schedule with each student. During briefings, a student spends thirty to sixty seconds telling (and showing) you what he or she has accomplished since the last briefing, so that you can monitor progress and provide support.

Suggested Content Modifications

SCIENCE

Formulate a campaign issue statement that relates to concepts you will cover in your textbook. Students could begin their research with the textbook and search for additional information on the Internet. For example, if you teach biology, the resolution could be: "The United States needs to allocate more money and resources for stem cell research." As in this project, students choose (or are assigned to) a candidate who either supports or refutes this statement and choose (or are assigned to) an area of expertise from which to present their arguments.

SOCIAL STUDIES

Choose a topic that focuses on the social studies standards that you teach, and write a resolution that incorporates this information. For example, if you teach economics, the resolution could be: "The North American Free Trade Agreement (NAFTA) should be revised to correct some of the problems that have resulted since it was implemented January 1, 1994."

MATH

Here is a sample math resolution: "For U.S. students to be more internationally competitive in mathematics, we should revamp our math curriculum so that fewer concepts are taught and they are covered more in-depth." For this resolution, you could ask your students to give each expert's perspective on the issue, and also to show how sample math problems from your curriculum might be covered more in-depth.

The Candidates' Debate
Introduction

Name: _____ **Date:** _____

This project asks you to take a position on a current issue by writing a research paper. Your perspective will be that of a political adviser with a specific area of expertise. In that role, your task is to compose and present a position paper for a presidential candidate.

Project Scenario

There is a presidential election approaching, and you have decided to actively support a candidate whose beliefs and positions closely align with your own. The campaign manager (a.k.a. your teacher) has selected teams of people to focus on various targeted issues. Because of your writing skills, area of expertise, and commitment to your candidate, you have been assigned to one of these teams and asked to prepare a paper that will help the candidate make his or her case to the American people. When it is finished, you will present the paper orally to the manager and the campaign team (a.k.a. your class). Everything in the paper must be clear, correct, and convincing. Its purpose is to help get your candidate elected!

This is the campaign issue statement:

Resolved: "That _____

_____

_____."

I have joined the campaign staff of:

☐ Candidate A, who supports the issue as it is stated above.

☐ Candidate B, who opposes the issue as it is stated above.

Assignment

1. Participate in a discussion with your campaign team to identify examples, points of view, and supporting details for both sides of the issue. The purpose of this discussion is to clearly establish the point of view of each candidate. Your opinions are important during this discussion, so please share them. There is no right or wrong position, but it is critical to determine what the two candidates believe as they go into the campaign. It will be your job as a political adviser to choose a side to support with a researched position paper.

continues ☞

2. Decide what kind of expert you want to be for this project. Each area of expertise requires a different type of position paper, and each has its own assignment sheet. You may examine the assignment sheets before choosing. The assignment sheets provide more detailed information about project requirements and expectations. For this project, you may choose to be a:

☐ Statistician

☐ Screenwriter

☐ Journalist

☐ Politician

☐ Scientist

☐ Sociologist

3. Conduct research to locate accurate information that supports the position you are taking.

- If you are expected to follow specific research guidelines, your campaign manager will provide them.

- Use at least two reliable Internet resources with correct citations.

4. Complete the Position Paper Proposal on your assignment sheet and have it approved by your campaign manager before writing your paper.

5. Write a position paper based on the tasks outlined on your assignment sheet.

6. Present your paper orally to the campaign team.

The Candidates' Debate

Assignment Sheet
Area of Expertise: Statistician

Name: _____ I Support Candidate: _____ Date: _____

As a statistician you will write a paper that includes at least one table, chart, or graph that your candidate can use to illustrate and support points during speeches and presentations. The candidate wants to be able to show voters why his or her position is sound, and data presented in visual form will help with this. Along with the visual representation of data, your paper should provide a clear written explanation of what the information shows and how it supports the candidate's position. After completing the position paper, you will present it orally. This will be your opportunity to support the candidate's perspective with researched data, not just opinion.

Complete the Position Paper Proposal and turn it in to the campaign manager (a.k.a. your teacher) for approval. Once approval has been given, you may begin writing the paper and preparing for your presentation.

Position Paper Proposal

List three descriptive keywords or phrases that are directly related to the issue.

1. _____

2. _____

3. _____

For this project you are required to use the Internet as a resource. Find at least two specific online sources that provide useful information about your topic and cite them below. Use only reputable Web sites for your research.

INTERNET SOURCE #1

1. Name of author and/or editor: _____

2. Title of the work:_____

3. Date of electronic publication or posting (month, day, year):_____

4. Name of publisher:_____

5. Date that you accessed information on the site (month, day, year):_____

6. The Web site URL (address):_____

continues ☛

INTERNET SOURCE #2

1. Name of author and/or editor: _____

2. Title of the work: _____

3. Date of electronic publication or posting (month, day, year): _____

4. Name of publisher: _____

5. Date that you accessed information on the site (month, day, year): _____

6. The Web site URL (address): _____

Record the three strongest reasons you can think of for a voter to support your candidate's position on this issue:

1. _____

2. _____

3. _____

Choose at least one of the reasons and describe what kinds of data you will use to help your candidate make his or her case.

_____

_____

How do you intend to represent the data (table, chart, graph, other)?

_____

_____

On a separate sheet of paper, make a sketch of the table, chart, or graph that you will create. Show its layout and what title and labels you will use. You do not need to include the actual data on this sketch.

Compose a campaign slogan that conveys the candidate's stand on the issue. The slogan must be seven words or fewer. Use the slogan as the title of your paper.

Slogan: _____

Approval to write this position paper is granted by: _____

The Candidates' Debate
Assignment Sheet
Area of Expertise: Screenwriter

Name: _____ **I Support Candidate:** _____ **Date:** _____

As a screenwriter you will compose a paper that describes a scene from a play or TV show that supports your candidate's position. The paper will incorporate important points and present key information to make your candidate's position clear and compelling. For example, you might design a scene in which characters who know about the topic discuss it in a setting such as an interview, telephone conversation, news broadcast, or debate. After completing the paper, you will present it (or perform it) for the campaign team (a.k.a. your class), with help from other campaign members if necessary. This will be your opportunity to support the candidate's perspective with researched data, not just opinion.

Complete the Position Paper Proposal and turn it in to the campaign manager (a.k.a. your teacher) for approval. Once approval has been given, you may begin writing the paper and preparing for your presentation.

Position Paper Proposal

List three descriptive keywords or phrases that are directly related to the issue.

1. _____

2. _____

3. _____

For this project you are required to use the Internet as a resource. Find at least two specific online sources that provide useful information about your topic and cite them below. Use only reputable Web sites for your research.

INTERNET SOURCE #1

1. Name of author and/or editor: _____

2. Title of the work:_____

3. Date of electronic publication or posting (month, day, year):_____

4. Name of publisher:_____

5. Date that you accessed information on the site (month, day, year):_____

6. The Web site URL (address):_____

continues ☞

INTERNET SOURCE #2

1. Name of author and/or editor: _____

2. Title of the work:_____

3. Date of electronic publication or posting (month, day, year):_____

4. Name of publisher:_____

5. Date that you accessed information on the site (month, day, year):_____

6. The Web site URL (address):_____

Record the three strongest reasons you can think of for a voter to support your candidate's position on this issue:

1. _____

2. _____

3. _____

Choose one of the reasons for supporting the candidate's position and describe the key points you will build into your paper to help convince an audience that this reason is powerful and believable.

_____

_____

What is the setting for the scene (for example, a news broadcast or a science conference)?

_____

_____

On a separate sheet of paper, describe the characters who will be in the scene and explain how you will have them present information to an audience using dialogue, setting, props, and so forth.

Compose a campaign slogan that conveys the candidate's stand on the issue. The slogan must be seven words or fewer. Use the slogan as the title of your paper.

Slogan:_____

Approval to write this position paper is granted by: _____

The Candidates' Debate

Assignment Sheet
Area of Expertise: Journalist

Name: _____ **I Support Candidate:** _____ **Date:** _____

As a journalist you will write a paper in the form of a newspaper editorial that favors your candidate's position while still offering an unbiased analysis of the issue. Your candidate wants to see how his or her position might be described in the media. Being "unbiased" means that when you discover information that supports an opposing or differing view from that of your candidate, you should mention it. Your job is to present the issue from the perspective of a journalist who has an opinion but still looks at the issue from all sides. After completing the position paper, you will present it orally. This will be your opportunity to support the candidate's perspective with researched data, not just opinion.

Complete the Position Paper Proposal and turn it in to the campaign manager (a.k.a. your teacher) for approval. Once approval has been given, you may begin writing the editorial and preparing for your presentation.

Position Paper Proposal

List three descriptive keywords or phrases that are directly related to the issue.

1. _____

2. _____

3. _____

For this project you are required to use the Internet as a resource. Find at least two specific online sources that provide useful information about your topic and cite them below. Use only reputable Web sites for your research.

INTERNET SOURCE #1

1. Name of author and/or editor: _____

2. Title of the work: _____

3. Date of electronic publication or posting (month, day, year): _____

4. Name of publisher: _____

5. Date that you accessed information on the site (month, day, year): _____

6. The Web site URL (address): _____

continues ☞

INTERNET SOURCE #2

1. Name of author and/or editor: _____

2. Title of the work:_____

3. Date of electronic publication or posting (month, day, year):_____

4. Name of publisher:_____

5. Date that you accessed information on the site (month, day, year):_____

6. The Web site URL (address):_____

Record the three strongest reasons you can think of for a voter to support your candidate's position on this issue:

1. _____

2. _____

3. _____

Choose one of the reasons for supporting the candidate's position and describe the key points you will build into your paper to help convince an audience that this reason is powerful and believable.

_____

_____

On a separate sheet of paper, record the who, what, when, why, and how information that you intend to include in your paper.

Compose a campaign slogan that conveys the candidate's stand on the issue. The slogan must be seven words or fewer. Use the slogan as the headline or title of your paper.

Slogan:_____

Approval to write this position paper is granted by: _____

The Candidates' Debate
Assignment Sheet
Area of Expertise: Politician

Name: _____ **I Support Candidate:** _____ **Date:** _____

As a politician you will write a "take a stand" paper that strongly and positively supports your candidate's position while also pointing out some of the weaknesses of the position taken by the other candidate. This paper could be used as a political speech. Its purpose is to develop an effective argument, support the argument with solid evidence, and present the evidence in a convincing manner. You want voters to read the paper (or hear the speech) and say, "I agree with that!" After completing the position paper, you will present it orally. This will be your opportunity to support the candidate's perspective with researched data, not just opinion.

Complete the Position Paper Proposal and turn it in to the campaign manager (a.k.a. your teacher) for approval. Once approval has been given, you may begin writing the paper and preparing for your presentation.

Position Paper Proposal

List three descriptive keywords or phrases that are directly related to the issue.

1. _____

2. _____

3. _____

For this project you are required to use the Internet as a resource. Find at least two specific online sources that provide useful information about your topic and cite them below. Use only reputable Web sites for your research.

INTERNET SOURCE #1

1. Name of author and/or editor: _____

2. Title of the work: _____

3. Date of electronic publication or posting (month, day, year): _____

4. Name of publisher: _____

5. Date that you accessed information on the site (month, day, year): _____

6. The Web site URL (address): _____

continues ☞

INTERNET SOURCE #2

1. Name of author and/or editor: _____

2. Title of the work:_____

3. Date of electronic publication or posting (month, day, year):_____

4. Name of publisher:_____

5. Date that you accessed information on the site (month, day, year):_____

6. The Web site URL (address):_____

Record the three strongest reasons you can think of for a voter to support your candidate's position on this issue:

1. _____

2. _____

3. _____

Choose one of the reasons for supporting the candidate's position and describe the key points you will build into your paper to help convince an audience that this reason is powerful and believable.

_____

_____

On a separate sheet of paper, describe the best argument you can think of that will help convince voters that your candidate's opponent is wrong on this issue. Include this argument in your paper.

Compose a campaign slogan that conveys the candidate's stand on the issue. The slogan must be seven words or fewer. Use the slogan as the title of your paper.

Slogan:_____

Approval to write this position paper is granted by: _____

The Candidates' Debate

Assignment Sheet
Area of Expertise: Scientist

Name: _____ I Support Candidate: _____ Date: _____

As a scientist you will write a paper that provides a factual, scientific basis for your candidate's position. The opposition will likely cite scientific evidence to back up its arguments, so your candidate wants to be well informed about such things as key theories, discoveries, ideas, background knowledge, and the potential for scientific advancement related to this campaign issue. It is important your candidate be prepared to debate the issue with clear, accurate information that supports his or her position. After completing the position paper, you will present it orally. This will be your opportunity to support the candidate's perspective with researched data, not just opinion.

Complete the Position Paper Proposal and turn it in to the campaign manager (a.k.a. your teacher) for approval. Once approval has been given, you may begin writing the report and preparing for your presentation.

Position Paper Proposal

List three descriptive keywords or phrases that are directly related to the issue.

1. _____

2. _____

3. _____

For this project you are required to use the Internet as a resource. Find at least two specific online sources that provide useful information about your topic and cite them below. Use only reputable Web sites for your research.

INTERNET SOURCE #1

1. Name of author and/or editor: _____

2. Title of the work: _____

3. Date of electronic publication or posting (month, day, year): _____

4. Name of publisher: _____

5. Date that you accessed information on the site (month, day, year): _____

6. The Web site URL (address): _____

continues ☛

INTERNET SOURCE #2

1. Name of author and/or editor: _____

2. Title of the work:_____

3. Date of electronic publication or posting (month, day, year):_____

4. Name of publisher:_____

5. Date that you accessed information on the site (month, day, year):_____

6. The Web site URL (address):_____

Record the three strongest reasons you can think of for a voter to support your candidate's position on this issue:

1. _____

2. _____

3. _____

Choose one of the reasons for supporting the candidate's position and describe the key points you will build into your paper to help convince an audience that this reason is powerful and believable.

_____

_____

On a separate sheet of paper, record two areas of science (examples include astronomy, ecology, biology, chemistry, physics, climatology, geology, archeology, medicine, technology, and so forth) and explain how the candidate's position is related to each area. Use this information in the paper.

Compose a campaign slogan that conveys the candidate's stand on the issue. The slogan must be seven words or fewer. Use the slogan as the title of your paper.

Slogan:_____

Approval to write this position paper is granted by: _____

The Candidates' Debate
Assignment Sheet
Area of Expertise: Sociologist

Name: _____ I Support Candidate: _____ Date: _____

As a sociologist you will write a paper that looks at the social implications of the issue and how your candidate's position will affect specific groups of people, or Americans in general. This is likely to be a positive impact that benefits people if it is to encourage voters to support your candidate, although you may point out negative impacts as well. Your candidate wants to connect at an emotional level with voters, and this paper will help. It is important to be prepared to debate the issue with clear, accurate information that supports his or her position. After completing the position paper, you will present it orally. This will be your opportunity to support the candidate's perspective with researched data, not just opinion.

Complete the Position Paper Proposal and turn it in to the campaign manager (a.k.a. your teacher) for approval. Once approval has been given, you may begin writing the paper and preparing for your presentation.

Position Paper Proposal

List three descriptive keywords or phrases that are directly related to the issue.

1. _____

2. _____

3. _____

For this project you are required to use the Internet as a resource. Find at least two specific online sources that provide useful information about your topic and cite them below. Use only reputable Web sites for your research.

INTERNET SOURCE #1

1. Name of author and/or editor: _____

2. Title of the work: _____

3. Date of electronic publication or posting (month, day, year): _____

4. Name of publisher: _____

5. Date that you accessed information on the site (month, day, year): _____

6. The Web site URL (address): _____

continues ☞

INTERNET SOURCE #2

1. Name of author and/or editor: _____

2. Title of the work:_____

3. Date of electronic publication or posting (month, day, year):_____

4. Name of publisher:_____

5. Date that you accessed information on the site (month, day, year):_____

6. The Web site URL (address):_____

Record the three strongest reasons you can think of for a voter to support your candidate's position on this issue:

1. _____

2. _____

3. _____

Choose one of the reasons for supporting the candidate's position and describe the key points you will build into your paper to help convince an audience that this reason is powerful and believable.

_____

_____

On a separate sheet of paper, identify two demographics (groups of people who share one or more of the following characteristics: gender, ethnicity, age, income level, health status, education level, type of employment, religion, residence, and so forth) and explain how your candidate's position affects each group. Use this information in the report.

Compose a campaign slogan that conveys the candidate's stand on the issue. The slogan must be seven words or fewer. Use the slogan as the title of your paper.

Slogan:_____

Approval to write this position paper is granted by: _____

The Candidates' Debate
Assessment Sheet

Name: _____ **Date:** _____

Area of Expertise: _____

POSITION PAPER PROPOSAL

- ☐ Chose a candidate to support, based on the candidate's position on a clearly defined issue.

- ☐ Identified three keywords or phrases directly related to the issue.

- ☐ Discovered two reliable Internet sources that provide accurate, useful information about the issue.

- ☐ Cited each Internet source, using a correct citation form for each source.

- ☐ Recorded three convincing reasons for voters to support the candidate's position.

- ☐ Chose one reason and described key points that correctly and appropriately support it.

- ☐ Included required information on the Position Paper Proposal.

- ☐ Developed an appropriate, descriptive campaign slogan of seven words or less.

POSITION PAPER

- ☐ Composed a well-written research paper appropriate for a specific audience.

- ☐ Included accurate information about the issue.

- ☐ Sequenced information in ways that make it clear and easy to understand.

- ☐ Included recognizable, appropriate organizational patterns.

- ☐ Exhibited a personal writing style that enhances the message.

- ☐ Used a variety of grammatical structures.

- ☐ Used correct spelling conventions.

- ☐ Produced a persuasive piece that effectively presents the candidate's position on the issue.

ORAL PRESENTATION

- ☐ Opened the presentation with an interesting and engaging beginning.

- ☐ Presented enough accurate, well-organized information to thoroughly cover the topic.

- ☐ Used correct vocabulary and understood what all words meant.

- ☐ Spoke loudly and clearly enough for everyone in the audience to hear and understand.

- ☐ Spoke slowly and distinctly, using an expressive tone of voice.

- ☐ Maintained regular eye contact with a variety of people in the audience.

- ☐ Demonstrated appropriate posture, body movement, and facial expressions.

- ☐ Ended the presentation with a well-developed conclusion statement.

- ☐ Provided a concise, thoughtful description of the central idea when asked.

Project Planner

Continental Cubing Competition

Content Focus: English/Language Arts
Class Periods: 3

Project Scenario

Students are part of three-member teams that are preparing to compete at the annual Continental Cubing Competition in the area of literature. You are their coach. Each team member rolls a die (cube) to find out which individual task he or she will complete for the competition.

Project Synopsis

The project's focus is on reading and analyzing literature. Each possible assignment at the cubing competition asks students to think critically about some aspect of the literature they have read. There is a wide range of choice for creating a final product, including creating a two-column chart, composing an essay, or identifying a global theme in the literature. Students must be prepared to complete any of the tasks, since the rolling of a die (chance) determines what they must work on.

Differentiation Strategies

- Flexible grouping
- Tiered assignments
- Cubing

Student Forms

- Introduction
- Assignment Sheet 1
- Assignment Sheet 2
- Assignment Sheet 3
- Assessment Sheet

Content Standards*

Note: The task a student is assigned (with the roll of the die) determines which standards are covered.

1. Students read a wide range of print and nonprint texts to build an understanding of texts, of themselves, and of the cultures of the United States and the world; to acquire new information; to respond to the needs and demands of society and the workplace; and for personal fulfillment. Among these texts are fiction and nonfiction, and classic and contemporary works.

2. Students read a wide range of literature from many periods in many genres to build an understanding of the many dimensions (e.g., philosophical, ethical, aesthetic) of human experience.

3. Students apply a wide range of strategies to comprehend, interpret, evaluate, and appreciate texts. They draw on their prior experience, their interactions with other readers and writers, their knowledge of word meaning and of other texts, their word-identification strategies, and their understanding of textual features (e.g., sound-letter correspondence, sentence structure, context, graphics).

4. Students adjust their use of spoken, written, and visual language (e.g., conventions, style, vocabulary) to communicate effectively with a variety of audiences and for different purposes.

5. Students employ a wide range of strategies as they write and use different writing-process

---

*Standards for the English Language Arts are from the National Council of Teachers of English (NCTE).

Continental Cubing Competition | **Project Planner** *continued*

elements appropriately to communicate with different audiences for a variety of purposes.

6. Students apply knowledge of language structure, language conventions (e.g., spelling and punctuation), media techniques, figurative language, and genre to create, critique, and discuss print and nonprint texts.

7. Students participate as knowledgeable, reflective, creative, and critical members of a variety of literacy communities.

8. Students use spoken, written, and visual language to accomplish their own purposes (e.g., for learning, enjoyment, persuasion, and the exchange of information).

How to Use This Project

1. Assign each student a piece of literature to read as homework. Be sure to select a story or passage that has multiple characters, since one of the tasks asks students to analyze relationships among characters. *Note:* You may choose to assign all students the same story or assign different stories based on reading level. (See "Methods of Differentiation" for more detail.)

2. Put students into groups of three, based on reading proficiency or by readiness to tackle analytical tasks.

3. Before presenting the project to students, examine the requirements for Tasks #2 and #3 on each assignment sheet. You will see that students have to choose topics from a list of options for each of these tasks. You may want to narrow their choice based on what you expect them to focus on in your literature class. If so, cross off the options that are not available to them.

4. Review the Introduction in a class discussion.

5. Give students in each group the Assessment Sheet and the appropriate assignment sheet. Assignment Sheet 1 is the lowest complexity; Assignment Sheet 3 is the highest. Go over the

points on the Assessment Sheet so that students understand how the project will be graded.

6. Model the cubing process and rules by having a three-student team demonstrate in front of the class how to determine each member's task according to the directions in the Introduction (see "Competition Rules for Team Cubing" on pages 88–89): In turn, each of the three members rolls the die, decides to accept the task that coordinates with the number on the die (or to pass the task to a willing teammate and roll again), and records the assigned task on the assignment sheet.

7. Inform students about the time requirements for the project. A typical time frame is three class periods (not including time spent reading the story):

- Period 1: Students learn about the project, form groups, examine their group's assignment sheet, discuss the rules, and observe the cubing process as it is modeled for the class.

- Period 2: During the second period, each group goes through the cubing process to identify a specific task for each group member and then devotes the rest of the period to working on the assigned tasks.

- Period 3: Students complete their work and their Assessment Sheets. (See the sample assessment rubric for this project included on page 49.)

Methods of Differentiation

Cubing is a popular differentiation strategy that is used either to let students examine a single topic from six different perspectives (the six levels of Bloom's taxonomy, for example) or to let students randomly select one of six different topics to study. Each face of a cube represents a specific task. Students determine which assignments they will complete by rolling the cube. Cubing provides novelty because students do not know which assignment they will "roll." It also adds variety because the randomness of rolling a cube means that six different assignments will be worked on simultaneously in the classroom.

Tiered assignments are also used as a differentiation method in this project. Tiering is accomplished by grouping students homogeneously, according to their readiness to learn or apply skills. Assignments or tasks are typically tiered for three levels: struggling learners, on-target learners, and advanced learners. Tiered assignments may be organized in at least three different ways for this project through the use of flexible grouping:

1. **Differentiate by reading level.** Using the assessment and observation data at your disposal, group students by their reading proficiency and assign appropriate reading material to each team of three. This means that the project will be conducted using a variety of texts. All students are expected to complete the same tasks (for example, use Assignment Sheet 2 with all groups), but the difficulty of the reading material will vary, depending on the assigned reading.

2. **Differentiate by task complexity.** Have everyone read the same text, but group students by their readiness to analyze what they have read. In this case, some teams will work from Assignment Sheet 1 (least complex and challenging), others will work from Assignment Sheet 2 (more complex and challenging), and the rest will work from Assignment Sheet 3 (highest level of complexity and challenge).

3. **Differentiate by both reading level and task complexity.** In this case, the least proficient readers are grouped in teams and will read simple texts and work from Assignment Sheet 1. Teams of more-proficient readers will read more-difficult texts and work from Assignment Sheet 2. The best readers will read texts at their level and work from Assignment Sheet 3.

Ideas for Extending or Modifying the Project

1. Eliminate the team component and conduct the project as an individual cubing activity. Each student rolls the die to identify an assigned task and has the option of rolling a second time to select a different task.

2. Conduct the project multiple times during the year. Require students to do a different task each time, and keep a chart to record the tasks students have completed over a semester or the year.

3. Use large foam dice to make the cubing process more interesting.

4. Add a presentation component to the project. Have each team develop a presentation for the class that incorporates the work of all three team members. This will require additional time.

Suggested Content Modifications

SCIENCE

After studying a complex, multi-sided issue related to science, such as global warming, stem cell research, or genetic engineering, compose a debate-like resolution that can be either agreed with or disagreed with. For example: "Resolved: That global warming is real and is caused primarily by carbon emissions produced by human beings." Have students take a stand (agree or disagree with the resolution) and roll a cube showing these six questions to be answered from a scientific standpoint:

1. What evidence supports your stand on this issue?

2. Why is this issue important?

3. What should we do (or not do) about this issue?

4. What do others think about this issue?

5. What counterarguments could be used against your stand?

6. What is your prediction for the future?

Continental Cubing Competition | **Project Planner** *continued*

MATH

Give students a math problem and have them provide a solution in one of the six following ways, determined by a roll of the cube:

1. Explain the solution with pictures or drawings.

2. Explain the solution in writing, using complete sentences.

3. Demonstrate the solution with manipulatives.

4. Show two different ways the problem could be solved.

5. Solve the problem, then show why the answer is reasonable.

6. Present the solution orally in any way you choose.

SOCIAL STUDIES

After studying a historical or current topic related to social studies, such as the Louisiana Purchase, the Emancipation Proclamation, the North American Free Trade Agreement, or American military involvement in the Middle East, ask students to explain the topic from a perspective selected by the roll of a cube that shows these six tasks:

1. Explain the topic from the perspective of economics.

2. Explain the topic from the perspective of history.

3. Explain the topic from the perspective of geography.

4. Explain the topic from the perspective of civics.

5. Explain the topic from the perspective of inquiry. (Why did this happen?)

6. Explain the topic from any perspective you choose.

Continental Cubing Competition
Introduction

Name: _____ Date: _____

This project focuses on reading and analyzing literature. It uses a process called "cubing" (rolling labeled dice) to identify required tasks, so your specific assignment will remain a mystery until the project actually begins. Selecting tasks based on chance adds challenge and interest, but the main purpose of the project is to let you demonstrate your understanding of the reading you have done.

Project Scenario

Your school has decided to enter a team in this year's Continental Cubing Competition. This is an annual event that brings teams together from all over the North American continent to compete in the academic areas of science, social studies, mathematics, and literature. You and your teammates will participate in the literature competition and have gathered together to begin practicing.

Assignment

The competition works like this:

1. Teams receive a piece of literature to read before the competition starts.

2. At the beginning of the competition, team members roll a die to randomly identify a task to complete (this is where the term *cubing* comes from—a die is a cube). There are six numbers on a die, and there are six tasks, numbered 1 to 6. When a team member rolls the die, the number that is rolled determines the assigned task. Competition rules for team cubing are provided below.

3. The competition is timed, so it's important to understand the task quickly, organize ideas effectively, and think on your feet.

4. When time is up, each team member's finished work is turned in to a judge to be scored.

5. A very high priority is placed on correctly interpreting the task and producing a final product that clearly accomplishes what the task prompt asks for.

Your team coach (a.k.a. your teacher) is ready to begin practice rounds. Use the following competition rules for team cubing to prepare for the Continental Cubing Competition.

Competition Rules for Team Cubing

A team consists of three members. In some special cases a team may have two or four members.

1. Team members receive an assignment sheet at the beginning of the project. The assignment sheet describes each task (numbered 1 to 6) and explains what must be done to complete it.

continues ☞

2. Team Member A rolls the die. Whatever number comes up becomes the assigned task.

3. Now a decision must be made. The team has one minute to choose Option 1, 2, or 3:

- Option 1: Team Member A may accept the assigned task.

- Option 2: Team Member A may give the task to another willing team member and roll again, but he or she must accept the next roll. (*Note:* If the same number comes up on the second throw, roll the die again.)

- Option 3: Team Member A may decline the task and roll again, but he or she must accept the next roll. (*Note:* If the same number comes up on the second throw, roll the die again.)

4. Team Member B rolls the die. Whatever number comes up becomes that person's assigned task. (*Note:* This may not be the same number as Team Member A's task, or the same number as any task Team Member A passed to other team members. If it is, roll the die again.)

5. Another decision must be made. The team has one minute to choose Option 1, 2, or 3:

- Option 1: Team Member B may accept the assigned task.

- Option 2: Team Member B may give the task to the remaining team member (if he or she does not already have a task and is willing to take it) and roll again. The next roll must be accepted by Team Member B. (*Note:* If the same number comes up on the second throw, or if the same number is rolled as another team member's task, roll the die again.)

- Option 3: Team Member B may decline the task and roll again, but he or she must accept the next roll. (*Note:* If the same number comes up on the second throw, or if the same number is rolled as another team member's task, roll the die again.)

6. Team Member C rolls the die if he or she still does not have an assigned task. This may not be the same number as the task of Team Member A or Team Member B. If it is, roll the die again. Team Member C may decline the task and roll again, but he or she must accept the next roll. (*Note:* If the same number comes up on the second throw, or if the same number is rolled as another team member's task, roll the die again.)

7. Following this cubing process, each group member has a different assigned task to complete.

8. Team members may collaborate, but each person must turn in his or her own final product.

Continental Cubing Competition
Assignment Sheet 1

Name: _____ **Date:** _____

Put a check mark next to the task you will complete. If you are working in a team, you may not have the same task as any of your teammates. Your coach (a.k.a. teacher) will tell you how much time you have.

☐ Task 1: **Compose an essay** that describes how at least two characters in the story formed opinions about one another. Tell what their opinions of each other were, how they arrived at their opinions, and why these opinions were fair or unfair. Provide details and examples from the story to support your ideas.

☐ Task 2: **Create a two-column chart** and use it to analyze the role of any three of these story elements: dialogue, plot, theme, major characters, minor characters, climax, antagonist, protagonist, internal conflict, external conflict, rising and falling action, minor characters in relation to conflict, and credibility of the narrator. Choose three of these elements and put them in the left column of the chart. In the right column, explain how the author used each element to develop the story.

☐ Task 3: **Design a graphic organizer** to show how the author used any two of the following storytelling techniques to develop the plot: dialogue, imagery, understatement, overstatement, theme, antagonists, protagonists, exaggeration, symbolism, imagery, and consistency. Write "author's craft" in the center of a piece of unlined paper, posterboard, or computer screen. Draw two large spaces on either side of the words to frame your explanations—you can use circles, squares, ovals, or any other shape you want. In each space, record one of the storytelling techniques and explain how the author used it to develop the plot of the story.

☐ Task 4: **Construct a concept map** or web that shows connections between you and the story you have read. On a piece of unlined paper, posterboard, or on a computer, record two key themes that you have identified in the story. Leave plenty of room around each item. Then, record at least two of your own experiences, beliefs, or ideas that are related to each theme and use lines to show the connections. Explain your reasons for making each connection.

☐ Task 5: **Produce a series of at least 5 drawings** to summarize the story. This is not an art project, but you may use sketches, cartoon drawings, computer images, or stick figures if that is more comfortable. Use the drawings to show the order in which events took place, and to highlight important parts of the story. If necessary, use writing on each drawing to make your meaning clear. Put your finished drawings in correct order to summarize the story, either as a booklet or as a storyboard that can be displayed on a wall.

☐ Task 6: **Identify a global theme** or universal truth in the story and describe how it is presented in the story. In other words, provide evidence that the theme or truth you have described really is an important part of the story. Include in your final product a simple explanation of what is meant by the terms "global theme" and "universal truth." You may use any method you want to complete this task: art, multimedia, writing, poetry, graphic organizer, chart, or another method of your choice.

Continental Cubing Competition
Assignment Sheet 2

Name: _____ **Date:** _____

Put a check mark next to the task you will complete. If you are working in a team, you may not have the same task as any of your teammates. Your coach (a.k.a. teacher) will tell you how much time you have.

☐ Task 1: **Compose an essay** about the tensions between at least two characters in the story, and tell how they are related to your own experiences. Explain what caused tensions among the characters and describe how those tensions are similar to ones you have observed among others, including in yourself. Provide details and examples from the story to support your ideas.

☐ Task 2: **Create a 3-column chart** and use it to analyze the role of any three of these story elements: dialogue, plot, theme, major characters, minor characters, climax, antagonist, protagonist, internal conflict, external conflict, rising and falling action, minor characters in relation to conflict, and credibility of the narrator. Enter the three elements in the left column of the chart. In the middle column, explain how the author used each story element to develop the story. In the last column, cite a specific example from the text to support your claim.

☐ Task 3: **Design a graphic organizer** to show how the author used any three of the following story-telling techniques to develop the plot: dialogue, imagery, understatement, overstatement, theme, antagonists, protagonists, exaggeration, symbolism, imagery, and consistency. Write "author's craft" in the center of a piece of unlined paper, posterboard, or computer screen. Draw three large spaces near the words to frame your explanations—you can use circles, squares, ovals, or any other shape you want. In each space, record one of the techniques and explain how the author used it to develop the story.

☐ Task 4: **Construct a concept map** or web that shows connections between you and the story you have read. On a piece of unlined paper, posterboard, or on a computer, record two key themes that you have identified in the story. Leave plenty of room around each item. Then, record at least two examples from the story and two of your own experiences, beliefs, or ideas and that are related to each theme, and use lines to show the connections.

☐ Task 5: **Produce a series of 5 drawings** to summarize the story. This is not an art project, but you may use sketches, cartoon drawings, computer images, or stick figures if that is more comfortable. Use the drawings to show the order in which events took place, and to highlight important parts of the story. If necessary, use writing on each drawing to make your meaning clear. Identify three of the drawings as key events, and briefly explain the importance of each one. Put your finished drawings in correct order to summarize the story, either as a booklet or as a storyboard that can be displayed on a wall.

☐ Task 6: **Identify a global theme** or universal truth in the story. Explain why it should be considered global or universal, and provide evidence that it is an important part of the story. You may use any method you want to complete this task: art, multimedia, writing, poetry, graphic organizer, chart, or another method of your choice.

Continental Cubing Competition
Assignment Sheet 3

Name: _____ **Date:** _____

Put a check mark next to the task you will complete. If you are working in a team, you may not have the same task as any of your teammates. Your coach (a.k.a. teacher) will tell you how much time you have.

☐ Task 1: **Compose an essay** about the use of distortion or stereotypes to highlight individual differences among characters, such as those associated with gender, race, culture, age, dress, class, physical size, intelligence, social status, economic standing, and religion. Explain how these individual differences are represented in the story and why they are distortions or stereotypes. Provide details and examples from the story to support your ideas.

☐ Task 2: **Create a 4-column chart** to analyze the role of any three of these story elements: dialogue, plot, theme, major characters, minor characters, climax, antagonist, protagonist, internal conflict, external conflict, rising and falling action, minor characters in relation to conflict, and credibility of the narrator. In Column 1 enter the elements you have chosen. In Column 2 explain what role each element played in the story. In Column 3 cite specific examples from the text. In Column 4 rate the author's effective use of the element on a 5-point scale (5 = high; 1 = low).

☐ Task 3: **Design a graphic organizer** to show how the author used any four of the following storytelling techniques to develop the plot: dialogue, imagery, understatement, overstatement, theme, antagonists, protagonists, exaggeration, symbolism, imagery, and consistency. Write or type "author's craft" in the center of a piece of unlined paper, posterboard, or computer screen. Draw four large spaces near the words to frame your explanations—you can use circles, squares, ovals, or any other shape you want. In each space, record one of the techniques and explain how the author used it to develop the story.

☐ Task 4: **Construct a concept map** or web that shows connections between you and the story you have read. On a piece of unlined paper, posterboard, or on a computer, record two key themes that you have identified in the story. Leave plenty of room around each item. Then, record at least two of your own experiences, beliefs, or ideas that are related to each theme and use lines to show the connections. For each connection that you make, provide an example from the story and explain why your experience is similar to the example.

☐ Task 5: **Produce a series of 5 drawings** to summarize the story. This is not an art project, but you may use sketches, cartoon drawings, computer images, or stick figures if that is more comfortable. Use the drawings to show the order in which events took place, and to highlight important parts of the story. If necessary, use writing to make your meaning clear. Identify three of the drawings as key events, and briefly explain the importance of each one. Label one of the key events as the "central event" and tell why this is the most important event in the story. Put your finished drawings in correct order to summarize the story, either as a booklet or as a storyboard that can be displayed on a wall.

continues ☞

☐ Task 6: **Identify a global theme** or universal truth in the story. Explain why it should be considered global or universal, and provide evidence that it is an important part of the story. Identify a real-world example of the same theme or truth and include it in your final product. You may use any method you want to complete this task: art, multimedia, writing, poetry, graphic organizer, chart, or other method of your choice.

Continental Cubing Competition
Assessment Sheet

Name: _____ **Date:** _____

TASK 1: COMPOSE AN ESSAY

☐ Wrote an essay that is well organized and supports the key ideas.

☐ Demonstrated a clear understanding of assignment guidelines and requirements.

☐ Described accurately the relationships among characters as called for by the assignment.

☐ Provided details and examples from the story to support ideas in the essay.

☐ Demonstrated a commitment to quality.

TASK 2: CREATE A COLUMN CHART

☐ Created a column chart that is well organized and focuses on appropriate topics.

☐ Demonstrated a clear understanding of assignment guidelines and requirements.

☐ Analyzed correctly the role of three story elements used by the author.

☐ Provided details and examples from the story to support ideas recorded on the chart.

☐ Demonstrated a commitment to quality.

TASK 3: DESIGN A GRAPHIC ORGANIZER

☐ Created a graphic organizer that is well designed and focuses on appropriate topics.

☐ Demonstrated a clear understanding of assignment guidelines and requirements.

☐ Described accurately examples of the author's craft.

☐ Provided details and examples from the story to support ideas recorded on the organizer.

☐ Demonstrated a commitment to quality.

TASK 4: CONSTRUCT A CONCEPT MAP

☐ Constructed a concept map or web that is well designed and focuses on appropriate topics.

☐ Demonstrated a clear understanding of assignment guidelines and requirements.

☐ Identified correctly two themes from the story.

☐ Made logical connections between the themes and personal experiences, beliefs, or ideas.

☐ Demonstrated a commitment to quality.

continues ☞

TASK 5: PRODUCE A SERIES OF DRAWINGS

☐ Produced five drawings that focus on appropriate topics and are properly sequenced.

☐ Demonstrated a clear understanding of assignment guidelines and requirements.

☐ Summarized the story correctly by choosing key events to illustrate with drawings.

☐ Provided details, examples, and explanations with the drawings to help summarize the story.

☐ Demonstrated a commitment to quality.

TASK 6: IDENTIFY A GLOBAL THEME

☐ Completed the task using a method that is well designed and focuses on appropriate topics.

☐ Demonstrated a clear understanding of assignment guidelines and requirements.

☐ Described correctly and completely a global theme or universal truth from the story.

☐ Provided details and examples to show that the theme or truth is an important part of the story.

☐ Demonstrated a commitment to quality.

Math Investment Plan

Content Focus: Math

Class Periods: Varies with the length of the unit being compacted or amount of time available for anchor activities

Project Scenario

Students are math entrepreneurs who have "investment options" within the math curriculum. You are their investment adviser.

Project Synopsis

"Math Investment Plan" introduces the concepts of curriculum compacting and anchor activities to students through economic metaphors. In a typical classroom, all students spend class time completing the same required tasks. In this project, students may make personal investments in math by "buying back" class time and spending it more profitably. This makes them math entrepreneurs. They can increase dividends by earning the right to spend their time differently. The project's title implies that a student can improve his or her prospects by learning math, and that a carefully planned investment in math can strengthen a person's life-preparation portfolio. Handouts are provided for one fully developed example of an alternative math project (or "investment option"). called "Time of My Life." You will provide materials for the remaining investment options. (See the schematic on page 98 for more detail on investment options.)

Differentiation Strategies

- Curriculum compacting
- Anchor activities

Student Forms

- Introduction
- "Time of My Life" Chart 1: School Days
- "Time of My Life" Chart 2: Weekends and Vacation Days

- "Time of My Life" Chart 3: Student Poll
- "Time of My Life" Chart 4: Graph-a-Day
- "Time of My Life" Charts 5 & 6: Charting the Future
- "Time of My Life" Chart 7: Changes Over Time
- Assessment Sheet

Content Standards*

Standards taught with the "Time of My Life" investment option are listed below. For the investment options that you provide for students, you will identify standards.

1. Students understand numbers, ways of representing numbers, relationships among numbers, and number systems. Expectation: Students work flexibly with fractions, decimals, and percents to solve problems.

2. Students understand meanings of operations and how they relate to one another. Expectation: Students understand the meaning and effects of arithmetic operations with fractions, decimals, and integers.

3. Students compute fluently and make reasonable estimates. Expectations:

   - Students develop and analyze algorithms for computing with fractions, decimals, and integers, and develop fluency in their use.

   - Students develop, analyze, and explain methods for solving problems involving proportions, such as scaling and finding equivalent ratios.

Principles and Standards for School Mathematics are listed with the permission of the National Council of Teachers of Mathematics (NCTM). NCTM does not endorse the content or validity of these alignments.

4. Students understand measurable attributes of objects and the units, systems, and processes of measurement. Expectation: Students understand relationships among units and convert from one unit to another within the same system.

How to Use This Project

This project may be used to compact the curriculum for advanced students who test out of an upcoming unit, and it also provides a basis for offering anchor activities to students who don't initially test out of the unit, but end up having time available as they demonstrate understanding of the math being covered. (See "Methods of Differentiation" on page 99 for more detail.)

Examine the diagram on the following page. In general, the diagram illustrates the concept of curriculum compacting and shows one way to think about how you would organize the system in your class. Following is a step-by-step explanation of how to complete the Math Investment Plan Organizer that is provided on the Introduction handout, along with an explanation of the example investment project titled "Time of My Life."

Using the Introduction handout, follow these steps to complete a math investment plan with a student who is a candidate for curriculum compacting or anchor activities:

1. Analyze the pretest results or completed coursework, and record the key concepts that have been mastered.

2. Record evidence of mastery. This may be as simple as writing, "Scored 95% on the chapter pretest," or "Completed planned coursework."

3. Analyze the pretest results or completed coursework to determine whether there are any gaps in knowledge and understanding. If any are discovered, record them under "Still Needs Work."

4. Reach agreement with the student on what tasks need to be done to help bridge the identified gaps, and record them under "Assignments/Tasks to Be Completed."

5. Help the student choose a project in which to invest his or her available time during math class (e.g., the "Time of My Life" project, which is included in this project as an example; see below).

6. Record evidence of success at the completion of the project. This may take many forms, depending on how the student has chosen to invest his or her time.

7. If the student chose to complete the "Time of My Life" project, or parts of it, have him or her fill out the Assessment Sheet.

The alternative math project (or "investment option"), "Time of My Life," focuses on fractions, decimals, percents, and ratios. It provides six data charts; students may complete one or any number in various combinations. The student instructions make each chart self-explanatory, which means that each one can easily be used as an anchor activity for students following the regular curriculum.

- "Time of My Life" Charts 1 and 2 ask the student to record personal activities, determine what fraction of a school day or a vacation day each activity represents, and then calculate what percent of a day the activity takes.

- "Time of My Life" Chart 3 asks the student to collect data from other students about their daily activities, and calculate for each activity the average and the percent of a day that the average represents.

- "Time of My Life" Chart 4 asks the student to graph data from one of the other charts.

- "Time of My Life" Chart 5 asks the student to use ratios to determine how many minutes, hours, days, and years are devoted to daily activities over extended periods of time.

- "Time of My Life" Chart 6 asks the student to form a calculation and chart a percentage increase in time spent on homework over ten years in school.

COMPACTING THE CURRICULUM FOR "MATH INVESTMENT PLAN"

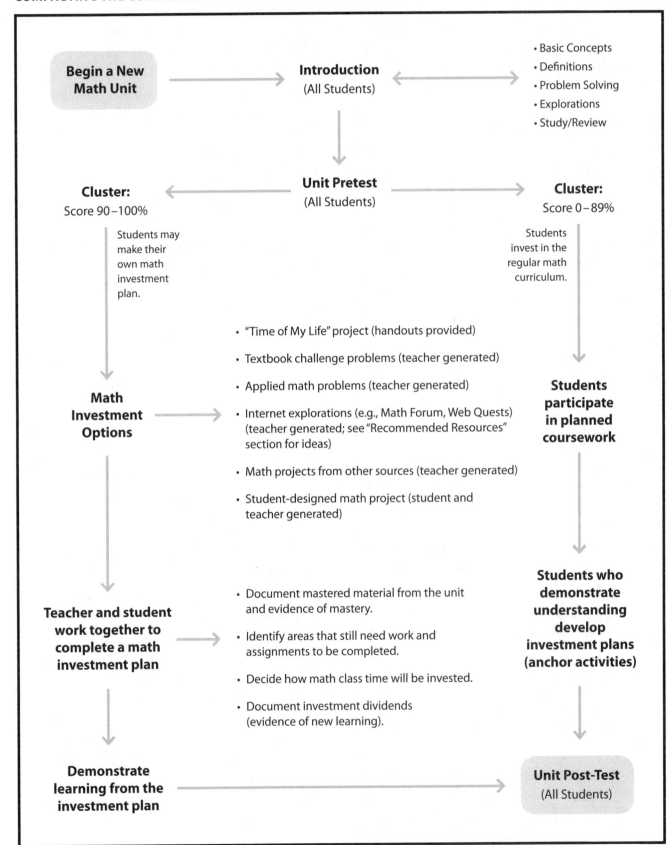

Begin a New Math Unit

Introduction (All Students)

- Basic Concepts
- Definitions
- Problem Solving
- Explorations
- Study/Review

Unit Pretest (All Students)

Cluster: Score 90–100%

Students may make their own math investment plan.

Cluster: Score 0–89%

Students invest in the regular math curriculum.

Math Investment Options

- "Time of My Life" project (handouts provided)
- Textbook challenge problems (teacher generated)
- Applied math problems (teacher generated)
- Internet explorations (e.g., Math Forum, Web Quests) (teacher generated; see "Recommended Resources" section for ideas)
- Math projects from other sources (teacher generated)
- Student-designed math project (student and teacher generated)

Students participate in planned coursework

Teacher and student work together to complete a math investment plan

- Document mastered material from the unit and evidence of mastery.
- Identify areas that still need work and assignments to be completed.
- Decide how math class time will be invested.
- Document investment dividends (evidence of new learning).

Students who demonstrate understanding develop investment plans (anchor activities)

Demonstrate learning from the investment plan

Unit Post-Test (All Students)

Math Investment Plan | Project Planner *continued*

Methods of Differentiation

Curriculum compacting in this project is based on the premise that if a student can demonstrate mastery of the skills, problem-solving procedures, and concepts for a given unit, he or she should have the opportunity to pursue other challenging or interesting areas of math. Mastery is determined through careful pre-assessment. Students who test out of the upcoming unit can create a math investment plan to show how they intend to spend their "currency" (time) wisely. Meanwhile, students who still need to learn the math concepts work with the teacher to establish a sound base for an investment in their future.

Anchor activities do not depend on pretests. They are used when students demonstrate, at any point during a unit, that they have mastered the concepts being taught and are ready to engage in a math investment plan. Rather than bypassing a unit entirely and investing all of their time in a new venture, students who use anchor activities turn their attention to their investment plans periodically. In the context of this project, anchor activities are the equivalent of small investments made whenever there is sufficient capital (time) to do so.

Ideas for Extending or Modifying the Project

1. Think of fun, frivolous things kids do with their time and plug them into the "Time of My Life" Chart 5: Charting the Future. For example, chewing gum. How many minutes does a student chew gum per day? How many "chews" are made per minute? Using this data, how many "chews" will this student make in a lifetime?

2. Use the "Time of My Life" data charts with the entire class, as an instructional unit rather than as a project for students who have compacted out of the regular curriculum.

3. Focus entirely on anchor activities and drop the focus on compacting. In this case, students create math investment plans and

work on projects such as "Time of My Life" at various points during a unit whenever they have earned the time to do so.

Suggested Content Modifications

Here are some alternate learning activities for students who have had the curriculum compacted for them based on a pre-assessment, or who demonstrate mastery of the required curriculum at any point during a unit and have extra time available.

SCIENCE INVESTMENT PLAN

- Ask an "I wonder" question related to topics being covered in class. Then develop a hypothesis based on the question and devise an experiment to test the hypothesis. Report the experimental results and conclusions to the class, or prepare a written report.

- Conduct an advanced investigation or experiment provided by the teacher. Demonstrate the experimental procedure used and describe the results to the class.

- Conduct research to identify real-world applications of concepts, principles, theories, and topics being covered in class. Prepare a report or presentation titled "Why Do We Need to Know This?" to show how the curriculum is connected to life outside the classroom.

- Choose a topic of interest from the curriculum being studied and investigate career opportunities related to that topic. What careers require an understanding of the topic? How does a student prepare himself or herself for one of these careers?

SOCIAL STUDIES INVESTMENT PLAN

- Focus on a specific country and analyze social science data such as population, infant mortality, life expectancy, annual income, imports and exports, GDP (gross domestic product), education, and so forth. Develop tables, charts, and graphs to demonstrate how these data have changed over the past twenty-five years, up to the present. Citing trends indicated in the data,

Math Investment Plan | Project Planner   *continued*

make predictions about the country ten years from now.

- Conduct a current-events study with an emphasis on cause and effect. Choose a current event and create a historical timeline to trace some of the important reasons (causes) why the event happened (effect). The timeline culminates with the chosen current event and shows key factors leading up to it.

- Look at human geography from a local perspective. Interview local adults to develop a "map" of human movement over two or more generations. What brought them to the community? Where did they come from? Were they (or their parents or grandparents or even great-grandparents) "pushed" or "pulled" into the community? How do the things learned about local community residents apply to human populations in general?

- Choose an economics term such as *opportunity cost* or *supply and demand,* and develop a way of illustrating the concept on a micro-scale (yourself) and a macro-scale (the nation). Use real examples to show what the term means and how it is the same and different on a personal level and on a national level.

ENGLISH/LANGUAGE ARTS INVESTMENT PLAN

- Read a novel and develop an analysis of the author's craft. Identify when, how, and why the author used devices such as antagonists and protagonists, distortion, stereotypes, rising and falling action, symbolism, dialogue, imagery, minor characters, internal and external conflict, themes, universal truths, and so forth.

- Choose a method of representing information about the author's craft within the context of the novel. For example, create a timeline for the novel, indicate key points in the story where various devices were used, and explain how and why they were used.

- Choose a local community issue and take a stand on it. Conduct research to gather supporting ideas, information, and data. Compose an essay that supports your position on the issue and submit it to a local newspaper, magazine, or Internet blog.

- Create a book of original writings: essays, short stories, poetry, opinion editorials, and so forth.

- Develop a dramatic presentation of a scene from a novel, short story, or play. Create a script based on the scene that will be performed with actors (classmates), props, costumes, and so forth.

Math Investment Plan
Introduction

Name: _____ **Date:** _____

This project is built on a model taken from economics. The purpose of a thoughtful, well-developed investment in the world of economics is to make a profit. What would you predict is the purpose of a math investment? To participate in this project, you must first demonstrate that you understand the material that will be (or has been) taught in a unit or textbook chapter. Since you are reading this handout, you have likely taken a pretest and done quite well on it, or you have worked to master the unit material and have extra time available. You are now ready to develop a new learning plan for yourself. Take this process seriously. After all, you are preparing to make a personal investment in math!

Project Scenario

You are a math entrepreneur with a goal of increasing the dividends you earn from your math class. The currency in this class is time. In most classes students spend their time doing the same things at the same times. In this class, however, you may demonstrate your understanding of math to buy back time and spend it more profitably. Your investment in math class begins with a productive plan for your time. Once a reasonable plan is in place, you should begin receiving greater returns on your investment.

Assignment

Work with your investment adviser (a.k.a. your teacher) to build a math investment plan, using the planning organizer on this handout. Keep these things in mind as you complete the plan:

1. You and your teacher will first determine your level of mastery of the material that will be (or has been) covered in class.

2. The plan will identify alternative "investment options," such as problem-solving tasks, projects, or activities for you to complete in place of (or in addition to) the regular curriculum.

3. The plan may also include areas of the regular curriculum that you still need to work on.

4. When you complete the plan, you will be assessed. You will be held accountable for quality work, and you will be expected to demonstrate that you understand and can apply the concepts you have studied.

continues ☞

Math Investment Plan Organizer

Mastered Concepts:

Still Needs Work:

Evidence of Mastery:

Assignments/Tasks to Be Completed:

How Student Will Invest Time in Math Class:

Investment Dividends
(Evidence of New Learning):

Math Investment Plan
"Time of My Life" Chart 1: School Days

Name: _____ **Date:** _____

On this handout is a list of common activities that young people do over a typical 24-hour period during the school week. There are nine activities listed, plus an "Everything else" category at the bottom of the chart. Your first task is to add four more school-day activities from your own life. After adding your own activities, follow these guidelines to complete the assignment:

1. Record at the top of the chart the number of minutes in a day.

2. Estimate and record how many minutes you spend on each activity in the list on a typical 24-hour period during the school week.

3. Record in the space titled "Everything else" how many minutes remain in a typical day after you subtract the time you spend on all of the other activities on the list. This means that if you add up the amount of time you have recorded on all lines, it will equal the number of minutes in a day.

4. Record (in lowest terms) what fraction of a day each activity takes.

5. Calculate the decimal equivalent to show in a different way how much of a day each activity takes. Round the decimal to the nearest hundredth.

6. Calculate the percent of a day each activity takes.

7. Add the percents to get a total. What should the total be? Why might it be slightly off?

continues ☞

"Time of My Life" Chart 1: School Days

Reference: 1 day = _____ minutes

Activity	Minutes Spent in 1 Day	Fraction of 1 Day (lowest terms)	Decimal Equivalent (rounded to nearest hundredth)	Percent of 1 Day
Sleeping				
Eating				
Watching TV				
Playing video games				
Talking on the phone and/or text messaging				
Using a computer				
Exercising or playing sports				
Doing homework				
Riding in a car and/or a bus or train				
Everything else				
	Total:			**Total:**

Math Investment Plan
"Time of My Life" Chart 2: Weekends and Vacation Days

Name: _____ **Date:** _____

On this handout is a list of common activities that young people do over a typical 24-hour period when there is no school. There are nine activities listed, plus an "Everything else" category at the bottom of the chart. Your first task is to add four more typical weekend and vacation-day activities from your own life. After adding your own activities, follow these guidelines to complete the assignment:

1. Record at the top of the chart the number of minutes in a day.

2. Estimate and record how many minutes you spend on each activity on a typical weekend or vacation day.

3. Record in the space titled "Everything else" how many minutes remain in a day after you subtract the time you spend on all of the other activities on the list. This means that if you add up the amount of time you have recorded on all lines, it will equal the number of minutes in a day.

4. Record (in lowest terms) what fraction of a day each activity takes.

5. Calculate the decimal equivalent to show in a different way how much of a day each activity takes. Round the decimal to the nearest hundredth.

6. Calculate the percent of a day each activity takes.

7. Add the percents to get a total. What should the total be? Why might it be slightly off?

continues ☞

"Time of My Life" Chart 2: Weekends and Vacation Days

Reference: 1 day = _____ minutes

Activity	Minutes Spent in 1 Day	Fraction of 1 Day (lowest terms)	Decimal Equivalent (rounded to nearest hundredth)	Percent of 1 Day
Sleeping				
Eating				
Watching TV				
Playing video games				
Talking on the phone and/or text messaging				
Using a computer				
Exercising or playing sports				
Doing homework				
Riding in a car and/or a bus or train				
Everything else				
	Total:			Total:

Math Investment Plan
"Time of My Life" Chart 3: Student Poll

Name: _____ **Date:** _____

Follow these guidelines to complete the assignment on this handout:

1. Record at the top of the chart the number of minutes in a day.

2. Identify up to 14 activities that students are likely to do on a typical day, and record them along the left side of the chart.

3. Identify five students to poll, and record their names across the top of the chart.

4. Poll each student and record the number of minutes he or she spends doing each activity on a typical day.

5. Calculate the average number of minutes per day the five students spend doing each activity. Round the answer to the nearest tenth.

6. Calculate what percentage of a day the average for each activity represents.

continues

"Time of My Life" Chart 3: Student Poll

Reference: 1 day = _____ minutes

Activity	Name: minutes/day	Name: minutes/day	Name: minutes/day	Name: minutes/day	Name: minutes/day	average minutes/day	average % of 1day

Math Investment Plan
"Time of My Life" Chart 4: Graph-a-Day

Name: _____ **Date:** _____

Follow these guidelines to complete the assignment:

1. Construct a graph on a piece of graph paper, using data from your own life or the lives of students you have polled. You may make a larger graph on posterboard if you want, or you may enter the data into a spreadsheet and create a graph electronically. You your teacher may also agree that you should construct more than one graph.

Choose one of these options for the graph:

A. Construct a pie graph that shows how you spend time on a typical school day.

B. Construct a pie graph that shows how you spend time on a typical weekend or vacation day.

C. Construct a pie graph that shows the average time spent on activities by students you have polled.

D. Construct a bar graph that shows how much time you spend on school-day activities compared to how much time you spend on the same activities during weekend and vacation time.

E. Construct a bar graph that shows how much time each student you have polled spends on activities compared to the time other students in the poll devote to the same activities.

F. Construct a bar graph that shows how much time you spend on activities compared to the average time students you have polled spend on the same activities.

G. Propose to your teacher a different type of graph to show the data you have collected.

2. Use correct graphing techniques, including an emphasis on accuracy and appropriate use of color, labels, legend, and title.

3. Be prepared to explain what your graph shows and why it is constructed the way it is.

Math Investment Plan
"Time of My Life" Charts 5 & 6: Charting the Future

Name: _____ **Date:** _____

Follow these guidelines to complete the assignment on this handout:

1. Choose an activity that you typically do daily and will likely continue to do for the rest of your life. Examples include sleeping, eating dinner, watching television, brushing your teeth, listening to music, taking a bath or shower, exercising, talking on the phone, instant messaging, reading, and so forth. Write this activity at the top of Chart 5.

2. Record in the "minutes/day" cell of Chart 5 how many minutes per day you devote to the activity.

3. Use your knowledge of ratios to complete the chart, using minutes/day as the starting point.

4. Round all decimals to the nearest hundredth.

5. For the "lifetime" category, assume you will live to be 90 years old. Even though you didn't do the activity when you were a baby, use 90 years as the basis for your calculations.

6. For the "school time" category, count the number of years from now until you graduate from high school or college or vocational/technical school (your choice). Count the current year as a full year.

7. Choose a second activity and repeat the process by completing Chart 6.

8. You may complete additional charts if you want.

continues ☞

"Time of My Life" Chart 5: Charting the Future

Day	minutes/day =	hours/day =		
Week	minutes/week =	hours/week =		
Year	minutes/year =	hours/year =	days/year =	
Schooltime (_____ years)	minutes/schooltime =	hours/schooltime =	days/schooltime =	
Lifetime (90 years)	minutes/lifetime =	hours/lifetime =	days/lifetime =	years/lifetime =

"Time of My Life" Chart 6: Charting the Future

Day	minutes/day =	hours/day =		
Week	minutes/week =	hours/week =		
Year	minutes/year =	hours/year =	days/year =	
Schooltime (_____ years)	minutes/schooltime =	hours/schooltime =	days/schooltime =	
Lifetime (90 years)	minutes/lifetime =	hours/lifetime =	days/lifetime =	years/lifetime =

Math Investment Plan

"Time of My Life" Chart 7: Changes Over Time

Name: _____ **Date:** _____

Follow these guidelines to complete the assignment on this handout:

1. Imagine that you will be a student for the next 10 years, through high school and college or vocational/technical school.

2. Assume also that you will do increasingly more homework each year for the next 10 years.

3. Record below an estimate of how many minutes you spend on homework each day this year.

4. Complete the chart to show how much time you will devote to homework each year, given a 10 percent increase each year over the previous year.

5. Show in the space provided how you will set up a calculation to determine how much time you will spend in the second year on homework if it is 10 percent more time than this year. Use this same formula to calculate time spent on homework for each of the next 10 years.

6. Make a line graph based on your data to see whether there is a recognizable pattern over time.

7. Use correct graphing techniques, including an emphasis on accuracy and appropriate use of color, labels, legend, and title.

8. Be prepared to explain how you calculated the increase in time for each year and why your graph looks like it does.

Estimated minutes/day spent on homework this year (Year 1) = _____

Annual percent increase in minutes/day = 10%

Show how to calculate the minutes/day for Year 2:

continues ☞

"Time of My Life" Chart 7: Changes Over Time

Year 1 = _____ minutes/day

Year 2 = _____ minutes/day

Year 3 = _____ minutes/day

Year 4 = _____ minutes/day

Year 5 = _____ minutes/day

Year 6 = _____ minutes/day

Year 7 = _____ minutes/day

Year 8 = _____ minutes/day

Year 9 = _____ minutes/day

Year 10 = _____ minutes/day

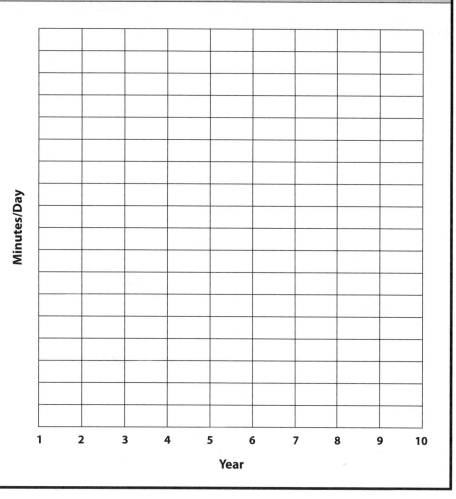

Minutes/Day

1 2 3 4 5 6 7 8 9 10

Year

Math Investment Plan
Assessment Sheet

Name: _____ **Date:** _____

Fill out the following checklists for the charts you have completed.

"TIME OF MY LIFE" CHART 1: SCHOOL DAYS

☐ Calculated the correct number of minutes in a day.

☐ Converted minutes/day for each activity into a correct fraction in lowest terms.

☐ Converted each fraction to its decimal equivalent.

☐ Converted each decimal to its percent equivalent.

☐ Completed the chart accurately and correctly.

☐ Demonstrated a commitment to quality.

"TIME OF MY LIFE" CHART 2: WEEKENDS AND VACATION DAYS

☐ Calculated the correct number of minutes in one day.

☐ Converted minutes/day for each activity into a correct fraction in lowest terms.

☐ Converted each fraction to its decimal equivalent.

☐ Converted each decimal to its percent equivalent.

☐ Completed the chart accurately and correctly.

☐ Demonstrated a commitment to quality.

"TIME OF MY LIFE" CHART 3: STUDENT POLL

☐ Identified at least five activities.

☐ Polled five students and correctly recorded initial polling data on the chart.

☐ Calculated the correct number of minutes in a day.

☐ Calculated the average minutes/day for each activity.

☐ Converted average minutes/day to average percent of one day for each activity.

☐ Completed the chart accurately and correctly.

☐ Demonstrated a commitment to quality.

continues ☞

"TIME OF MY LIFE" CHART 4: GRAPH-A-DAY

☐ Selected a graph type that matches the data.

☐ Represented data accurately.

☐ Used correct graphing techniques.

☐ Explained what the graph shows.

☐ Demonstrated a commitment to quality.

"TIME OF MY LIFE" CHARTS 5 & 6: CHARTING THE FUTURE

☐ Represented data accurately.

☐ Converted ratio quantities between different systems (minutes/day to years/lifetime).

☐ Performed calculations correctly.

☐ Completed two charts accurately and correctly.

☐ Demonstrated a commitment to quality.

"TIME OF MY LIFE" CHART 7: CHANGES OVER TIME

☐ Demonstrated an understanding of how to calculate percent increases.

☐ Performed calculations correctly.

☐ Graphed data correctly and accurately.

☐ Demonstrated a commitment to quality.

Project Planner

The Mathematute

Content Focus: Math
Class Periods: 4

Project Scenario

Students assume the role of mathematicians who solve a problem and then present the solution at a "Mathematute" workshop. You are the workshop leader.

Project Synopsis

After solving problems individually, students work in teams, each person assuming a different role on the team, to develop a presentation about the problem they solved. The project can be focused on any math content that you choose to assign (see "Contents Standards" below).

Differentiation Strategies

- Tiered assignments
- Bring-something-to-the-group
- Multiple intelligences

Student Forms

- Introduction
- Assignment Sheet
- Assessment Sheet

Content Standards*

"The Mathematute" project can be used to have students demonstrate mastery of almost any math content standard. Suggested workshop titles are shown here with examples of standards that could be used with each title.

Principles and Standards for School Mathematics are listed with the permission of the National Council of Teachers of Mathematics (NCTM). NCTM does not endorse the content or validity of these alignments.

THE X-Y EQUATIONS AND GRAPHING EXPOSITION

1. Students represent and analyze mathematical situations and structures using algebraic symbols. Expectations:

   - Students explore relationships between symbolic expressions and graphs of lines, paying particular attention to the meaning of intercept and slope.

   - Students use symbolic algebra to represent situations and to solve problems, especially those that involve linear relationships.

2. Students use mathematical models to represent and understand quantitative relationships. Expectation: Students model and solve contextualized problems using various representations, such as graphs, tables, and equations.

SYMPOSIUM ON RATES, RATIOS, AND PROPORTIONS

1. Students understand numbers, ways of representing numbers, relationships among numbers, and number systems. Expectation: Students work flexibly with fractions, decimals, and percents to solve problems.

2. Students understand measurable attributes of objects and the units, systems, and processes of measurement. Expectation: Students understand relationships among units and convert from one unit to another within the same system.

3. Students compute fluently and make reasonable estimates. Expectation: Students develop, analyze, and explain methods for solving problems involving proportions, such as scaling and finding equivalent ratios.

4. Students apply appropriate techniques, tools, and formulas to determine measurements.

The Mathematute | Project Planner *continued*

Expectation: Students solve simple problems involving rates and derived measurements for such attributes as velocity and density.

A MEETING OF THE MINDS ON FRACTIONS, DECIMALS, AND PERCENTS

1. Students understand numbers, ways of representing numbers, relationships among numbers, and number systems. Expectation: Students work flexibly with fractions, decimals, and percents to solve problems.

2. Students understand meanings of operations and how they relate to one another. Expectation: Students understand the meaning and effects of arithmetic operations with fractions, decimals, and integers.

3. Students compute fluently and make reasonable estimates. Expectation: Students develop and analyze algorithms for computing with fractions, decimals, and integers, and develop fluency in their use.

THE EXPONENT ZONE: EXPLORING THE POWERS AND ROOTS OF MATHEMATICS

1. Students understand meanings of operations and how they relate to one another. Expectation: Students understand and use the inverse relationships of addition and subtraction, multiplication and division, and squaring and finding square roots to simplify computations and solve problems.

2. Students understand numbers, ways of representing numbers, relationships among numbers, and number systems. Expectation: Students develop an understanding of large numbers and recognize and appropriately use exponential, scientific, and calculator notation.

FOCUS ON PYTHAGORAS

1. Students analyze characteristics and properties of two- and three-dimensional geometric shapes and develop mathematical arguments about geometric relationships. Expectation: Students create and critique inductive and deductive arguments concerning geometric

ideas and relationships, such as congruence, similarity, and the Pythagorean relationship.

PLANE GEOMETRY FORUM

1. Students analyze characteristics and properties of two- and three-dimensional geometric shapes and develop mathematical arguments about geometric relationships. Expectations:

- Students precisely describe, classify, and understand relationships among types of two- and three-dimensional objects using their defining properties.

- Students understand relationships among the angles, side lengths, perimeters, areas, and volumes of similar objects.

2. Students apply transformations and use symmetry to analyze mathematical situations. Expectations:

- Students describe sizes, positions, and orientations of shapes under informal transformations such as flips, turns, slides, and scaling.

- Students examine the congruence, similarity, and line or rotational symmetry of objects using transformations.

PERIMETER, AREA, AND VOLUME

1. Students apply appropriate techniques, tools, and formulas to determine measurements. Expectations:

- Students develop and use formulas to determine the circumference of circles and the area of triangles, parallelograms, trapezoids, and circles, and develop strategies to find the area of more-complex shapes.

- Students develop strategies to determine the surface area and volume of selected prisms, pyramids, and cylinders.

INVESTIGATING DATA ANALYSIS

1. Students formulate questions that can be addressed with data and collect, organize, and display relevant data to answer them. Expectation: Students select, create, and use appropriate graphical representations of data, including histograms, box plots, and scatter plots.

2. Students select and use appropriate statistical methods to analyze data. Expectations:

- Students find, use, and interpret measures of center and spread, including mean and interquartile range.

- Students discuss and understand the correspondence between data sets and their graphical representations, especially histograms, stem-and-leaf plots, box plots, and scatter plots.

3. Students develop and evaluate inferences and predictions that are based on data. Expectation: Students make conjectures about possible relationships between two characteristics of a sample on the basis of scatter plots of the data and approximate lines of fit.

PROBING PROBABILITY

1. Students understand and apply basic concepts of probability. Expectations:

- Students understand and use appropriate terminology to describe complementary and mutually exclusive events.

- Students use proportionality and a basic understanding of probability to make and test conjectures about the results of experiments and simulations.

- Students compute probabilities for simple compound events, using such methods as organized lists, tree diagrams, and area models.

How to Use This Project

The Mathematute is designed to be an assessment of understanding of specific math skills and concepts. Follow these steps to implement the project:

1. Choose a math unit on which to focus the project. This project may be used with virtually any unit that you teach.

2. Plan to use the project as a final activity that will allow students to demonstrate problem-solving proficiency and mastery of the key concepts and skills from the unit.

3. Assign the project a more specific workshop-like title to indicate what math content the students will cover with their presentations. There is a place on the student Assignment Sheet to record the workshop title. Some suggested titles are listed along with the content standards.

4. Give students the Introduction, Assignment Sheet, and Assessment Sheet. Review all materials together so that students know what will be expected of them.

5. Assign each student a problem to solve. These may be problems from the textbook, problems found on the Internet, or problems that you have collected from other sources. In order to make this project fit snugly into your curriculum, the problems that students complete must be provided by you. It is important to identify problems that are challenging and that have some degree of real-world application. Students will gain the most from the project if they can transfer processes and solutions to other aspects of their lives, or at least recognize that the math concepts they are working with are useful and have value outside of the classroom.

No more than four or five students should receive the same problem, and these problems may be differentiated at your discretion (see "Methods of Differentiation" on the following page). Record the problem in the space provided on each student's Assignment Sheet. For example, for four of your students you may write in this space "Challenge Problem 4.8, page 53." Try to identify complex problems that can be approached in more than one way or that require multiple steps to solve. This will add to the richness of students' discussions and final presentations.

6. Collect the finished problems and check them. Place students who turn in a finished problem and demonstrate an understanding of the problem-solving process in a presentation group (see Step 7). Put students who do not turn in acceptable solutions or procedures in a group that you lead. These students will work directly with you to complete the project. As group leader, you will guide them through the steps for solving their assigned problems, and help them prepare a presentation to demonstrate the problem-solving process.

7. Create presentation groups of four or five students. Group together all students who successfully solved the same problem, or who demonstrated an understanding of how the problem should be solved. It is not necessary for students to actually solve the problem correctly; they only need to prove that when working in a group, they can contribute with a reasonable level of understanding. Their task is to meet, discuss how each person approached the problem, and develop a presentation, assuming the roles listed on the Assignment Sheet, to explain basic concepts and demonstrate how the problem is solved.

8. Conduct the Mathematute like a mini-conference: Develop a presentation schedule, provide a moderator (this could be you, a colleague, or a student volunteer), and give each small group an opportunity to present its problem-solving "session." By limiting the presentations to about seven minutes each, you should be able to complete them all in one class period.

This project requires three to four class periods to complete:

- Period 1: Give each student an assigned problem to solve, with class time to work on it.
- Period 2: Assign groups; provide time for groups to work on presentations.
- Period 3: Provide another class period for group work (optional).
- Period 4: Conduct the Mathematute; students complete their Assessment Sheets.

Methods of Differentiation

The first method of differentiation, tiered assignments, is based on the problems you assign to individual students. Through observation and student performance, you have a very good idea at the end of a unit what level of challenge each student in your class is capable of handling. You may create as many tiered levels as you want or as the range of mastery in your class warrants. A typical tiering model provides three levels for students who are advanced, on-target, and struggling. By choosing problems that fit into these categories, you are differentiating for three student readiness levels. And by assigning students specific problems, you are using your judgment to group students into teams that are most likely to work well together. For example:

Level I: Advanced

- Assign Problem A to Students 1, 2, 3, and 4.
- Assign Problem B to Students 5, 6, 7, and 8.

Level II: On-Target

- Assign Problem C to Students 9, 10, 11, and 12.
- Assign Problem D to Students 13, 14, 15, and 16.
- Assign Problem E to Students 17, 18, 19, and 20.

Level III: Struggling

- Assign Problem F to Students 21, 22, 23, and 24.
- Assign Problem G to Students 25, 26, 27, and 28.

Given this arrangement for a class of twenty-eight students, the Mathematute will offer seven presentations covering three different challenge levels, all focused on the content of the unit just completed.

The second method of differentiation is called "bring-something-to-the-group." Students are assigned to a team whose job is to develop ways in which the solution to their common problem may be presented to an audience of colleagues. Thus, if there are seven problems, for example, there will be seven groups. However, there is an important stipulation. In order to become a member of a presentation team, each student must first submit a solution to the teacher and have it checked to verify that he or she has something to contribute to the group. This means that everyone who joins a group already has a solution (or at least has demonstrated an understanding of the required problem-solving process). Students do not need to know beforehand that the problems they are assigned are also a specific means of grouping them. This can be explained later.

Once the students are grouped, their task is to collaboratively decide how to present their problem-solving procedure. There is a good chance that the problems, especially for the advanced students, can be solved in multiple ways. This means that the presentation must go beyond the right answer and get closer to the essence of good mathematics: the thinking process that goes into problem solving. The bring-something-to-the-group strategy ensures everyone in the group already has a viable solution, thus collaborative learning is much easier to achieve.

Meanwhile, there will likely be students who either can't solve the problem they are assigned, or simply don't turn in a solution. These students become a separate (eighth) group with you as their leader. Your task with these students is to carefully help them recognize and articulate the procedure that is necessary to find an answer to each one's problem, and guide them to think of ways to share that procedure with the class.

The final method of differentiation is based on the idea of multiple intelligences. If you examine the roles that are outlined on the Assignment Sheet, you will see that they represent different intelligence types. There are five roles listed, and at least one student must assume each role:

- Team Leader: Interpersonal
- Graphics Director: Visual/Spatial
- Script Writer: Verbal/Linguistic
- Presenter: Verbal/Linguistic
- Mathematics Manager: Logical/Mathematical

Establish a rule early on that the Team Leader is the only person who can bring questions to the teacher. This is an important classroom-management strategy, especially if you are leading your own group of students who did not complete the initial problem-solving assignment. If anyone other than the Team Leader asks you a question, your response should be, "I need to hear this from your leader. That's his/her job."

Ideas for Extending or Modifying the Project

1. Develop a comprehensive Mathematute for the end of a semester or term, and use it to review all of the units that were covered.

2. Put students who solved different problems into the same group, and have the presentations focus on comparing and contrasting the strategies used for solving each problem.

3. Make the project an interdisciplinary team effort by involving teachers of other content areas. Encourage colleagues who teach science or social studies to join your Mathematute to demonstrate the use of mathematics in other content areas.

4. Rather than reviewing and assessing material from a completed unit, use the Mathematute to introduce students to areas of math ordinarily not covered in the regular curriculum.

5. Use the project as an anchor activity. See "Anchor Activities" on pages 38–41 for more detail.

6. Allow students to find or construct their own problems (as opposed to being assigned problems by you). Give students specific content expectations or benchmarks to focus on, and instruct them to turn in both a problem and a solution. In small groups, these students will develop presentations to describe the problems they have chosen and also explain how to solve them.

The Mathematute | **Project Planner** *continued*

Suggested Content Modifications

SCIENCE

- Give the project a new name, such as "The Science Symposium."

- Organize the project around one of the following three ideas:

  - Give students general, big-idea questions related to topics being studied, and have them collaborate to present explanations to the class. For example, "Photosynthesis: How important is it, really?" or "Why does nature like cycles?"

  - Assign students specific problems or questions from the science textbook or other curriculum materials.

  - Have students conduct observations and/or experiments and use the project as a way to report results.

SOCIAL STUDIES

- Give the project a new name, such as "The Sociatute."

- Organize the project around one of the following three ideas:

  - Give students general, big-idea questions related to topics being studied, and have them collaborate to present explanations to the class. For example, "Supply and demand: How important are they, really?" or "Push–pull: What gets humans going?"

  - Assign students specific problems or questions from the social studies textbook or other curriculum materials.

  - Have students take a stand on specific current or historical issues being studied and present their position.

ENGLISH/LANGUAGE ARTS

- Give the project a new name, such as "The Literatute."

- Organize the project around one of the following three ideas:

  - Have students analyze literature for global themes and universal truths, and present connections between their lives and the stories they read.

  - Have students examine how authors develop relationships among characters. Students present their insights by giving examples from the literature they read, and by drawing parallels between the stories and their own lives.

  - Assign all students to read a specific short story. Divide the class into groups of four or five and have each small group read a second short story. Each small group should read a different second story than the other small groups. The students in each small group compare and contrast the original story with their second story and present their analysis to the class.

The Mathematute
Introduction

Name: _____ **Date:** _____

This project involves working in a small group to develop a presentation that shows how to solve a math problem. You will first work on a problem independently and turn it in to be checked. Then you will be assigned to a group to complete the project.

Project Scenario

You are an esteemed member of a mathematics institute called the Mathematute. At an upcoming Mathematute workshop, you and a group of fellow mathematicians are scheduled to present the solution to a problem you have been working on. Your team's task is to demonstrate for your colleagues in the audience the problem-solving procedures you used to arrive at a solution to the problem.

Assignment

1. Solve the problem that the Mathematute leader (a.k.a. your teacher) assigns to you and turn it in. Keep detailed notes that explain how you tackled the problem.

2. Join a small team after demonstrating that you understand how to solve the assigned problem.

3. Decide which person on your team will take each of the jobs on this handout and record their names on the Assignment Sheet you will receive. Each job must have at least one person assigned to it. A job may have more than one person, and a person may have more than one job. However, there can only be one Team Leader.

4. Work together as a team to develop a presentation that shows clearly how to solve the problem.

5. Present the solution at the Mathematute workshop.

continues ☞

Job	Description
Team Leader	The Team Leader is responsible for seeing that the project follows the assignment and is done on time. This person is in charge of quality control. The only person who can take questions to the teacher is the Team Leader.
Graphics Director	The Graphics Director is responsible for the quality and accuracy of all the drawings and illustrations that will be used to show how the problem is solved. Other group members may contribute, but the Graphics Director has the final say on which graphics are included in the presentation.
Script Writer	The Script Writer is responsible for the quality and accuracy of what is said during the presentation. The presentation may be written out completely, or it can be outlined. Either way, it is the Script Writer's job to produce the document that will guide the presentation.
Presenter	The Presenter is responsible for talking to the audience during the presentation. There may be contributions from other team members, but it is the Presenter's job to follow the script and present the illustrations to explain how the problem is solved.
Mathematics Manager	The Mathematics Manager is responsible for ensuring that the math concepts and problem-solving steps used in the presentation are correct and logical. This person is also responsible for identifying a real-world application of the math concepts to include in the presentation.

The Mathematute
Assignment Sheet

Name: _____ **Date:** _____

Project Title: _____

Assigned Problem: _____

Record who will be responsible for each job on your team:

Team Leader		
Graphics Director		
Script Writer		
Presenter		
Mathematics Manager		

The presentation must include the following things:

1. A step-by-step verbal description of the problem and the process used to solve it.

2. Definitions and explanations of math terms that are used to describe the problem and its solution.

3. Drawings or other graphics to help describe the problem and illustrate its solution.

4. A written script, outline, or set of notes for the presenter to follow. This will be turned in.

5. Descriptions of alternate methods of solving the problem.

6. An example of a real-world application of the math concepts in the problem.

The Mathematatute
Assessment Sheet

Name: _____ **Date:** _____

INDIVIDUAL WORK

☐ Turned in the assigned problem on time.

☐ Kept detailed notes to explain how the assigned problem was solved.

☐ Provided evidence of mastery in the area of math being covered.

☐ Accepted the responsibility of being a contributing member of a team.

☐ Completed the required tasks of the job assumed on the team.

☐ Demonstrated an understanding of the necessary problem-solving process.

☐ Demonstrated a commitment to quality.

GROUP WORK

☐ Offered a well-designed, step-by-step presentation that was clear and easy to follow.

☐ Included definitions and explanations of critical math terms.

☐ Included enough information to make the problem-solving process understandable.

☐ Provided well-designed graphics that described the problem and the process used to solve it.

☐ Developed a well-written script, outline, or set of notes to guide the presentation.

☐ Described at least one alternate method of solving the problem.

☐ Provided an example of a real-world application of the math concepts in the problem.

☐ Worked well together as a team.

Project Planner

Life on Planet X

Content Focus: Life Science
Class Periods: 10

Project Scenario

Students are biologists, part of a scientific space-exploration team. The team has been sent to study and document the plant and animal life on a new planet that was just discovered in our solar system. You are the head biologist.

Project Synopsis

All students work to complete basic requirements, creating documents about plant and animal life forms discovered on Planet X for a publication titled *The Biologist's Guide to Planet X.* Students who finish early can choose additional project activities from a choice board. Students choose project activities from the board based on interest and number of days left to work on the project.

Differentiation Strategies

- All-most-some
- Choice board
- Anchor activities

Student Forms

- Introduction
- *The Biologist's Guide to Planet X* Document 1: Plant-Eating Animal
- *The Biologist's Guide to Planet X* Document 2: Green Plant the Animal Eats
- *The Biologist's Guide to Planet X* Document 3: Adaptations of the Animal
- *The Biologist's Guide to Planet X* Document 4: Body Systems of the Animal
- Planet X Choice Board
- Choice Board Activity 1: Design an Ecosystem

- Choice Board Activity 2: Luck of the Draw
- Choice Board Activity 3: Investigate Invertebrates
- Choice Board Activity 4: Flowering Plants
- Choice Board Activity 5: Meat Eater
- Choice Board Activity 6: The Big Picture
- Choice Board Activity 7: Biologist's Journal
- Choice Board Activity 8: All in the Family
- *The Biologist's Guide to Planet X* Assessment Sheet
- Planet X Choice Board Assessment Sheet

Content Standards*

1. Students develop an understanding of matter, energy, and organization of living things.
2. Students develop an understanding of the structure and function in living systems.
3. Students develop an understanding of the interdependence of organisms.

How to Use This Project

"Life on Planet X" is designed to be used as a wrap-up or assessment project at the close of a semester or term, as it assumes students are already familiar with the concepts and vocabulary terms included.

Follow these steps to implement the project:

1. Hand out the Introduction and *The Biologist's Guide to Planet X* Assessment Sheet, and explain the project goals and expectations. Students will work within the context of the project scenario to produce entries for *The*

---

*National Science Education Standards are from the National Research Council (NRC).

Biologist's Guide to Planet X. Each assignment sheet is a document, focused on a specific aspect of life, which will be included in the guide if it is completed at an acceptable level of quality. Students will complete four assignment sheets to fulfill the basic requirements of the project. Sufficient resources must be available for students to complete each document independently. Designate a three-ring notebook or other repository to represent *The Biologist's Guide to Planet X.* This is where completed documents will be stored and made available for reference by future biologists.

2. Give each student Document 1. Record the classes of vertebrate animals (fish, amphibian, reptile, bird, mammal) on slips of paper, one slip per student, and put them in a hat. For example, if there are thirty students in the class, put six slips per vertebrate class in the hat. Have each student draw a slip from the hat to determine which vertebrate class his or her animal will belong to. The animal the student invents must be given appropriate classification characteristics. Each student may choose a unique habitat for the animal—aquatic, arboreal, or terrestrial. It may live in any of the five climates listed on Document 1, under any other conditions the student wants to specify.

3. At this point the project begins to differentiate. As students work independently, they will inevitably complete tasks at different rates. When students finish Document 1, they hand it in to be checked. If a student's Document 1 is done correctly with enough quality, you will give him or her Document 2 to begin working on. If not, you will return Document 1 to the student with notes (or a brief conference) to explain what still needs to be done. If you return the document for continued work, you may also specify additional learning support that is needed, such as an assigned reading, textbook references, or a mini-lesson with you to help clear up misunderstandings. The remaining assignment sheets (Documents 2,

3, and 4) are self-explanatory. Repeat this process for each sheet.

4. The obvious result of this process is that some students will complete Document 4 well before the rest of the class, as others finish at a staggered rate. The specified time frame for the project is two weeks, or ten class periods, and some students may require all of this time to demonstrate mastery of the focused science expectations. But for the early finishers, this project provides anchor activities. The anchor activities are designed to provide meaningful work that will engage students for the rest of the project. Each activity is described on the Planet X Choice Board handout on page 139.

5. Give students who finish Document 4 the Planet X Choice Board handout and the Planet X Choice Board Assessment Sheet. Review the activities listed on the handout and the items on the assessment checklist. Allow each student to choose one of the anchor activities listed and give him or her the accompanying assignment sheet. The activity must *not* require more days to complete than remain in the project, but it *may* require fewer days. In other words, if there are three days remaining in the project, a student may choose a three-, two-, or one-day activity, but not the four-day activity. Upon successfully completing the chosen activity, a student may choose another activity to fill the remaining time.

6. Be sure to familiarize yourself with all of the choice board assignment sheets so that you can support students as they undertake the required tasks. You may need to provide additional resources, such as reference materials and art supplies.

Methods of Differentiation

This project models the all-most-some differentiation strategy. *All* students are expected to demonstrate understanding of the material presented on the four assignment sheets (Documents 1, 2, 3, and 4). Students are not allowed to simply complete a set of worksheets and be done. If an assignment is turned in that does not clearly demonstrate understanding, the student must continue working on it, with teacher feedback and extra support if necessary. Plenty of time is allocated to ensure that all students learn this material.

A critical component of this differentiation model is the idea of anchor activities, which take the form of a choice board in this project. Students working toward mastery will naturally require differing amounts of time to get there. Those who complete the basic assignments ahead of schedule need something meaningful that will challenge, motivate, and engage them. Thus, there are ten anchor activities provided that are directly connected to the original project scenario, each with an assignment sheet and an estimated completion time. Students may choose any combination of activities from the choice board, based on how much time they have available. *Most* students will participate in anchor activities at least minimally, and *some* students will take extensive advantage of them.

Ideas for Extending or Modifying the Project

1. Increase the basic requirements by choosing one or more anchor activities and assigning them as documents for *The Biologist's Guide to Planet X.*

2. Decrease the basic requirements by choosing one of the documents and changing it to an anchor activity.

3. Use the "Life on Planet X" concept to teach other areas of science, such as cell biology, genetics, the rock cycle, weather, or the hydrosphere.

Suggested Content Modifications

MATH

- Develop a mathematical description of Planet X that includes radius, diameter, circumference, area, and volume.

- Develop a coordinate system for a continent on Planet X, and use coordinate pairs to locate places where new animal and plant species have been discovered.

- Use lines, angles, and measurements to locate life forms on the continent.

SOCIAL STUDIES

- Develop a map of a continent on Planet X and show where major landforms, rivers, and bodies of water are located. Have students tell where human colonies should be located and explain their reasoning.

- Tell students that Planet X has plentiful natural resources, and that modern technology has developed a way to transport these resources to Earth. Have students predict what would happen economically if the United States were to receive a large infusion of oil, gold, rare metals, and so forth.

ENGLISH/LANGUAGE ARTS

- Have students write stories about discovering and exploring Planet X.

- Have students write news articles about Planet X in the voice of a journalist.

- Have students write essays about the positive and negative implications of humans colonizing Planet X.

- Organize oral presentations around the idea of returning astronauts who have stories to tell about their exploits and discoveries.

Life on Planet X
Introduction

Name: _____ **Date:** _____

This is a life science project that focuses on the classification of living things, animal systems, and how organisms acquire energy from the sun. You will have two weeks to successfully complete all of the assignments for the "Life on Planet X" project. If you finish the requirements in less time, you will work on optional activities to add depth or a new perspective to your project.

Project Scenario

A new planet has been recently discovered in our solar system. Referred to by astronomers as "Planet X," it is in the same orbit as Earth, but we have never seen the planet because the sun is always directly between us. You are a biologist who is part of a scientific space-exploration team that has been sent to investigate Planet X. What you discover is a world that is very much like Earth: same size, same distance from the sun, same atmosphere, same climate, plenty of water, and lots of plant and animal life. It doesn't take long to realize that the animals of Planet X belong to the same classes as animals on Earth, and that green plants convert the sun's energy to food, just like on Earth. Your team's job is to carefully record observations of the organisms that you discover, and create a research document for scientists on Earth titled *The Biologist's Guide to Planet X.*

Assignment

The basic requirement for this project is to develop documents for *The Biologist's Guide to Planet X.* Each document is an assignment sheet that you will receive from the head biologist (a.k.a. your teacher). To produce documents for the guide, you will work on seven tasks that must be completed before moving on to optional activities. Here is a brief description of the required tasks:

- Task 1: Invent a plant-eating vertebrate animal that has been discovered on Planet X.
- Task 2: Classify the animal as a fish, amphibian, reptile, bird, or mammal.
- Task 3: Invent a green plant, discovered on Planet X, that is your animal's primary food source.
- Task 4: Describe how your plant produces and stores food.
- Task 5: Describe adaptations that allow your animal to survive in its environment.
- Task 6: Describe how your animal acquires energy from the sun.
- Task 7: Explain how at least two systems or processes work together in your animal.

The project will last two weeks, or ten class periods. The assignment sheets will provide clear directions and expectations for completing each of the required tasks.

continues ☞

Choice Board

If you complete the required tasks before the end of the two weeks, you will be allowed to enhance the project with optional activities chosen from the Planet X Choice Board. There are eight activities on the choice board, requiring one to four class periods to complete. Your choices will be determined by which options are most interesting to you and by the number of remaining class periods for the project. For example, if you finish the basic project requirements in six class periods, you will have four more periods available to complete optional activities from the choice board.

The Biologist's Guide to Planet X

The project scenario leads to the creation of a research document titled *The Biologist's Guide to Planet X,* for scientists on Earth. Your work will be included in this document if it achieves an acceptable level of accuracy and quality. The guide may be produced as a book, or it may be developed in other ways, such as a wall display or through class presentations, depending on decisions made by the head biologist.

Life on Planet X
The Biologist's Guide to Planet X Document 1: Plant-Eating Animal

Name: _____ **Date:** _____

For this task, record your observations of a plant-eating animal found on Planet X.

Animal Name: _____

Vertebrate Class:

☐ Fish

☐ Amphibian

☐ Reptile

☐ Bird

☐ Mammal

List four general characteristics that you used to classify this animal. (For example, feathers would be a general characteristic of an animal in the class of birds.)

Describe your observations about the animal's natural habitat.

Choose the type of habitat in which your animal lives:	Choose the type of climate in which your animal lives:	Include any additional details about the animal's habitat:
☐ Aquatic ☐ Arboreal ☐ Terrestrial	☐ Tropical ☐ Dry ☐ Temperate ☐ Cold ☐ Polar	

continues ☛

Make a sketch of the animal, to show what it looks like:

Life on Planet X
The Biologist's Guide to Planet X Document 2: Green Plant the Animal Eats

Name: _____ **Date:** _____

For this task, record observations of a green plant that is your animal's primary food source.

Animal Name: _____ **Plant Name:** _____

Produce an illustration of the plant in its natural environment. Label the part that your animal eats.

continues 👉

Make a diagram to show how your plant makes food and stores it. Be sure to clearly illustrate the process of photosynthesis, and include these terms: *sunlight, chlorophyll, chloroplast, stomata, carbon dioxide, oxygen, water, transport, xylem, phloem, sugar, starch, roots, stems,* and *fruit.*

Life on Planet X
The Biologist's Guide to Planet X Document 3: Adaptations of the Animal

Name: _____ **Date:** _____

Animal Name: _____

In the table below, record four adaptations that help your animal survive in its natural habitat. Think about protection from predators, staying warm (or cool), movement, communication, the five senses, and so forth. Follow the format in the example to describe each adaptation. Include at least one adaptation for finding, getting, and/or eating the part of the plant that you labeled on Document 2.

	Descriptor	**Body Part**	**Purpose**
Example	*long, flexible, elastic*	*proboscis*	*for breathing while hiding underwater to escape predators*
Adaptation 1 (eating)			
Adaptation 2			
Adaptation 3			
Adaptation 4			

continues ☞

Make a diagram that shows how the animal gets energy for sustaining its life. Use key terms correctly, such as *light energy, photosynthesis, producer,* and *consumer.* Using arrows, show the flow of energy from its source to the animal. Explain whether this flow is a direct or indirect transfer of energy.

Is this a direct or indirect transfer of energy? Explain why.

_____

_____

_____

_____

Life on Planet X
The Biologist's Guide to Planet X Document 4: Body Systems of the Animal

Name: _____ **Date:** _____

Animal Name: _____

Choose two body systems that work together in your animal. Choose from this list: digestion, circulation, respiration, endocrine, reproduction, skeletal, muscular, nervous, excretion, transport, growth, and repair. Describe each system in the spaces below, using illustrations and written explanations. Explain the purpose of the system and tell how it works in the animal.

Body System: _____	**Body System:** _____

continues ☞

Using illustrations and written explanations, describe how the two systems are related and how they work together.

Life on Planet X
Planet X Choice Board

Name: _____ Date: _____

The Planet X Choice Board offers activities that are available only after you have successfully completed the basic requirements of the "Life on Planet X" project. After receiving permission to proceed, you may choose any combination of activities that can be completed in the time remaining. The choice board shows about how much time is needed for each activity. For example, if you have four class periods remaining for the project, you may choose one of the following options:

- 1 four-period activity
- 1 three-period activity and 1 one-period activity
- 2 two-period activities
- 1 two-period activity and 2 one-period activities

Look at the following choice board to see the activities you may choose from. When you select an activity, your teacher will provide its accompanying assignment sheet to help guide your work.

Time	Name	Activity
4 Periods	Design an Ecosystem	Invent new animals and plants to create a detailed food web. You may work alone or with a partner.
3 Periods	Luck of the Draw	Invent a new animal based on random factors. Draw factors from a hat and build them into an animal.
3 Periods	Investigate Invertebrates	Invent an arachnid, insect, mollusk, or other invertebrate. Choose an invertebrate, do some research, and start inventing.
2 Periods	Flowering Plants	Invent a new flowering plant and document its life cycle. Show the reproduction process in a flowering plant.
2 Periods	Meat Eater	Invent a top predator with adaptations for hunting. Tell how it captures and kills its prey.
1 Period	The Big Picture	Create a large drawing of the Planet X animal you invented. Produce a large, color image with details.
1 Period	Biologist's Journal	Compose a journal describing your discoveries on Planet X. Use the voice of a biologist writing in a daily log.
1 Period	All in the Family	Describe the male, female, and young of the animal you invented for this project. Show what they look like and tell how they behave.

Life on Planet X

Choice Board Activity 1: Design an Ecosystem

Class Periods: 4

Name: _____ **Date:** _____

You may work with a partner on this activity, but each person must contribute equally. For two people, double the requirements below. Remember, you have earned the right to work independently, and your teacher will assume that you intend to accept the responsibility of putting all of your time and effort into completing this assignment to the best of your ability.

Goal:

Design a detailed Planet X food web that includes the plant and animal you already invented, in addition to new ones. Make small drawings of all the organisms you create for the ecosystem, and connect them with arrows to show the flow of energy, beginning with the sun. The new animals and plants don't have to be detailed like the ones you already invented; the primary goal is to show the flow of energy from the sun to the top predator in your food web.

Requirements:

The food web should contain at least twelve animals and four plants (including the plant and animal you already invented). You may add any other organisms you want, such as insects, arachnids, fungi, or even bacteria. Give each additional organism a name. Only one of the animals can be the top predator; two may be intermediate predators; three may be omnivores; and the rest must be herbivores. No animal may eat more than three organisms. Some organisms may have only one or two food sources. After completing the food web, choose one of the new organisms and predict what would happen to your animal if this organism were eliminated from the food web. Support your prediction with evidence. Be prepared to do the same thing for any of the new organisms.

Complete these tables as a starting point. Use a separate piece of paper if you need more space.

Plant Name	Eaten By			

continues ☞

For the table below, use the following Diet abbreviations: TP = Top Predator, IP = Intermediate Predator, O = Omnivore, H = Herbivore

Animal Name	Class	Diet	Eats				Eaten By			

Life on Planet X
Choice Board Activity 2: Luck of the Draw
Class Periods: 3

Name: _____ **Date:** _____

Remember, you have earned the right to work independently, and your teacher will assume that you intend to accept the responsibility of putting all of your time and effort into completing this assignment to the best of your ability.

Goal:

Invent an animal with appropriate adaptations and characteristics for a random set of factors.

Requirements:

Cut the five rows of factors on the next page into individual slips of paper. Put the slips one row at a time into a bowl, and draw a slip to determine what adaptations and characteristics need to be designed into an imaginary animal. Create an illustration of the animal with written explanations to show how each factor has been accounted for. Understand that it is possible to get a strange combination of factors, like a nocturnal, arboreal, polar fish that is an herbivore. You will need all of your imagination to figure out how to design such a creature! If you don't like what you draw from bowl, you may choose to do one redraw, but you must redraw all of the factors, not just a selected few. If you decide to redraw, you will return the slips to the bowl and draw again for each factor. Whatever you draw on the second try is what you will work from.

Be sure to provide a full explanation for all factors. For example, if your animal is an amphibian living in a polar climate, you must explain how a cold-blooded (endothermic) animal will be able to maintain body heat. Or, if you draw an arboreal fish, how will the animal breathe?

My Animal:

Class:	Climate:	Diet:	Habitat	Activity Period:

continues ☞

Factor Number 1: Classification

Fish	Amphibian	Reptile	Bird	Mammal

Factor Number 2: Climate

Tropical	Dry	Temperate	Cold	Polar

Factor Number 3: Diet

Carnivore	Herbivore	Omnivore

Factor Number 4: Habitat

Aquatic	Terrestrial	Arboreal

Factor Number 5: Activity Period

Diurnal	Nocturnal	Crepuscular

Life on Planet X

Choice Board Activity 3: Investigate Invertebrates

Class Periods: 3

Name: _____ **Date:** _____

Remember, you have earned the right to work independently, and your teacher will assume that you intend to accept the responsibility of putting all of your time and effort into completing this assignment to the best of your ability.

Goal:

Choose a type of invertebrate animal to focus on. Learn as much as possible about this type of animal, and then invent one that lives on Planet X.

Requirements:

Choose one of the four examples of invertebrate animals (insect, arachnid, mollusk, crustacean), and then conduct research to discover as much as possible about it. Find information about these areas: finding, eating, and digesting food; breathing mechanism; circulation; reproduction; body structure; movement; and behavior. If necessary, study a specific species to get more detailed information. For example, for mollusks you could study squid. After studying the animal, create an imaginary version that has been discovered on Planet X. Use illustrations and written explanations to describe the animal's classification, body structure, systems, habitat, diet, and so forth. You may include special adaptations. Finally, document a link between this animal and the first animal you invented for *The Biologist's Guide to Planet X*. For example, perhaps one is a predator of the other, or a competitor for the same food source.

Life on Planet X
Choice Board Activity 4: Flowering Plants
Class Periods: 2

Name: _____ **Date:** _____

Remember, you have earned the right to work independently, and your teacher will assume that you intend to accept the responsibility of putting all of your time and effort into completing this assignment to the best of your ability.

Goal:

Learn about flowering plants, then invent a new flowering plant and document its life cycle.

Requirements:

Conduct research to learn about the parts and processes of flowering plants. Then invent a flowering plant that has been discovered on Planet X, using illustrations and written explanations. Describe in detail the life cycle of the plant. Use these terms correctly in your description: *roots, stems, leaves, flower, stamen, pistil* (or *carpel*), *fruit, seeds, embryo, pollen, ovary, egg cell, germination,* and *fertilization.* Your final product should answer this question: How does the flowering plant you have invented reproduce itself?

Life on Planet X

Choice Board Activity 5: Meat Eater

Class Periods: 2

Name: _____ **Date:** _____

Remember, you have earned the right to work independently, and your teacher will assume that you intend to accept the responsibility of putting all of your time and effort into completing this assignment to the best of your ability.

Goal:

Invent a top predator with adaptations for hunting. This animal hunts the plant eater you invented for *The Biologist's Guide to Planet X*.

Requirements:

Design an animal that is built to hunt, kill, and eat other animals. Include these things in a carefully developed drawing of the animal:

- Classification as a fish, amphibian, reptile, bird, or mammal
- At least five specific adaptations that allow the animal to be a successful hunter
- A detailed description of one adaptation, with enlarged illustrations and written explanations
- A description of the animal's habitat
- A description of its home (den, burrow, nest, hive, cave, and so forth)
- An explanation or description of how it hunts and kills the plant-eating animal you invented

Life on Planet X
Choice Board Activity 6: The Big Picture
Class Periods: 1

Name: _____ **Date:** _____

Remember, you have earned the right to work independently, and your teacher will assume that you intend to accept the responsibility of putting all of your time and effort into completing this assignment to the best of your ability.

Goal:

Create a large drawing of the animal you invented for *The Biologist's Guide to Planet X.*

Requirements:

On a piece of posterboard or drawing paper, or on a computer, make a large color drawing of your animal. Include the animal's name, classification, habitat, and as much detail as possible. Provide labels to explain important features of the animal.

Life on Planet X

Choice Board Activity 7: Biologist's Journal

Class Periods: 1

Name: _____ **Date:** _____

Remember, you have earned the right to work independently, and your teacher will assume that you intend to accept the responsibility of putting all of your time and effort into completing this assignment to the best of your ability.

Goal:

Compose a journal describing your discoveries on Planet X.

Requirements:

Using the voice of a biologist, produce a daily journal that documents your discoveries as you explored Planet X. Include entries for at least three days. They do not need to be long, but they should all relate to show what you did on, and learned about, Planet X during that three-day period. Include in the entries details about your discovery of the animal you created for *The Biologist's Guide to Planet X*. Describe where and how you found the animal, and what you learned about it.

Life on Planet X

Choice Board Activity 8: All in the Family
Class Periods: 1

Name: _____ **Date:** _____

Remember, you have earned the right to work independently, and your teacher will assume that you intend to accept the responsibility of putting all of your time and effort into completing this assignment to the best of your ability.

Goal:

Describe the adult male, the adult female, and the young of the animal you invented for *The Biologist's Guide to Planet X.*

Requirements:

Produce a color drawing of what each animal (male, female, young) looks like. Focus on how the adults take care of the young. Include written explanations of what their family life is like. For example:

- What the family's home is like (burrow, den, nest, cave, and so on)
- How many young are born at a time
- Whether the mother or father is primarily responsible for "day care"
- What the young eat
- How the young are protected when a predator is nearby
- How the young are taught to take care of themselves

Life on Planet X

The Biologist's Guide to Planet X Assessment Sheet

Name: _____ Date: _____

DOCUMENT 1: PLANT-EATING ANIMAL

☐ Gave the animal an acceptable name.

☐ Recorded the correct classification for the animal.

☐ Described accurately a classification characteristic for the animal.

☐ Described accurately a second classification characteristic for the animal.

☐ Described accurately a third classification characteristic for the animal.

☐ Described accurately a fourth classification characteristic for the animal.

☐ Recorded the correct habitat for the animal.

☐ Recorded a climate in which the animal lives.

☐ Produced a carefully developed sketch of the animal.

☐ Demonstrated a commitment to quality.

DOCUMENT 2: GREEN PLANT THE ANIMAL EATS

☐ Gave the plant an acceptable name.

☐ Produced a carefully developed sketch of the plant in its natural habitat.

☐ Labeled the part of the plant the animal eats.

☐ Produced a carefully developed diagram to show how the plant makes and stores food.

☐ Explained correctly the process of photosynthesis.

☐ Included all of the required terms.

☐ Used correctly terms for describing the process of photosynthesis.

☐ Demonstrated a commitment to quality.

continues ☞

DOCUMENT 3: ADAPTATIONS OF THE ANIMAL

☐ Developed an adaptation accurately, using the form provided.

☐ Developed a second adaptation accurately, using the form provided.

☐ Developed a third adaptation accurately, using the form provided.

☐ Developed a fourth adaptation accurately, using the form provided.

☐ Produced a carefully developed diagram to show how the animal gets energy.

☐ Used key terms correctly.

☐ Showed on the diagram the flow of energy, from its source to the animal.

☐ Specified whether the flow of energy to the animal is a direct or indirect transfer.

☐ Explained correctly why the transfer of energy is either direct or indirect.

☐ Demonstrated a commitment to quality.

DOCUMENT 4: BODY SYSTEMS OF THE ANIMAL

☐ Chose from the list two body systems that work together in the animal.

☐ Described correctly one of the systems with drawings and written explanations.

☐ Described correctly the second system with drawings and written explanations.

☐ Explained clearly and accurately how the two systems are related.

☐ Explained clearly and accurately how the two systems work together in the animal.

☐ Used key terms correctly.

☐ Demonstrated a commitment to quality.

Life on Planet X
Planet X Choice Board Assessment Sheet

Name: _____ **Date:** _____

Choice Board Activity: _____ **Class Periods Required:** _____

Fill out the checklist below for each choice board activity that you completed.

- ☐ Followed activity requirements carefully.
- ☐ Completed activity requirements fully.
- ☐ Made productive use of time.
- ☐ Worked well independently.
- ☐ Functioned well in the classroom without interfering with others' work.
- ☐ Made decisions without requiring extensive help from the teacher.
- ☐ Found materials and resources to support his or her work.
- ☐ Produced a final product that is well designed and organized.
- ☐ Produced a final product that contains appropriate and accurate information.
- ☐ Demonstrated a commitment to quality.

Project Planner

Message in a Capsule

Content Focus: Earth/Space Science
Class Periods: 13

Project Scenario

A scientific research team develops materials about our solar system for an interstellar communication capsule. You are the lead researcher.

Project Synopsis

Using the clock partners grouping strategy (see "Methods of Differentiation"), students first meet with their 12 o'clock partners to choose a topic to address for the space capsule. They then meet successively with their 3, 6, and 9 o'clock partners to study how Earth supports life, to compare and contrast another planet with Earth, and to explain how the solar system works. Finally, they reunite with their 12 o'clock partners to complete the final product for inclusion in the capsule.

Differentiation Strategies

- Clock partners
- Choice-as-motivator

Student Forms

- Introduction
- Assignment Sheet 1: 12 O'Clock Partner
- Assignment Sheet 2: 3 O'Clock Partner
- Assignment Sheet 3: 6 O'Clock Partner
- Assignment Sheet 4: 9 O'Clock Partner
- Assignment Sheet 5: 12 O'Clock Partner
- Clock Partners Form
- Assessment Sheet

Content Standards*

1. Students develop an understanding of the structure of the earth system.

2. Students develop an understanding of Earth in the solar system.

How to Use This Project

Follow these steps to implement the "Message in a Capsule" project:

1. Introduce the concept of clock partners to the class, and hand out the Clock Partners Form on page 166. (A suggested method of partner assignation for this project is provided under "Methods of Differentiation.") Note that the clock partners grouping strategy may be used for all kinds of activities that require pairs of students to work together. For this reason, you may want to introduce clock partners well before the project begins, and use it in other contexts so that students are used to the idea of joining their clock partners for various lessons, assignments, and activities.

2. Conduct whatever pre-teaching and class work you feel is necessary to prepare students for the project. It is a good idea to provide background information about all of the major topics covered in the five assignments before students begin working in pairs.

3. Students begin working through the assignments with their clock partners. This will require about ten class periods. You may need to modify the amount of time devoted to the project based on how well your students know the material and to what depth you want to take their investigations. Each assignment is unique and focuses on a different aspect of the study of the solar system. It is critical to the success of

---

National Science Education Standards are from the National Research Council (NRC).

the project that you provide plenty of reference materials and resources, including Internet access if possible. Here are specific instructions related to each of the five assignments:

Assignment 1

- Pair students with their 12 o'clock partners.

- Give them the Introduction and Assessment Sheet and discuss the project scenario and the requirements and expectations for each assignment.

- Give them Assignment Sheet 1 and allow them to study the questions. Their first task is to prioritize the questions in order of preference, from the question they would most like to study to their least favorite.

- Ask each pair to write their names on a slip of paper and give it to you.

- Place all of the slips in a bowl and randomly draw one. This pair gets to choose any question from the list. Be sure to write down the question they select for your own reference, and have the students circle their question on the Assignment Sheet 1.

- Draw another slip from the bowl. This pair may choose any question other than the one already claimed. Repeat this process until each pair has chosen and circled a question to answer during the project.

- Explain that time will be provided later in the project for 12 o'clock partners to conduct research and develop answers to each pair's question. Meanwhile, they will meet with their other clock partners to complete assignments that contribute to the final product. Along the way, they are likely to come across information that is related to their question, which is why this part of the project was done first.

Assignment 2

- Pair students with their 3 o'clock partners.

- Give them Assignment Sheet 2, and allow them to study the statements provided on the sheet about supporting life on Earth.

- Each pair will choose to study any two of the statements.

Assignment 3

- Write the names of the planets (do not include Earth) on slips of paper, and make two more slips than there are pairs of students. For example, if there are fourteen pairs, make sixteen slips (two per planet).

- Pair students with their 6 o'clock partners and give them Assignment Sheet 3.

- Put the slips in a bowl and randomly draw one for each pair.

- After each drawing, have the students check with their 12 o'clock partners to be sure that they are not studying the same planet. Otherwise, they will draw again. This is necessary because one of the tasks 12 o'clock partners will do when they reunite for Assignment 5 is compare and contrast two *different* planets with Earth.

Assignment 4

- Pair students with their 9 o'clock partners and give them Assignment Sheet 4.

- Each pair chooses one of four sets of terms that are provided and completes the assignment.

Assignment 5

- Pair students again with their 12 o'clock partners and give them Assignment Sheet 5.

- Each 12 o'clock pair must complete six tasks, as described on Assignment Sheet 5. Be sure to establish specific expectations for final products and presentations.

4. Provide time for final presentations. Decide how formal or informal you want the presentations to be.

5. This project is estimated to require thirteen class periods to complete:

- Period 1: Introduction and Assignment 1—12 O'Clock Partner

- Period 2: Assignment 2—3 O'Clock Partner

- Period 3: Assignment 2—3 O'Clock Partner
- Period 4: Assignment 3—6 O'Clock Partner
- Period 5: Assignment 3—6 O'Clock Partner
- Period 6: Assignment 4—9 O'Clock Partner
- Period 7: Assignment 4—9 O'Clock Partner
- Period 8: Assignment 5—12 O'Clock Partner
- Period 9: Assignment 5—12 O'Clock Partner
- Period 10: Assignment 5—12 O'Clock Partner
- Period 11: Final presentations
- Period 12: Final presentations
- Period 13: Final presentations; students complete Assessment Sheets

Methods of Differentiation

"Message in a Capsule" utilizes two differentiation strategies: choice-as-motivator and clock partners. The purpose of clock partners is to have a quick, easy system for putting students together in pairs for collaborative learning activities. The strategy also ensures that students work with several different partners during the course of the project. While it is possible for each student to have up to twelve clock partners, this project utilizes four: a 12 o'clock, 3 o'clock, 6 o'clock, and 9 o'clock partner. There are many ways to determine who these partners will be. Below is one method that you may want to try. (More suggestions are in "Clock Partners" on pages 28–30.)

1. Before students come to class, divide the room into quadrants, with an even number of seats in each quarter of the room. For example, if there are twenty-eight students in the class, put eight seats in two quadrants and six seats in the other two, rather than seven in each. If there is an odd number of students in the class, one quadrant will have an odd number of chairs. Be sure that the four quadrants are clearly marked or defined with space between them.

2. When the students come to class, tell them to sit anywhere they want, but they may not move the seats out of position. The assumption here is that students will sit with their friends.

3. Explain what clock partners are and how they will be used. Give students the Clock Partners Form on page 166.

4. Tell students that you will assign their 12 o'clock partners. Use whatever criteria you want to make these assignments, such as students who get along well, or students with similar learning readiness levels, or students with different learning readiness levels, or students with similar interests. If there is an odd number of students in the class, there will be one group of three. Have students record their 12 o'clock partners' names in the appropriate place on the form.

5. Have students choose their 3 o'clock partners. These partners must be sitting together in the same quadrant of the classroom, which means they will likely be friends. They cannot, however, choose somebody who is already their 12 o'clock partner. If one of the quadrants has an odd number of students, there will be one group of three. Students record their 3 o'clock partners on the form.

6. Have students choose 6 o'clock partners. These must be new partners who are not sitting in the same quadrant of the classroom. After a short time, ask who does not have a 6 o'clock partner. Have those students meet with you to make quick partner assignments. Again, if there is an odd number of students in the class, there will be one group of three. Students record their 6 o'clock partners on the handout.

7. Have students choose 9 o'clock partners. As with 6 o'clock partners, these must be new partners who are not sitting in the same quadrant of the classroom. Follow Step 6 for choosing 9 o'clock partners.

8. Make a record of everyone's clock partners for your own reference. An easy way to do this is to use a form with students' names along the left side and four columns for the four clock partners. Send the form around the class and have each student record their clock partners on the appropriate lines next to his or her name.

Choice-as-motivator is the second differentiation strategy used with this project. Students make at least four key choices as they work with their clock partners; each choice allows them to pursue topics of interest and contributes to the uniqueness of the final product. They make their choices in this order:

- 12 o'clock partners choose a question about the solar system to research.

- 3 o'clock partners choose two statements about how Earth supports life, and then develop an explanation of each statement.

- 9 o'clock partners choose a set of terms related to the motion of objects in the solar system to define and describe.

- 12 o'clock partners choose a final product (poster, model, multimedia, and so forth) as a means of presenting their information.

Each time a student makes a choice, the project becomes more personally interesting and relevant. As choices are made, the student is increasingly vested in the project and motivated to complete it.

Ideas for Extending or Modifying the Project

1. Select Assignment Sheet 1, 2, 3, or 4 to use for the entire project, and have each pair of clock partners focus on different aspects of it. For example, each pair of clock partners could choose a different question from Assignment Sheet 1. Or, the project focus could be on how Earth supports life, and each pair of clock partners could look at two different statements from Assignment Sheet 2. Each pair could study a different planet by completing Assignment Sheet 3, or partners could explain each set of terms from Assignment Sheet 4.

2. Use one or more of Assignment Sheets 1–4 with the entire class, without using clock partners. Students have choice built into each assignment as a way of differentiating the project.

3. Change the focus of the project from astronomy to a different science topic. The "message in a capsule" scenario can be used for just about any topic in biology, earth science, physics, or chemistry.

Suggested Content Modifications

MATH

- Choose an area of mathematics (for example, linear algebra or coordinate geometry) and have students write descriptions, explanations, and examples to include in the capsule.

- Have students write carefully developed solutions to math problems taken from the textbook or other sources to include in the capsule.

SOCIAL STUDIES

- Develop a list of social studies topics on which students can focus their space-capsule materials. Some examples include the following:

  - A description of the American government system, or a review of types of government systems around the world

  - A collection of population maps, with explanations of where people live and why they live there

  - Definitions and examples of the world's economic systems

  - Descriptions of cultures from various regions of the world

  - Compare/contrast charts that show similarities and differences among the world's human inhabitants

ENGLISH/LANGUAGE ARTS

- Have students produce book reports or story reviews that will provide space creatures with an idea of what the "literature of Earth" is like.

- Assign students to write essays, poetry, short stories, and so forth to include in the capsule.

- Have students write letters, journals, or other types of documents addressed to beings not of this world, for inclusion in the space capsule.

Message in a Capsule
Introduction

Name: _____ **Date:** _____

This is an astronomy project in which you will work with several partners to investigate the solar system and produce a final product. The work that each pair of partners will do is outlined on this sheet.

Project Scenario

A scientific research team has received a signal from deep space, indicating the existence of intelligent life. The team has decided to develop a special interstellar communication capsule called Life Finder. This capsule will transmit a continuous signal to attract the attention of intelligent beings. The information contained in the capsule will help whoever finds it understand who we are on Earth and what we know about our planet and its solar system. You will work with a primary partner and several research partners to assemble and organize information to include in the capsule. The method of partnering used by your research team is called the "clock partner system," which is explained in detail below.

Assignment

You will be paired with four different partners, named for times on a clock: a 12 o'clock partner, a 3 o'clock partner, a 6 o'clock partner, and a 9 o'clock partner. Your team's lead researcher (a.k.a. your teacher) will explain how these partnerships are formed. Write your partners' names below.

12 o'clock partner: _____

3 o'clock partner: _____

6 o'clock partner: _____

9 o'clock partner: _____

Working with these partners, you will complete the following five assignments:

Assignment 1: You and your 12 o'clock partner will choose a question from a pool of questions concerning our knowledge of the solar system and Earth's place in it. Each pair of 12 o'clock partners will answer a different question. The answer you and your partner provide by the end of the project will be a key part of the information included in the space capsule.

Assignment 2: You and your 3 o'clock partner will focus on how Earth supports life. It is very important to describe the uniqueness of our planet to an interested alien audience. Why is Earth the only planet in

continues ☞

our solar system that has life? What are the features and characteristics of Earth that allow life to exist here? What do we know is necessary for life to thrive, and how does Earth provide those things?

Assignment 3: You and your 6 o'clock partner will be randomly assigned a planet to compare and contrast with Earth in terms of physical data (atmosphere, gravity, temperature, and so forth) and the ability to support life. This will help an alien scientist understand how Earth is similar to and different from other planets in the solar system.

Assignment 4: You and your 9 o'clock partner will address the question "How does the solar system work?" by describing the types of objects found in the solar system (for example, planets, moons, comets, asteroids) and explaining their positions and motions in space.

Assignment 5: Finally, you will reunite with your 12 o'clock partner to complete the project by developing materials for the Life Finder capsule. You will compose an answer to the question you and your partner chose at the beginning of the project. You will also combine the information each of you gathered when working on the assignments with other partners to produce documents, diagrams, descriptions, explanations, and examples that demonstrate what the solar system looks like, how it works, and how our planet supports life.

Message in a Capsule
Assignment Sheet 1: 12 O'Clock Partner

Name: _____ **12 O'Clock Partner:** _____

Discuss the questions below with your 12 o'clock partner and decide which ones would be most interesting to investigate. Your team's lead researcher (a.k.a. your teacher) is going to draw the names of partner pairs from a container. The first pair drawn may choose any question from the list. The next pair drawn may choose any question that has not already been selected, and so on until each pair has chosen its own unique question. When the lead researcher draws your and your partner's names, select a question and circle it on this sheet as a reminder. You and your partner will later develop an answer to this question, to be included in the Life Finder interstellar communication capsule.

Questions About the Solar System

1. How do the four inner planets compare with the four outer planets? (Note: In 2006, Pluto was defined as a "dwarf planet," reducing the list of actual planets to eight.)

2. Why are there seasons on Earth?

3. Where do scientists find extreme physical conditions on Earth? How does the analysis of these extreme conditions on Earth help scientists understand conditions on other planets?

4. What is the definition of a day and a year? Why do different planets have days and years of different lengths?

5. What tools do astronomers use, and what do we learn from them?

6. Why does the moon go through phases, as viewed from Earth?

7. What was the ancient Greek astronomer Ptolemy's model of the universe, and what were the flaws in it?

8. Why do stars in the sky appear to change their position hourly, nightly, monthly, and seasonally?

9. What is the Milky Way?

10. What might our solar system look like to an observer in another solar system?

11. How has technology been used to help us learn more about the planets?

12. Why do we know more about Mars than any other planet?

13. Who was Nicolaus Copernicus, and what was his contribution to modern astronomy?

14. How can the planets be classified by (1) composition, (2) size, (3) position, and (4) history of discovery?

15. What makes Earth unique among the planets of the solar system?

16. What are planets, moons, comets, asteroids, and meteoroids? What are their similarities and differences?

17. What role does gravity play in the solar system?

18. How is Earth's atmosphere like and unlike other atmospheres in the solar system?

19. Why did ancient astronomers have difficulty explaining the differences between the motion of the planets and the motion of the stars in the night sky?

20. Why is the moon important to people on Earth?

Message in a Capsule
Assignment Sheet 2: 3 O'Clock Partner

Name: _____   3 O'Clock Partner: _____

For life to exist as we know it, certain conditions must be met, whether it's on Earth or elsewhere in the universe. One key question an alien scientist would be interested in is this: How does our planet support life? Work with your 3 o'clock partner to explain to an alien scientist any two of the following statements:

- Earth's atmosphere helps support life.

- The temperature on Earth helps support life.

- Earth's gravity helps support life.

- The process of photosynthesis helps support life on Earth.

- The existence of oxygen molecules on Earth helps support life.

- The existence of carbon molecules on Earth helps support life.

- The existence of water molecules on Earth helps support life.

- Earth's distance from the sun helps support life.

- Light provides energy that helps support life on Earth.

Use separate pieces of paper to show information that you learn about each of your two statements. You may use any combination of drawings, data, and written explanations to make your case. Be as complete and detailed as possible. Staple your finished pages to this sheet.

Message in a Capsule
Assignment Sheet 3: 6 O'Clock Partner

Name: _____ 6 O'Clock Partner: _____

Another key piece of information an alien scientist would be interested in is how Earth compares with other planets in our solar system. You and your 6 o'clock partner will follow the lead researcher's (a.k.a. your teacher's) instructions to select a planet to compare with Earth. Then, complete the table below. Provide two reasons why it is unlikely that life exists on the planet you have selected, and compare those reasons with conditions on Earth. *Note: You and your 12 o'clock partner may not study the same planet for this assignment.*

	Planet:	Planet: Earth
Size		
Atmosphere		
Geology		
Moon information		
Length of day		
Length of year		
Surface gravity		
Temperature range		
Distance from the sun		
Weather/Climate		

continues ☞

Give two reasons why it is unlikely that life exists on the planet you have selected.

Reason #1:	Compare this with conditions on Earth:
Reason #2:	Compare this with conditions on Earth:

Message in a Capsule
Assignment Sheet 4: 9 O'Clock Partner

Name: _____   **9 O'Clock Partner:** _____

Alien scientists will certainly be interested in how our solar system works. You and your 9 o'clock partner will describe and explain to an alien scientist the motion of objects in our solar system. Use the space below to create drawings, written explanations, graphic organizers, or other methods to explain one of the following sets of terms and how the terms within the set are connected:

- Set 1: orbit, rotation, axis, tilt, seasons
- Set 2: summer and winter solstices, spring and fall equinoxes, changes in duration of daylight
- Set 3: moon phases, solar eclipse, lunar eclipse, emitted light, reflected light
- Set 4: actual and perceived movement of the moon, planets, stars, comets, and meteors

Message in a Capsule
Assignment Sheet 5: 12 O'Clock Partner

Name: _____ **12 O'Clock Partner:** _____

Each pair of 12 o'clock partners on your research team will develop a unique product to include in the Life Finder capsule. Life Finder is designed to help alien scientists understand more about Earth and its solar system.

Work with your 12 o'clock partner to complete the tasks listed below. You each have met with other research partners to gather data and organize facts about Earth and the solar system. By combining this information, you will create a product that fulfills the goals of the Life Finder mission.

Remember your audience! You are preparing information for alien scientists who have no prior knowledge of our solar system. Take nothing for granted. It is very important that you think of ways to make the concepts and facts you present as clear and understandable as possible.

Task 1

Decide how to organize and present the information you will collect in Tasks 2–5. You may choose any combination of the following methods. You may also request permission from the lead researcher (a.k.a. your teacher) to use methods not found in the list if you have other ideas.

- Poster
- Model
- Written report
- Drawings/Illustrations
- Multimedia presentation
- Web page
- Movie
- Wall mural
- Book
- Other: _____

Task 2

Develop an answer to the question that you and your partner chose at the beginning of the project. This is a critical part of the final product and must be completed with the highest level of quality, accuracy, and completeness.

continues ☞

Task 3

Combine information from your 3 o'clock partner meetings to explain how Earth supports life. It is up to you to decide what information to use and how to present it. At a minimum, you should include two statements about how life is supported on Earth, with clear explanations of why each statement is true.

Task 4

Combine information from your 6 o'clock partner meetings to compare and contrast Earth with two other planets. You may organize information like it is on Assignment Sheet 3, or you may design your own way of comparing and contrasting the two planets with Earth.

Task 5

Combine information from your 9 o'clock partner meetings to describe how the solar system works. Your product should either (1) show how the motion of a planet results in seasons, or (2) explain the actual and perceived movement and appearance of objects in the solar system.

Task 6

Complete your final product and present it to your research team (a.k.a. the class). Use the voice of an astronomer presenting scientific research.

Message in a Capsule
Clock Partners Form

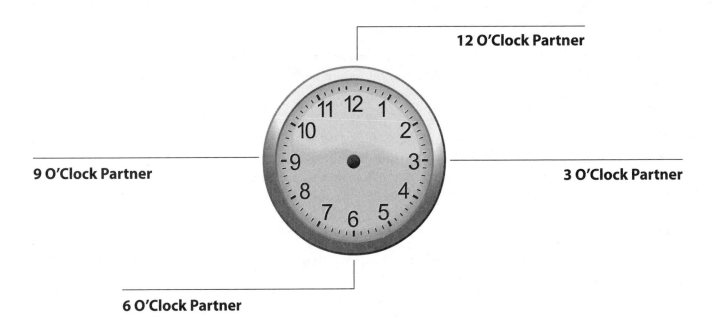

12 O'Clock Partner

9 O'Clock Partner

3 O'Clock Partner

6 O'Clock Partner

Date	Project/Activity	Partner	Completed

Message in a Capsule
Assessment Sheet

Name: _____ **Date:** _____

Complete the following checklists for Assignment Sheets 2–5. No assessment items are necessary for Assignment Sheet 1.

ASSIGNMENT SHEET 2: 3 O'CLOCK PARTNER: _____

☐ Supported Statement 1 with complete, accurate, detailed information.

☐ Supported Statement 2 with complete, accurate, detailed information.

☐ Explained information related to Statement 1 in a clear, understandable way.

☐ Explained information related to Statement 2 in a clear, understandable way.

☐ Worked well with a partner to complete required tasks.

☐ Demonstrated a commitment to quality.

ASSIGNMENT SHEET 3: 6 O'CLOCK PARTNER: _____

☐ Gathered enough data to make comparisons between Earth and another planet.

☐ Made accurate comparisons between characteristics of that planet and those of Earth.

☐ Recorded two valid reasons why it is unlikely that life exists on the planet.

☐ Compared each reason with related conditions that allow life to exist on Earth.

☐ Worked well with a partner to complete required tasks.

☐ Demonstrated a commitment to quality.

ASSIGNMENT SHEET 4: 9 O'CLOCK PARTNER: _____

☐ Chose one of four sets of terms related to the motion of objects in the solar system.

☐ Gathered enough data to describe and explain the motion of solar system objects.

☐ Defined and explained each term correctly.

☐ Explained clearly and accurately how the terms are connected.

☐ Worked well with a partner to complete required tasks.

☐ Demonstrated a commitment to quality.

continues ☛

ASSIGNMENT SHEET 5: 12 O'CLOCK PARTNER: _____

- ☐ Decided how to organize and present information about the solar system (Task 1).
- ☐ Chose a question from Assignment Sheet 1 that was acceptable to both partners (Task 2).
- ☐ Conducted research to find information about the chosen question (Task 2).
- ☐ Provided accurate, appropriate information in response to the question (Task 2).
- ☐ Provided a complete, well-developed answer to the question (Task 2).
- ☐ Included two correct statements about how life is supported on Earth (Task 3).
- ☐ Supported each statement with clear, accurate explanations (Task 3).
- ☐ Compared and contrasted Earth with two different planets in the solar system (Task 4).
- ☐ Gave valid reasons why there is likely no life on the two other planets (Task 4).
- ☐ Explained how planetary motion results in seasons (Task 5, Option 1)
- ☐ Explained the actual and perceived movement of objects in the solar system (Task 5, Option 2).
- ☐ Used an appropriate voice for the final product in keeping with the project scenario (Task 6).
- ☐ Completed a final product and presented it on the due date (Task 6).
- ☐ Worked well with a partner to complete required tasks.
- ☐ Demonstrated a commitment to quality.

Moments in Time

Content Focus: Social Studies
Class Periods: 9

Project Scenario

A company that develops interactive multimedia resources called "wall webs" (for large classroom viewing screens) has hired a team of social scientists to conduct research for a special series of "clickable" historical timelines. You are the lead researcher.

Project Synopsis

This project is divided into two parts. For Part I of the project, students first work on their own, then with a partner, and finally in a group of four to identify events to include on a historical timeline. They share these events in a class discussion. For Part II of the project, each student individually studies one event from the timeline in-depth and provides information about this event in a final design for a "Moments in Time" Wall Web (similar to an Internet Web site).

Differentiation Strategies

- 1-2-4 Present!
- Tiered assignments

Student Forms

- Introduction

PART I: CONSTRUCTING A TIMELINE

- Working on Your Own
- Working with a Partner
- Working in a Group of Four

PART II: CREATING A WALL WEB PAGE

- History: Red Assignment
- History: Blue Assignment

- History: Green Assignment
- Economics: Red Assignment
- Economics: Blue Assignment
- Economics: Green Assignment
- Inquiry: Red Assignment
- Inquiry: Blue Assignment
- Inquiry: Green Assignment

Content Standards*

This project focuses on three of the five basic social studies strands: history, economics, and inquiry. Virtually any content standards for these three strands can be taught using the project assignment sheets. Following are four sample content standards that align with the project, no matter which strand you choose to focus on.

1. Students use key concepts such as causality, change, conflict, and complexity to explain, analyze, and show connections among patterns of historical change and continuity.

2. Students describe selected historical periods and patterns of change within and across cultures, such as the rise in civilization, the development of transportation systems, the growth and breakdown of colonial systems, and others.

3. Students identify and use processes important to reconstructing and reinterpreting the past, such as using a variety of resources; providing, validating, and weighing evidence for claims; checking credibility of sources; and searching for causality.

---

*Expectations of Excellence: Curriculum Standards for Social Studies are from the National Council for the Social Studies (NCSS).

4. Students analyze group and institutional influences on people, events, and elements of culture.

How to Use This Project

Follow these steps to implement the "Moments in Time" project:

BEFORE YOU BEGIN

1. Identify specific beginning and end dates for the timeline.

2. Identify a region of the world as the area of emphasis.

3. Decide how to designate student groups and partners for Part I of the project. See the "Methods of Differentiation" section on page 172 for suggestions.

4. Choose *one* of the three social studies strands (history, economics, or inquiry) as the focus for Part II of the project. A set of three tiered assignment sheets is provided for each strand, and each assignment has a color designation: red (for struggling learners), blue (for on-target learners), and green (for advanced learners).

5. Select ten "lead researcher's choice" events for inclusion on the timeline. These events should relate primarily to the social studies strand on which Part II is focused. Don't announce these events to students until after they have constructed their timeline.

6. For Part II of the project, identify each student's level of learning readiness: struggling learner (red), on-target learner (blue), or advanced learner (green), using appropriate criteria. The readiness level determines which handout students receive. Students will work individually to complete their Part II assignment for the timeline.

7. Have on hand reference materials and resources that will support the project, especially the red assignment. A rich and varied collection of relevant resources is key to ensuring success for struggling learners.

8. Schedule class time for completing project requirements. The project is designed to last nine fifty-minute class periods:

- Period 1: Introduction; students work individually to identify events for the timeline (Working on Your Own).

- Period 2: Students share and combine events with partners. (Working with a Partner). Then, groups of four share and combine events (Working in a Group of Four).

- Period 3: The small groups of four contribute events to the timeline.

- Period 4: Class discusses the timeline; "lead researcher's choice" events are announced.

- Period 5: Students are given Part II assignments based on their readiness; the scenario is reiterated; assessment checklists for each assignment are reviewed; work begins.

- Period 6: Students work individually on Part II assignments.

- Period 7: Students complete Part II assignments.

- Period 8: Final wall web pages are presented and displayed.

- Period 9: Final wall web pages are presented and displayed; students complete the relevant assessment checklists on their Part II assignment sheets.

PART I: CONSTRUCTING A TIMELINE

1. Hand out the Introduction and explain the project. Students will work within the context of the project scenario to accomplish two primary tasks: Part I—produce a timeline; and Part II—create a page for the wall web that presents information about a specific event on the timeline.

2. Use the three separate Part I assignment sheets to conduct a 1-2-4 Present! timeline development process. This means that students first work on their own, then with a partner, and finally in a group of four to identify events to include on the timeline.

3. Each group of four contributes to the construction of a timeline by presenting its events to the class. For example:

   - Put a large timeline on a wall. Give groups of four sticky notes on which to record their events.

   - In a round-robin discussion, have each group of four present one event at a time until no new topics remain. As events are presented, have a student recorder attach the sticky notes to the timeline in the proper positions.

   - At this point, you may want to ask that each group of four send one representative to a "Timeline Convention." These students are responsible for finalizing the look and design of the timeline. Meanwhile, provide the rest of the class with an anchor activity related to the content being studied.

4. Announce your list of ten pre-selected "lead researcher's choice" events, and ask students who correctly predicted events on the list to stand and take a bow. (*Note:* see the student assignment sheets for more information on this.) You may want to enhance the prestige of this accomplishment by including these students' names on the timeline, or recognizing their powers of prediction in some other way.

5. Spend some time analyzing and discussing individual student contributions and the completed timeline. Acknowledge those who identified unique events that no one else thought of.

PART II: CREATING A WALL WEB PAGE

The expected results for each content strand's tiered assignments are very similar. At one end of the spectrum, red-level students receive significant support, primarily through your assigning them a timeline event, making resources available, and providing a graphic organizer. At the other end, green-level students are expected to operate at a more complex and independent level, and so they are often asked to develop their own way of representing information and to complete more of their assignment at the synthesis level of Bloom's taxonomy. In between, blue-level students are provided some support, but still have choices about which event to study and ways of representing information.

1. Give each student an assignment sheet, based on your chosen content strand and the student's designation as a struggling learner (red), on-target learner (blue), or advanced learner (green).

2. After students receive the appropriate assignment sheet, they will work on their own to complete the requirements for Part II.

3. Provide support for red-level students by assigning a carefully chosen event from the timeline and making sufficient resources available to help them complete the assignment. While red-level students are assigned an event to work with, blue- and green-level students are expected to choose an event that fits the assignment. By carefully pre-selecting your "lead researcher's choice" events, you can determine ahead of time which of these you will assign to red-level students and have plenty of appropriate resources on hand at the beginning of the project.

4. Plan a conclusion to the project that is in keeping with the scenario. For example:

   - Display the timeline on a wall. Then, connect timeline events and related student wall web pages with colored yarn to represent hyperlinks between Web site pages activated by a mouse click.

   - Create a three-ring binder that contains all of the students' assignments. On the first page is the timeline with a line connecting each event to a student's name and page number. To see the wall web page for that event, you would turn to the correct page to view the student's work.

- Have students actually create a page for the wall web on a computer, resulting in an authentic application of student work to the project scenario. You might even choose to have students add audio and/or video recordings of some of the assignments.

Methods of Differentiation

Part I of the project utilizes a grouping strategy called 1-2-4 Present! in which students work on their own, join a partner to share and combine information, and then collaborate in small groups of four before participating in a full class discussion. Do not use readiness as the criteria for grouping students in Part I, since it is used to determine which assignment students work on in Part II. Instead, use one of the following methods to identify partners for Part I:

1. Random selection: Using a set of shuffled index cards numbered 1 through the number of students in the class, randomly give each student a card. Assign students with numbers 1 and 2 to be partners. Do the same for students with numbers 3 and 4, 5 and 6, and so on. To form groups of four, combine pairs in any way you choose (for example, put Students 1 and 2 with Students 3 and 4). There are, of course, many ways to randomly select partners.

2. Pre-identified partners: Assign partners that have already been identified for previous class activities. For example, if students have clock partners, you can simply tell them that for this project they will work with their 3 o'clock partners (so long as this is not a readiness partner). To form groups of four, put index cards in a bowl with letters written on them: two cards with "A," two cards with "B," and so on. Have each pair draw a card from the bowl. The two pairs that draw the "A" cards form a group of four, and so on.

3. Mixed readiness: Intentionally pair students of different readiness levels, then form groups of four to include a range of readiness in each group.

4. Student choice: Allow students to choose their own partners, then use a method like the letter cards above to put the pairs into groups of four.

5. Teacher choice: Assign partners using criteria such as social compatibility, shared interests, potential for disruptive behavior, or creative thinking.

Part II of the project utilizes a readiness strategy called tiering, which means you will classify each student as a struggling learner, an on-target learner, or an advanced learner and provide each with an appropriately challenging assignment. Of course, you will not use this terminology with the students. Instead, you will give struggling learners the "red" assignment, on-target learners the "blue" assignment, and advanced learners the "green" assignment. Use appropriate criteria and the best available data to make readiness-level determinations. This might include such things as the following:

- Reading levels
- Current grades
- Formative observations and assessment data
- Past performance on individualized projects
- Demonstrated mastery of content knowledge
- Demonstrated mastery of research skills
- Your best judgment about the level of tiered support each student needs to be successful

You might also follow Diane Heacox's six methods of tiering: challenge, complexity, resources, outcome, process, and product (see the Sample Tiered Assignment Planner for "Moments in Time" on page 39).

Ideas for Extending or Modifying the Project

1. Expand the project by having students complete assignment sheets for more than one social studies strand.

2. Have small groups create specialized timelines for each social studies strand. For example,

one group might create a history timeline that focuses on political, military, and scientific events, while another group creates an economics timeline that focuses on supply and demand, resource allocation, and the role of economic institutions.

Suggested Content Modifications

MATH

- Have students look at social science data from the time period being studied. Have the students decide how to represent and interpret the data.

- Have students work with population data from various time periods to make charts, graphs, and tables that show trends, movement patterns, and composition (by age, race, gender, ethnicity, income, and so forth).

SCIENCE

- Have students focus on technological advances from a specific time period.

- Have students focus on scientific discoveries and accomplishments from a specific time period.

- Have students focus on the impact of science on important historical events on a timeline.

ENGLISH/LANGUAGE ARTS

- Use this project as the basis for a research assignment.

- Have students focus on the impact literature has had on important historical events on a timeline. Or, conversely, focus on the impact of historical events on classic works of literature.

- Create a timeline project for a work of historical fiction and have students produce pages for a wall web focused on events related to plot, theme, characters, setting, author's craft, and so forth.

Moments in Time
Introduction

Name: _____ **Date:** _____

This is a social studies project that focuses on historical timelines. Your teacher will assign a time period and a region of the world. Then, you will collaborate with your classmates to identify specific events that happened during the assigned period. After you and your classmates have created a timeline, you will examine one of the events from the perspective of history, economics, or inquiry, and develop a final product to show what you have learned.

Project Scenario

A company is developing computer software for school classrooms that will allow students to view and interact with information related to their lessons on a large flat-screen monitor. The company, Tech Learning Systems, is asking social scientists to help develop interactive timelines for specific historical time periods and regions of the world. You are part of a team that has been hired to create a prototype (sample product) for the company. Your job is to identify and research important and unique events to be included in an interactive timeline. The finished product will be called a "Moments in Time" Wall Web and will be similar to an Internet Web site. It will allow teachers or students to click on any event in a timeline with a remote laser mouse and view movie clips, historical documents, and photographs of people and places around the world. The goal is to present information and insight about historical events within a dynamic format.

Assignment

The assignment for this project is divided into two parts: In Part I, you will research events and construct a timeline. In Part II, you will create a product related to a specific event on the timeline. Assignment sheets will explain what you will do for each of these activities.

Here is a brief description of the required tasks for Part I and Part II of the assignment:

PART I: CONSTRUCTING A TIMELINE

The four tasks below represent a collaborative (shared) process for completing a job. This is an example of how experts might combine ideas to come up with a final product that everyone has contributed to and can agree on.

- Task 1: After the lead researcher (a.k.a. your teacher) specifies a time period and a world region to focus on, work on your own to identify five events that you think should be noted on the timeline.

- Task 2: Meet with a partner and combine the events that each of you has identified.

- Task 3: Join another pair to make a group of four, and share and combine your events.

- Task 4: Present your group's combined events in a discussion with your research team (a.k.a. your class), and develop a timeline as a team that includes all of the events identified by the groups of four.

continues

PART II: CREATING A WALL WEB PAGE

Part II involves only one task:

● Task 1: Research and create a design for a page of a "Moments in Time" Wall Web (like an Internet Web page) that focuses on one of the events from the timeline. The goal is to demonstrate your knowledge of a specific event by finding relevant information and organizing it in an interesting, practical way.

If you were to carry the project beyond this stage and actually create a wall web, your page design would become an important part of an interactive learning product that provides information about historic events with the click of a remote.

Moments in Time, Part I: Constructing a Timeline
Working on Your Own

Name: _____ **Date:** _____

Timeline Beginning Date: _____ **Timeline End Date:** _____

World Region Focus: _____

The lead researcher (a.k.a. your teacher) has made a list of ten events that will be included on the timeline. Below, predict two events that you think the lead researcher has included on the list. Then, briefly explain why you think each event should be included on the timeline.

For Events 3 and 4, record events that you believe should be included on the timeline, and briefly explain why.

For Event 5, identify an important event that you predict will not be included in anybody else's list. Then, briefly explain why you think this event should be on the timeline.

I predict that these two events will be on the lead researcher's list:

Event 1:

Date:

Why it should be included on the timeline:

Event 2:

Date:

Why it should be included on the timeline:

---

continues

I believe that these two events should be included on the timeline:

| **Event 3:** |
| **Date:** |
| **Why it should be included on the timeline:** |

| **Event 4:** |
| **Date:** |
| **Why it should be included on the timeline:** |

This in an important event that I predict will not be on anyone else's list:

| **Event 5:** |
| **Date:** |
| **Why it should be included on the timeline:** |

Moments in Time, Part I: Constructing a Timeline
Working with a Partner

Name: _____ **Partner:** _____ **Date:** _____

Timeline Beginning Date: _____ **Timeline End Date:** _____

World Region Focus: _____

Combine the events you have identified with those of your partner, and record them in the spaces below. Include each event only once, and tell who made each prediction.

Events we predict will be on the lead researcher's list:

Date	Event	Predicted by

continues

Other events we think should be on the timeline:

Date	Event

Events we predict will not be on anyone else's list:

Date	Event	Predicted by

Moments in Time, Part I: Constructing a Timeline
Working in a Group of Four

Group Members: **Date:** _____

_____   _____

_____   _____

Timeline Beginning Date: _____ **Timeline End Date:** _____

World Region Focus: _____

Combine the events you and your partner have identified with those of another pair, and record them in the spaces below. Include each event only once, and tell who made each prediction.

Events we predict will be on the lead researcher's list:

Date	Event	Predicted by

continues ☞

Other events we think should be on the timeline:

Date	Event

Events we predict will not be on anyone else's list:

Date	Event	Predicted by

Moments in Time, Part II: Creating a Wall Web Page
History: Red Assignment

Name: _____ **Date:** _____

You have been assigned an event from the timeline constructed by your research team (a.k.a. your class). Create a poster to show how you would design a page for the "Moments in Time" Wall Web that explains and illustrates what caused the event to happen. Include at least 4 significant causes (people or occurrences) that helped shape the event. The poster must include a diagram like the one below. You may include whatever additional material you want to make your page informative, interesting, and unique. Use the timeline, along with other resources provided by the lead researcher (a.k.a. your teacher), to complete the assignment. Then fill out the Assessment Checklist below.

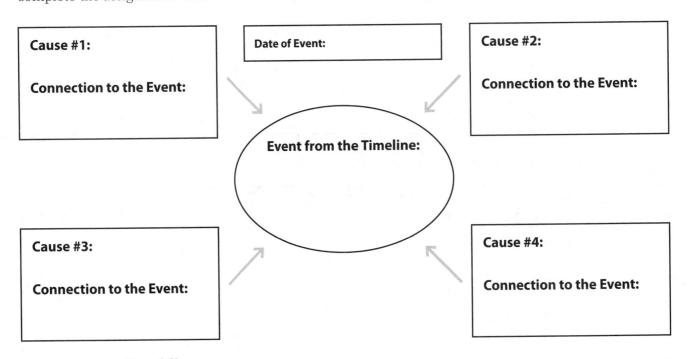

Cause #1:	Date of Event:	Cause #2:
Connection to the Event:		Connection to the Event:

Event from the Timeline:

Cause #3:		Cause #4:
Connection to the Event:		Connection to the Event:

Assessment Checklist

- ☐ Recorded Cause #1 clearly and correctly, with a direct connection to the assigned event.
- ☐ Recorded Cause #2 clearly and correctly, with a direct connection to the assigned event.
- ☐ Recorded Cause #3 clearly and correctly, with a direct connection to the assigned event.
- ☐ Recorded Cause #4 clearly and correctly, with a direct connection to the assigned event.
- ☐ Produced a poster that is accurate, contains appropriate information, and is well organized.
- ☐ Demonstrated an understanding of the concept of cause and effect.
- ☐ Demonstrated a commitment to quality.

Moments in Time, Part II: Creating a Wall Web Page
History: Blue Assignment

Name: _____ **Date:** _____

Choose an event from the timeline constructed by your research team (a.k.a. your class). Write a newspaper article from the perspective of a reporter who was at the event covering the story. The purpose of the article is to provide an answer to this question: Why did this event happen? It should include the five key elements of journalism (who, what, when, where, and why) and thoroughly explain how the event was shaped by people and earlier events. This is a historical document that will be posted on the "Moments in Time" Wall Web. Use the organizer below to prepare to write your article. You may develop illustrations, maps, diagrams, or other graphics to accompany your article if you wish. Finally, fill out the Assessment Checklist below.

Cause #1:	Date of Event:	Cause #2:

Event from the Timeline:

Cause #3:		Cause #4:

Assessment Checklist

☐ Described Cause #1 clearly and correctly, with a direct connection to the event.

☐ Described Cause #2 clearly and correctly, with a direct connection to the event.

☐ Described Cause #3 clearly and correctly, with a direct connection to the event.

☐ Described Cause #4 clearly and correctly, with a direct connection to the event.

☐ Produced an article that is accurate, contains appropriate information, and is well organized.

☐ Demonstrated an understanding of the concept of cause and effect.

☐ Demonstrated a commitment to quality.

183

Moments in Time, Part II: Creating a Wall Web Page
History: Green Assignment

Name: _____ **Date:** _____

Choose one of the events from the timeline constructed by your research team (a.k.a. your class). Analyze this event to develop an answer to this question: Why did this event happen? Using the voice of an expert, compose a lecture that could be made into a podcast. The podcast could then be posted on the "Moments in Time" Wall Web for visitors to download and listen to. Your lecture is designed to inform an audience of at least three key causes of the event, and should also explain what effect the event had on at least one later event. Produce a visual aid that illustrates and supports the cause-and-effect process that your lecture describes. You may use the graphic organizer provided below, or use one of your own design. Finally, fill out the Assessment Checklist on this handout.

Date of Event:

Cause #1:

Cause #2:

Cause #3:

Event from the Timeline:

A Result of This Event:

continues ☞

Assessment Checklist

☐ Described the timeline event fully and correctly within the text of the lecture.

☐ Described Cause #1 clearly and correctly within the text of the lecture.

☐ Described Cause #2 clearly and correctly within the text of the lecture.

☐ Described Cause #3 clearly and correctly within the text of the lecture.

☐ Described an effect of the timeline event clearly and correctly within the text of the lecture.

☐ Composed a lecture that is accurate, contains appropriate information, and is well organized.

☐ Produced a visual that clearly and accurately shows cause-and-effect relationships among events.

☐ Demonstrated an understanding of the concept of cause and effect.

☐ Demonstrated a commitment to quality.

Moments in Time, Part II: Creating a Wall Web Page
Economics: Red Assignment

Name: _____ **Date:** _____

You have been assigned an event from the timeline constructed by your research team (a.k.a. your class). Choose a market economy concept listed below that is related to the event, and learn about it by examining the materials provided by the lead researcher (a.k.a. your teacher). In the spaces below, show how you might design a page for the "Moments in Time" Wall Web that explains the relationship between the concept and the event. Then provide an example of how the same concept applies to your own life. You may wish to develop your ideas in a larger format on paper or posterboard. Finally, fill out the Assessment Checklist on this handout.

Date of Event: _____

Event: _____

Market Economy Concept:

_____ The problem of scarcity   _____ Supply and demand   _____ Incentives and profits

How is the concept related to the event?

continues ☞

How does the concept apply to your life?

Assessment Checklist

☐ Selected a market economy concept that is directly related to the assigned event.

☐ Demonstrated a basic understanding of the economic concept.

☐ Explained clearly and correctly how the economic concept is related to the assigned event.

☐ Described a specific example from real life that is related to the economic concept.

☐ Explained clearly and correctly how the economic concept is related to the real-life situation.

☐ Demonstrated a commitment to quality.

Moments in Time, Part II: Creating a Wall Web Page
Economics: Blue Assignment

Name: _____ **Date:** _____

Identify an event from the timeline constructed by your research team (a.k.a. your class). Choose two market economy concepts listed below that are directly related to the event. On a separate sheet of paper or posterboard, design a page for the "Moments in Time" Wall Web that explains how the two concepts combined to influence, or be influenced by, the event. Then, design a second wall web page to show how the same concepts combine to influence your life. Use the spaces below to brainstorm your ideas. Finally, fill out the Assessment Checklist on this handout.

Date of Event: _____

Event: _____

Market Economy Concepts (choose 2): _____ Problem of scarcity   _____ Supply and demand

_____ Incentives and profits   _____ Prices   _____ Production and distribution

Ideas for an Economics Wall Web Page
How did the concepts combine to influence the event?

continues ☞

How do the same concepts combine to influence your life?

Assessment Checklist

☐ Selected two market economy concepts that combined to influence the timeline event.

☐ Demonstrated a basic understanding of the two economic concepts.

☐ Explained clearly and correctly how the economic concepts are related to the timeline event.

☐ Described a specific example from real life that is related to both economic concepts.

☐ Explained clearly and correctly how the economic concepts are related to the real-life situation.

☐ Demonstrated a commitment to quality.

Moments in Time, Part II: Creating a Wall Web Page
Economics: Green Assignment

Name: _____ **Date:** _____

Identify an event from the timeline constructed by your research team (a.k.a. your class). Choose two market economy concepts that are directly related to the event. On a separate sheet of paper or posterboard, design a page for the "Moments in Time" Wall Web that explains how the two concepts combined to influence the event. Then, design a second wall web page to predict how the event would have changed if the economic conditions had been different. For example, you might develop a scenario in which the supply of a raw material was much smaller, and predict the effect this would have had on the event. Use the spaces below to brainstorm your ideas. Finally, fill out the Assessment Checklist on this handout.

Date of Event: _____

Event: _____

Market Economy Concepts (choose 2): _____ Problem of scarcity _____ Supply and demand

_____ Incentives and profits _____ Prices _____ Production and distribution

Ideas for an Economics Wall Web Page
How did the concepts combine to influence the event?

continues ☛

What economic conditions could have changed how this event developed?

Scenario:

Predicted effect:

Assessment Checklist

☐ Selected two market economy concepts that combined to influence the timeline event.

☐ Demonstrated a basic understanding of the two economic concepts.

☐ Explained clearly and correctly how the economic concepts are related to the timeline event.

☐ Developed a scenario in which an economic condition was different at the time of the event.

☐ Predicted convincingly the effect that altered economic conditions might have had on the event.

☐ Demonstrated a commitment to quality.

Moments in Time, Part II: Creating a Wall Web Page
Inquiry: Red Assignment

Name: _____ **Date:** _____

You have been assigned an event from the timeline constructed by your research team (a.k.a. your class). Follow guidelines provided by the lead researcher (a.k.a. your teacher) to compose a social science "Why?" question that is directly related to the event. Your task is to use available resources to gather and analyze information, develop an answer to the question, and organize the results of your investigation in a form that could be used on a "Moments in Time" Wall Web page. Finally, fill out the Assessment Checklist on this handout.

Date of Event: _____

Event: _____

1. With the lead researcher's help, compose a clearly stated "Why?" question that is directly related to your assigned event on the timeline:

   Why?

2. On a separate sheet of paper, follow the K-W-L (**k**now-**w**ant-**l**earned) format below to prepare to answer the "Why?" question.

continues ☞

What I **K**now	What I **W**ant to Know	What I **L**earned
From the timeline: From prior knowledge:	List of things to find out:	Important facts and information that I have discovered:

3. Using what you have learned, develop an answer to the "Why?" question and organize it in one of the following ways that could be included on a wall web page:

- Write a report that could be posted as text.

- Develop a chart, table, or graph to show data.

- Construct a diagram, illustration, concept map, or graphic organizer.

- Compose a lecture that could be presented orally and recorded as a podcast.

- Other: _____

Assessment Checklist

☐ Composed a specific, clearly stated "Why?" question that is directly related to the event.

☐ Documented relevant, accurate prior knowledge ("what I *know* right now").

☐ Produced an appropriate, carefully focused list of things to find out ("what I *want* to know").

☐ Gathered, classified, and organized newly acquired information ("what I *learned*").

☐ Developed a clear, accurate answer to the "Why?" question.

☐ Organized the answer as a final product that shows how it could be included on a page in a wall web page.

☐ Demonstrated a commitment to quality.

Moments in Time, Part II: Creating a Wall Web Page
Inquiry: Blue Assignment

Name: _____ **Date:** _____

Choose an event on the timeline constructed by your research team (a.k.a. your class). Then, develop a social science question that is directly related to it. Gather and analyze information, develop an answer to the question, and organize the results of your investigation in a form that could be used on a "Moments in Time" Wall Web page. Finally, fill out the Assessment Checklist on this handout.

Date of Event: _____

Event: _____

Follow this step-by-step procedure to complete the requirements of the project:

1. Think of a social science "Why?" question, and record it in the space below. The question must be related directly to the event on the timeline. "Why?" questions may come from a variety of categories, including:

   - Why did the event happen? (cause and effect)
   - Why did people believe something? (psychology)
   - Why is the event related to the way people lived? (social condition)
   - Why did people move/live/work where they did? (geography)

   Before moving on to Step 2, ask the lead researcher (a.k.a. your teacher) to check your question to make sure it is appropriate and consistent with the project assignment.

   Question:

   Lead Researcher Approval: _____

2. Gather information to help you answer the question. What prior knowledge do you already have about the topic? What other kinds of information will help you develop a solid answer? How will you find the information? How will you record it?

continues ☞

3. Sort and classify the information. If your answer is challenged, you need to be able to show evidence that your response to the "Why?" question is logical, reasonable, and supported with solid, documented, well-organized facts.

4. Analyze the information you have gathered and develop the best possible answer to the question.

5. Decide how to represent your answer on a wall web page. There are many possibilities. For example, you might write a report that could be posted as text; develop a chart, table, or graph to show data; construct a diagram, illustration, concept map, or graphic organizer; or compose a narration that could be made into a podcast.

Assessment Checklist

☐ Posed an acceptable, specific, clearly stated "Why?" question that is directly related to the event.

☐ Gathered relevant, accurate information, including personal prior knowledge.

☐ Sorted and classified newly acquired information.

☐ Developed a clear, accurate answer to the "Why?" question.

☐ Organized the answer as a final product that shows how it could be included on a wall web page.

☐ Demonstrated a commitment to quality.

Moments in Time, Part II: Creating a Wall Web Page
Inquiry: Green Assignment

Name: _____ **Date:** _____

Choose an event on the timeline constructed by your research team (a.k.a. your class). Then, develop a "Should?" question that is directly related to it. A "Should?" question can be answered with a yes or no, and requires an explanation to support the answer. An example would be this: "Should President Truman have ordered an atomic bomb to be dropped on Hiroshima?" A case can be made for answering either way, depending on the point of view. For this project, you will gather and analyze information, develop two opposing answers to the question, and organize the results of your investigation in a form that could be used on a "Moments in Time" Wall Web page. Finally, fill out the Assessment Checklist on this handout.

Date of Event: _____

Event: _____

Follow this step-by-step procedure to complete the requirements of the project:

1. Think of a social science "Should?" question, and record it in the space below. The question must be related directly to the event on the timeline. You will take both sides of the issue and provide an answer beginning with "Yes, because . . ." and an answer beginning with "No, because . . ." Before moving on to Step 2, ask the lead researcher (a.k.a. your teacher) to check your question to be sure that it is appropriate and consistent with the project assignment.

   Question:

   Lead Researcher Approval: _____

2. Gather information to help you answer the question. What prior knowledge do you already have about the topic? What other kinds of information will help you develop support for both a "Yes" and a "No" answer?

3. Sort and classify the information. If either the "Yes" or the "No" answer is challenged, you need to show evidence that your response is logical, reasonable, and supported with solid, documented, well-organized facts.

continues ☞

4. Analyze the information that you have gathered and develop the best possible "Yes" and "No" answer to the question.

5. Decide how to represent your two answers on a wall web page. There are many possibilities. For example, you might write a report that could be posted as text; develop a chart, table, or graph to show data; construct a diagram, illustration, concept map, or graphic organizer to represent arguments; or compose a narration that could be made into a podcast.

Assessment Checklist

☐ Posed an acceptable, specific, clearly stated "Should?" question that is directly related to the event.

☐ Gathered relevant, accurate information that supports the "Yes" answer.

☐ Gathered relevant, accurate information that supports the "No" answer.

☐ Sorted and classified newly acquired information.

☐ Developed a clear, accurate "Yes" answer to the question.

☐ Developed a clear, accurate "No" answer to the question.

☐ Organized the answers to show how they could be included on a wall web page.

☐ Demonstrated a commitment to quality.

One World

Content Focus: Social Studies
Class Periods: 10

Project Scenario

The U.S. host city of the next Summer Olympic Games has hired a team of social science experts to highlight the cultures, societies, histories, and national identities of participating countries around the world. The city's goal, as it hosts this "One World" event, is to promote understanding and appreciation of each country. You are the city's event manager.

Project Synopsis

A tic-tac-toe topic board provides the topic choices for this project; students choose any three topics that line up in a row. After receiving an assignment sheet for each of their three topics, students choose one assignment at Level I (knowledge), one at Level II (analysis), and one at Level III (synthesis). Level I assignments involve creating a fact organizer; Level II assignments involve creating and presenting a compare/contrast chart; and Level III assignments involve creating, or "publishing," unique products in a variety of formats.

Differentiation Strategies

- Tic-tac-toe
- Bloom's taxonomy
- Multiple intelligences

Student Forms

- Introduction
- Assignment Sheet, Topic 1: Languages
- Assignment Sheet, Topic 2: Global Regions
- Assignment Sheet, Topic 3: World Trade
- Assignment Sheet, Topic 4: Social Science Data
- Assignment Sheet, Topic 5: Your Choice
- Assignment Sheet, Topic 6: Religions
- Assignment Sheet, Topic 7: Current Problems
- Assignment Sheet, Topic 8: Economy
- Assignment Sheet, Topic 9: Government
- "Did You Know?" Fact Organizer
- "Analyze This" Compare/Contrast Chart

Content Standards*

1. Students compare similarities and differences in the ways groups, societies, and cultures meet human needs and concerns. (Topics 1 and 6)

2. Students explain and give examples of how language, literature, the arts, architecture, other artifacts, traditions, beliefs, values, and behaviors contribute to the development and transmission of culture. (Topics 1 and 6)

3. Students examine, interpret, and analyze physical and cultural patterns and their interactions, such as land use, settlement patterns, cultural transmission of customs and ideas, and ecosystem changes. (Topic 2)

4. Students use economic concepts to help explain historical and current developments and issues in local, national, or global contexts. (Topics 3 and 8)

5. Students identify and use processes important to reconstructing and reinterpreting the past, such as using a variety of resources; providing, validating, and weighing evidence for

---

Expectations of Excellence: Curriculum Standards for Social Studies are from the National Council for the Social Studies (NCSS).

claims; checking credibility of sources; and searching for causality. (Topics 4 and 7)

6. Students use key concepts such as causality, change, conflict, and complexity to explain, analyze, and show connections among patterns of historical change and continuity. (Topic 7)

7. Students differentiate among various forms of exchange and money. (Topic 8)

8. Students compare different political systems (their ideologies, structure, institutions, processes, and political cultures) with that of the United States, and identify representative political leaders from selected historical and contemporary settings. (Topic 9)

How to Use This Project

This project supports the study of countries and regions in both the Eastern and Western Hemispheres. A "One World" Topic Board (a version of a tic-tac-toe board) is provided on the Introduction handout. Each square on the board provides a different social studies topic related to the study of cultures, societies, regions, and nations. Students choose three squares in a row vertically, horizontally, or diagonally as the basis for their investigations.

Follow these steps to implement the "One World" project:

1. Assign each student a country on which to focus. This may be done in one of three ways: randomly, by student choice, or by teacher assignment. The country should be a part of a geographic region currently being studied. The region may be as large as a hemisphere, or it may be a smaller area, such as the Middle East or Central America.

2. Give students the Introduction handout and ask each student to record his or her assigned country on it. Discuss the project scenario. Allow students to spend time examining the "One World" Topic Board. To participate in the project, a student will select three topics in a row, vertically, horizontally, or diagonally.

This means that he or she will choose one of the eight possible tic-tac-toes (three-in-a-row line) on the board. For example, a student may work with the tic-tac-toe across the top row by choosing Topics 1 (languages), 2 (global regions), and 3 (world trade).

3. Explain that each topic on the "One World" Topic Board has its own separate assignment sheet. This means that a student who chooses Topics 1, 2, and 3 will receive the three corresponding assignment sheets. You might want to make copies available of all nine assignment sheets to help students choose their topics.

4. Have students record their three topics on the Introduction handout. Give them an assignment sheet for each topic they have chosen.

5. Walk students through the organization of the assignment sheets. Each sheet has three assignment levels to choose from (based on Bloom's taxonomy):

- Level I is constructed at the knowledge level. Students complete the "Did You Know?" Fact Organizer (see reproducible form on page 223) to provide basic information about their countries. Completed sheets will be displayed in a "Did You Know?" exhibit about countries that are participating in the Olympics.

- Level II is constructed at the analysis level. Students complete the "Analyze This" Compare/Contrast Charts (see reproducible form on page 224) that document similarities and differences between their countries and the United States. These charts are the basis for oral presentations.

- Level III is constructed either at the evaluation or synthesis level, depending on the topic. Students create unique products that represent information about their countries. These products will be included in a book titled *One World,* which will provide an eclectic look at the countries involved in the Olympics.

In addition, each level on an assignment sheet has its own assessment checklist, so that students know what will be expected of them.

6. Explain that each student will select and complete one Level I assignment, one Level II assignment, and one Level III assignment for the three topics he or she has chosen. Instruct students to circle on their Introduction handouts which assignment level they have decided to complete for each topic.

7. Prepare a wall space in the room to establish a "Did You Know?" exhibit to display the Level I fact organizers.

8. Establish clear guidelines for the Level II oral presentations. These presentations should take no more than two to three minutes each, unless you choose to increase their purpose and importance.

9. Make a plan for producing a *One World* collection of Level III assignments. This can be as simple as a large three-ring binder, or it can be something more elaborate, such as a bound book or a Web page.

10. This project requires ten class periods to complete, if all work is done during class time:

   • Period 1: Assign countries; give students the Introduction; discuss the project scenario; examine and discuss the "One World" Topic Board.

   • Period 2: Discuss the nine assignment sheets. Give each student the assignment sheets for the three squares he or she has chosen on the "One World" Topic Board.

   • Period 3: Students complete the Level I assignment and start work on Level II.

   • Period 4: Students finish the Level II assignment and start work on Level III.

   • Period 5: Students work on the Level III assignment.

   • Period 6: Students finish the Level III assignment.

   • Period 7: Students turn in their Level I "Did You Know?" Fact Organizers and begin Level II presentations.

   • Period 8: Students finish Level II presentations and turn in their compare/contrast charts.

   • Period 9: Students share and discuss Level III assignments as a class.

   • Period 10: Discuss with the class the project scenario with reference to all final products; have students complete the relevant assessment checklists on their three assignment sheets.

Methods of Differentiation

The first method of differentiation employed in this project is a tic-tac-toe board, a tool for offering choice. After examining the nine topics on the "One World" Topic Board, students choose one of the eight tic-tac-toe (three-in-a-row) options. The reason for requiring students to choose three in a row instead of just any three is to minimize the tendency of some students to simply identify the "easiest" topics. Some thought has been put into the organization of the topics on the topic board. By extension, some thought will be required of students as they decide which three topics to tackle.

The second method of differentiation employed in this project is based on Bloom's taxonomy. Students write Level I assignments at the knowledge level, Level II assignments at the analysis level, and Level III assignments at the evaluation or synthesis level, depending on the topic. One purpose of having three levels to choose from is so that everyone will be challenged and will experience some degree of success. Please note that you should never prevent a student from attempting a Level III assignment just because he or she struggles at Level I or Level II. All students should experience the challenge of Level III assignments. However, students who do not provide evidence of learning at Level III will still have the results of Levels I and II to help them earn a passing grade.

The third method of differentiation employed in this project is an emphasis on multiple intelligences. This is not a full-blown multiple intelligences project, but students will find that, to a certain extent, their intelligence preferences are met. The key intelligences that are accommodated are verbal/linguistic, visual/spatial, and logical/mathematical.

- Level I assignments are simple verbal/linguistic representations of basic facts. They may take on additional visual/spatial emphasis if students choose to create their own "templates" for presenting the facts they collect. However, there is no requirement that they do so.

- Level II assignments are more in the logical/mathematical category. They may also take on a visual/spatial emphasis if students want to create their own way of representing similarities and differences.

- Level III assignments have all three previously mentioned intelligences designed into the options that students are given for synthesizing information. At this level, students may choose a product that fits their preferred way of learning.

Ideas for Extending or Modifying the Project

1. Conduct the project with small groups. Create groups of three, and have each group be responsible for a series of three assignments at three levels. You may want to increase the requirement for Level I.

2. Create groups of three or four. No two students in the group may choose the same three topics from the topic board; each student must have a unique three-in-a-row (and each student will still be individually responsible for the assignment requirements). However, there may be intersections, and when these occur, those students may work together to complete one assignment. For

example, Student 1 chooses Topics 1, 2, and 3 across the top row. Student 2 chooses Topics 3, 6, and 9 vertically on the right side of the board. These two students share Topic 3, which means that they may work together on that assignment. One stipulation is that the assignment they choose for Topic 3 must be Level II or III. If Student 3 chooses the diagonal of Topics 3, 5, and 7, he or she may join the other two students working on Topic 3, but now the group must do the Level III assignment. Finally, if Student 4 chooses the horizontal Topics 7, 8, and 9 along the bottom row, he or she may collaborate with Student 2 on Topic 9 and with Student 3 on Topic 7.

3. Focus more specifically on factual information by asking students to do the Level I assignment for all three of their chosen topics.

4. Focus more specifically on comparing and contrasting by asking students to do the Level II assignment for all three of their chosen topics. A possible final product would be an enlarged Venn diagram that incorporates similarities and differences for all three topics.

5. Focus more specifically on open-ended final products by asking students to do the Level III assignment for all three of their chosen topics. This will result in a substantial "book" about countries from the region. The scenario for this could be to create an encyclopedia of Olympic nations.

6. Change the Level II assignment to have students work in pairs to complete a compare/contrast chart for the countries each has studied, rather than comparing countries with the United States.

7. Have students use the assignment sheets independently, without incorporating the "One World" Topic Board. In this case, you have nine assignment sheets, any one of which may be used with the entire class at any level. For example, you might conduct a

One World | **Project Planner** *continued*

two-class-period activity by assigning everyone a different country and having each person do the Level II assignment for Topic 1.

8. If you choose to use this project every year, keep the Level III assignments in the *One World* book and allow them to accumulate over time. Previous years' work can serve as models for current students, and the book will begin to take on significance as a result of its bulk. To increase the quality and overall value of the book, cull the best products from each year's material.

9. Change the content focus from countries to time periods, such as the United States from 1788 to 1900. Modify the "One World" Topic Board and assignments to reflect different content benchmarks. The basic assignment levels will still work quite well, taking topics from areas such as history, geography, civics, economics, and inquiry. In this case, the Level II assignment would ask students to explain similarities and differences between two dates on the U.S. historical timeline. For example, compare and contrast the movement of people, goods, services, and information within and between regions of the United States from 1850 to 1880.

Suggested Content Modifications

MATH

● Collaborate with a social studies teacher and have students look at social science data for the countries they are assigned. Have students decide how to represent and interpret the data, and compare and contrast the data with similar U.S. data.

● Have students work with Olympic Games statistics.

SCIENCE

● Have students study the social and economic impact of science and technology on the countries they are assigned. Is the country a scientifically advanced country? What are its major uses of science and technology? What contributions have scientists from this country made? Does the country have environmental issues? Health issues? How could science and technology provide improved conditions in the country?

ENGLISH/LANGUAGE ARTS

● Use this project as the basis for a research assignment.

● Collaborate with a social studies teacher and have students focus on the literature from the countries they are assigned.

● Develop writing assignments that are related to world cultures and/or the Olympic Games.

One World
Introduction

Name: _____ **Date:** _____

This project allows you to learn about a country by choosing topics from a tic-tac-toe board. You will complete three assignments that line up in a row, just like a tic-tac-toe game. Be sure to look at all of the options carefully before making your choices, because you get to decide how you will complete this project.

Project Scenario

The International Olympic Committee recently announced that a major U.S. city has been selected as a future host of the Summer Olympics. The city's planning team has chosen the phrase "One World" as its theme. It has made a commitment to promote international understanding and cooperation by highlighting the cultures, societies, histories, and national identities of countries around the world. You are a social science expert who will help the host city prepare for these Olympics. You have been asked to choose topics of interest from a "One World" Topic Board developed by the planning team. Your job is to develop materials related to those topics that will help the host city and the general public gain a better understanding and appreciation of the guest nations participating in the Games.

Assignment

1. The host city's event manager (a.k.a. your teacher) will assign you a country. Record the name of the country in the space provided on this handout.

2. Examine the "One World" Topic Board. Choose any three squares that line up to make three-in-a-row. Record the numbers of the three topics in the spaces provided on this handout.

3. The event manager will give you the assignment sheets for the three topics you have selected. Decide which assignment level you want to do for each topic. You *must* do one Level I assignment, one Level II assignment, and one Level III assignment. Circle the assignment level you have chosen for each topic.

continues ☞

"One World" Topic Board

Topic 1 **Languages** Focuses on the languages spoken in your country.	**Topic 2** **Global Regions** Focuses on the world regions (cultural, climatic, economic, political, and physical) that your country is a part of.	**Topic 3** **World Trade** Focuses on how your country presently contributes to world trade, and how it might contribute in the future.
Topic 4 **Social Science Data** Focuses on interpreting social science information about your country (such as its population, life expectancy, unemployment, and literacy rate).	**Topic 5** **Your Choice** You may choose to focus on any aspect of your country, with permission.	**Topic 6** **Religions** Focuses on the religions observed in your country.
Topic 7 **Current Problems** Focuses on a current problem faced by the people in your country, and the history of that problem.	**Topic 8** **Economy** Focuses on using economic measurement (such as GDP, inflation rate, and external debt) as a way to describe your country.	**Topic 9** **Government** Focuses on the form of government found in your country.

My Country: _____

Topic Number: _____
Assignment Level (circle one):   Level I   Level II   Level III

Topic Number: _____
Assignment Level (circle one):   Level I   Level II   Level III

Topic Number: _____
Assignment Level (circle one):   Level I   Level II   Level III

One World
Assignment Sheet, Topic 1: Languages

Name: _____ **Date:** _____ **Country:** _____

You have chosen three topics from the "One World" Topic Board and received an assignment sheet for each topic. To fulfill the requirements of this project, you will complete a different assignment level (I, II, or III) from each sheet. Put a check mark on this sheet next to the assignment you intend to complete. When you are finished, fill out the Assessment Checklist for the assignment.

____ Assignment: Level I

Complete a "Did You Know?" Fact Organizer about languages spoken in your country. Discover the official or primary language of your country, record it in the center space of the fact organizer, and identify it clearly as the official language. Provide an explanation of why the majority of people have come to speak this language. In the remaining four spaces, identify the most common unofficial languages spoken in your country. Identify and briefly describe the subgroups of the country's population that speak each language. Because this fact organizer is intended for use in a public exhibit, you are expected to use complete sentences.

ASSESSMENT CHECKLIST

☐ Identified the country's official language.

☐ Explained why the majority of people speak the official language.

☐ Identified at least four of the country's unofficial languages.

☐ Described the subgroups that speak each unofficial language listed.

☐ Recorded entries on the fact organizer clearly and correctly, using complete sentences.

☐ Demonstrated a commitment to quality.

____ Assignment: Level II

Complete the "Analyze This" Compare/Contrast Chart to show the similarities and differences among languages spoken in your country and those spoken in the United States. Pay special attention to the official, or primary, language of each country. Make an oral presentation to explain what your chart shows about languages in the two countries. As part of your presentation, offer a recommendation about what language services people from your country will need when they come to the United States for the Olympic Games. Support your recommendation by referring to the data on your compare/contrast chart.

ASSESSMENT CHECKLIST

☐ Developed the chart to correctly show language similarities and differences.

☐ Presented information in a clear and understandable way.

continues ☞

☐ Made a recommendation that makes sense and is supported by data on the chart.

☐ Demonstrated a commitment to quality.

____ Assignment: Level III

Create an entry for the host city's *One World* book, which will be displayed during the upcoming Olympic Games. Title the entry "In Other Words." Choose an option from the list below.

1. Write an article in the voice of a social scientist, explaining why language is considered a main characteristic of culture. Use your country and its languages as examples.

2. Develop a chart showing how languages in your country are related to region, ethnicity, geography, religion, traditions, human migration, social status, or other categories you identify.

3. Compose a poem *or* write a story with a "One World" theme that includes words from a language spoken in your country. Include a simple glossary to provide definitions of the words you include.

4. Create a timeline that shows the history of languages in your country. What are the origins of the languages? When and how did the languages become part of the history of your country? Were different languages used during different time periods?

ASSESSMENT CHECKLIST

☐ Produced an original document that is clearly focused on languages.

☐ Included correct information.

☐ Presented information in a logical, understandable form.

☐ Followed the guidelines provided for the chosen option.

☐ Demonstrated a commitment to quality.

One World

Assignment Sheet, Topic 2: Global Regions

Name: _____ Date: _____ Country: _____

You have chosen three topics from the "One World" Topic Board and received an assignment sheet for each topic. To fulfill the requirements of this project, you will complete a different assignment level (I, II, or III) from each sheet. Put a check mark on this sheet next to the assignment you intend to complete. When you are finished, fill out the Assessment Checklist for the assignment.

___ Assignment: Level I

Complete a "Did You Know?" Fact Organizer about a global region in which your country can be found. Choose one of these types of regions to focus on: cultural region, economic region, political region, or physical region. Record it in the center space of the fact organizer. In the remaining four spaces, identify general characteristics that are commonly used to describe the type of region you have chosen. For example, if you entered "cultural region" in the center space, you might enter "language," "religion," "traditions," and "role of women" in the other four spaces. For "physical region," you might enter "climate," "landforms," "vegetation," and "bodies of water." For "political region," you might enter "government," "ethnic groups," "military," and "political parties." For "economic region," you might enter "per capita income," "transportation," "natural resources," and "primary industries." These are just examples—there are other options. Finally, beneath each of these general characteristics, provide specific information that describes your country's region. Because this graphic organizer is intended for use in a public exhibit, you are expected to use complete sentences.

ASSESSMENT CHECKLIST

☐ Chose a type of region to focus on.

☐ Identified general characteristics for the type of region.

☐ Provided specific information about each characteristic in relation to the country's region.

☐ Recorded entries on the fact organizer clearly and correctly, using complete sentences.

☐ Demonstrated a commitment to quality.

___ Assignment: Level II

Complete the "Analyze This" Compare/Contrast Chart to show the similarities and differences between your country and the United States with regard to global regions. Focus on at least one of the main types of regions: cultural, climatic, economic, political, or physical. Make an oral presentation to explain what your chart shows about the two countries. As part of your presentation, offer a recommendation about what the host city should understand about people from your country when they come to the United States for the Olympic Games, based on regional similarities and differences. Support your recommendation by referring to the data on your compare/contrast chart.

continues ☞

ASSESSMENT CHECKLIST

- ☐ Developed the chart correctly to show regional similarities and differences.
- ☐ Presented information in a clear and understandable way.
- ☐ Made a recommendation that makes sense and is supported by data on the chart.
- ☐ Demonstrated a commitment to quality.

____ Assignment: Level III

Create an entry for the host city's *One World* book, which will be displayed during the upcoming Olympic Games. Title the entry "Oh, the Places We Live." Choose an option from the list below.

1. Write an article in the voice of a social scientist, explaining what global regions are. Use your country and its regional characteristics as examples.

2. Develop a chart showing important characteristics of your country with regard to each major type of global region: cultural, climatic, economic, political, and physical.

3. Compose a poem *or* write a story with a "One World" theme that incorporates regional information about your country. Be sure to identify the global regions included in your writing to make it clear that your country is a part of each region described.

4. Create a timeline that shows the history of the region that your country is a part of. For example, what are the cultural origins of the culture? What is the political history? How has the physical region changed over time? Has the economy changed during different time periods?

ASSESSMENT CHECKLIST

- ☐ Produced an original document that is clearly focused on regions.
- ☐ Included correct information.
- ☐ Presented information in a logical, understandable form.
- ☐ Followed the guidelines provided for the chosen option.
- ☐ Demonstrated a commitment to quality.

One World
Assignment Sheet, Topic 3: World Trade

Name: _____ **Date:** _____ **Country:** _____

You have chosen three topics from the "One World" Topic Board and received an assignment sheet for each topic. To fulfill the requirements of this project, you will complete a different assignment level (I, II, or III) from each sheet. Put a check mark on this sheet next to the assignment you intend to complete. When you are finished, fill out the Assessment Checklist for the assignment.

___ Assignment: Level I

Complete a "Did You Know?" Fact Organizer about your country's involvement in world trade. In the two upper spaces, record your country's main import partner and main export partner. Explain in these spaces why your country trades with these countries. In the two lower spaces, record three key export commodities (products) and three key import commodities. Explain in these spaces why the country imports or exports these commodities. In the center space, record how much money your country spends on imports and how much it makes on exports. Because this fact organizer is intended for use in a public exhibit, you are expected to use complete sentences.

ASSESSMENT CHECKLIST

- ☐ Identified the country's main trade partners.
- ☐ Explained why the country trades with each partner.
- ☐ Identified at least three of the country's import and export commodities.
- ☐ Explained why the country imports or exports each commodity.
- ☐ Recorded how much money the country spends on imports and makes on exports.
- ☐ Demonstrated a commitment to quality.

___ Assignment: Level II

Complete the "Analyze This" Compare/Contrast Chart to show the similarities and differences between your country and the United States with regard to world trade. Focus on imports and exports. Make an oral presentation to explain what your chart shows about the two countries. As part of your presentation, offer a recommendation about what the U.S. host city should understand about your country, based on world trade similarities and differences. Support your recommendation by referring to the data on your compare/contrast chart.

ASSESSMENT CHECKLIST

- ☐ Developed the chart to correctly show import and export similarities and differences.
- ☐ Presented information in a clear and understandable way.

continues ☛

☐ Made a recommendation that makes sense and is supported by data on the chart.

☐ Demonstrated a commitment to quality.

____ **Assignment: Level III**

Create an entry for the host city's *One World* book, which will be displayed during the upcoming Olympic Games. Title the entry "You Need Me, I Need You." Choose an option from the list below.

1. Write an article in the voice of a social scientist, explaining what world trade is. Use your country and its imports, exports, and trading partners as examples.

2. Develop a chart showing information about your country's imports and exports.

3. Compose a poem *or* write a story with a "One World" theme that includes information about world trade. Explain what imports and exports are, and tell why it is important for your country to be able to trade with other countries.

4. Create a timeline that shows the history of trade between your country and other parts of the world. For example, when did your country begin trading? What commodities were traded? What countries have been trading partners with your country over the years? Has your country been involved in conflicts or war over trade?

ASSESSMENT CHECKLIST

☐ Produced an original document that is clearly focused on world trade.

☐ Included correct information.

☐ Presented information in a logical, understandable form.

☐ Followed the guidelines provided for the chosen option.

☐ Demonstrated a commitment to quality.

One World

Assignment Sheet, Topic 4: Social Science Data

Name: _____ **Date:** _____ **Country:** _____

You have chosen three topics from the "One World" Topic Board and received an assignment sheet for each topic. To fulfill the requirements of this project, you will complete a different assignment level (I, II, or III) from each sheet. Put a check mark on this sheet next to the assignment you intend to complete. When you are finished, fill out the Assessment Checklist for the assignment.

___ Assignment: Level I

Complete a "Did You Know?" Fact Organizer with social science data about your country. Choose five of the following categories of social science data: total population, birth rate, death rate, infant mortality, life expectancy, per capita income, population below the poverty line, literacy rate, migration rate, unemployment rate, labor force (by occupation), and inflation rate. Locate data for your country in the categories you choose, and record and label it in the five spaces on the fact organizer.

Choose for the center space the data you think would be most useful in helping people understand your country, and briefly explain why. Because this fact organizer is intended for use in a public exhibit, you are expected to use complete sentences.

ASSESSMENT CHECKLIST

- ☐ Identified five categories of social science data.
- ☐ Located actual data in each category for the country.
- ☐ Chose data for the center space of the fact organizer, and explained why.
- ☐ Recorded entries on the fact organizer clearly and correctly, using complete sentences.
- ☐ Demonstrated a commitment to quality.

___ Assignment: Level II

Complete the "Analyze This" Compare/Contrast Chart to show the similarities and differences between your country and the United States with regard to social science data. See the Level I Assignment above for types of data that you might use. As part of your presentation, offer a recommendation about what the host city should understand about people from your country when they come to the United States for the Olympic Games, based on these similarities and differences. Support your recommendation by referring to the data on your compare/contrast chart.

ASSESSMENT CHECKLIST

- ☐ Developed the chart to correctly show similarities and differences in social science data.
- ☐ Presented information in a clear and understandable way.

continues ☞

☐ Made a recommendation that makes sense and is supported by data on the chart.

☐ Demonstrated a commitment to quality.

____ Assignment: Level III

Create an entry for the host city's *One World* book, which will be displayed during the upcoming Olympic Games. Title the entry "We Are Who We Are." Choose an option from the list below.

1. Write an article in the voice of a social scientist, explaining the types of data that are collected to describe the people of a nation. Use your country and its social science data as examples.

2. Develop a chart showing important social science data for your country.

3. Compose a poem *or* write a story with a "One World" theme that includes social science information about your country. It is not necessary to cite specific percentages. The purpose of your writing is to demonstrate what the social science data tells us about the country's people.

4. Create a graph that shows how a type of social science data for your country has changed over time. For example, you might graph unemployment rate, literacy rate, total population, inflation rate, or per capita income. Your graph should cover a time period of at least 20 years.

ASSESSMENT CHECKLIST

☐ Produced an original document that is clearly focused on social science information.

☐ Included correct information.

☐ Presented information in a logical, understandable form.

☐ Followed the guidelines provided for the chosen option.

☐ Demonstrated a commitment to quality.

One World
Assignment Sheet, Topic 5: Your Choice

Name: _____ **Date:** _____ **Country:** _____

You have chosen three topics from the "One World" Topic Board and received an assignment sheet for each topic. To fulfill the requirements of this project, you will complete a different assignment level (I, II, or III) from each sheet. Put a check mark on this sheet next to the assignment you intend to complete. When you are finished, fill out the Assessment Checklist for the assignment.

___ Assignment: Level I

Choose any aspect of your country on which to focus, and okay it with the event manager (a.k.a. your teacher) before proceeding. Complete a "Did You Know?" Fact Organizer about the topic you have chosen. Record the topic in the center space, along with a brief explanation or description of it. Find four interesting and informative facts about your country that are directly related to the topic. Because this fact organizer is intended for use in a public exhibit, you are expected to use complete sentences.

ASSESSMENT CHECKLIST

☐ Identified an appropriate topic and recorded it in the center space.

☐ Provided a brief description or explanation of the topic.

☐ Identified four facts related to the topic.

☐ Recorded entries on the fact organizer clearly and correctly, using complete sentences.

☐ Demonstrated a commitment to quality.

___ Assignment: Level II

Choose any aspect of your country on which to focus, and okay it with the event manager (a.k.a. your teacher) before proceeding. Complete the "Analyze This" Compare/Contrast Chart about the topic you have chosen, to show similarities and differences between your country and the United States. Make an oral presentation explaining what your chart shows about the topic and the two countries. As part of your presentation, offer a recommendation about what the U.S. host city should understand about your country, based on these similarities and differences. Support your recommendation by referring to the data on your compare/contrast chart.

ASSESSMENT CHECKLIST

☐ Developed the chart to correctly show similarities and differences involving the chosen topic.

☐ Presented information in a clear and understandable way.

☐ Made a recommendation that makes sense and is supported by data on the chart.

☐ Demonstrated a commitment to quality.

continues ☞

___ Assignment: Level III

Choose any aspect of your country on which to focus, and okay it with the event manager (a.k.a. your teacher) before proceeding. Create an entry for the host city's *One World* book, which will be displayed at the upcoming Olympic Games. Give the entry an appropriate title. Choose an option from the list below.

1. Write an article in the voice of a social scientist, explaining why the topic is important for understanding people, cultures, and countries. Use your country and its culture and people as examples.

2. Develop a chart showing data or key information about your country.

3. Compose a poem *or* write a story with a "One World" theme that describes or explains what the topic tells us about your country's people.

4. Create a timeline or graph that shows information about the topic. What are the origins of the topic? When and how did the topic become part of the history of your country? Who were some famous people related to the topic, and when were they involved? What historical events are connected to the topic?

ASSESSMENT CHECKLIST

☐ Produced an original document that is clearly focused on the chosen topic.

☐ Included correct information.

☐ Presented information in a logical, understandable form.

☐ Followed the guidelines provided for the chosen option.

☐ Demonstrated a commitment to quality.

One World
Assignment Sheet, Topic 6: Religions

Name: _____ **Date:** _____ **Country:** _____

You have chosen three topics from the "One World" Topic Board and received an assignment sheet for each topic. To fulfill the requirements of this project, you will complete a different assignment level (I, II, or III) from each sheet. Put a check mark on this sheet next to the assignment you intend to complete. When you are finished, fill out the Assessment Checklist for the assignment.

___ Assignment: Level I

Complete a "Did You Know?" Fact Organizer about religion in your country. Discover the primary religion of your country, record it in the center space of the fact organizer, and identify it clearly as the primary religion. Include a brief explanation of how this came to be the primary religion in the country. In the remaining four spaces, record the most common other religions practiced in your country. Tell what percent of the population practices each religion. Because this fact organizer is intended for use in a public exhibit, you are expected to use complete sentences.

ASSESSMENT CHECKLIST

☐ Identified the country's primary religion.

☐ Explained how it came to be the primary religion.

☐ Identified at least four other religions practiced in the country.

☐ Stated the percent of the population that practices each of the other religions listed.

☐ Recorded entries on the fact organizer clearly and correctly, using complete sentences.

☐ Demonstrated a commitment to quality.

___ Assignment: Level II

Complete the "Analyze This" Compare/Contrast Chart to show the similarities and differences in religions practiced in your country and those practiced in the United States. Pay special attention to the primary religion of each country. Make an oral presentation to explain what your chart shows about religions in the two countries. As part of your presentation, offer a recommendation about what religious considerations people from your country will require when they come to the U.S. host city for the Olympic Games. Support your recommendation by referring to the data on your compare/contrast chart.

ASSESSMENT CHECKLIST

☐ Developed the chart to correctly show religious similarities and differences.

☐ Presented information in a clear and understandable way.

continues ☞

☐ Made a recommendation that makes sense and is supported by data on the chart.

☐ Demonstrated a commitment to quality.

___ Assignment: Level III

Create an entry for the host city's *One World* book, which will be displayed at the upcoming Olympic Games. Title the entry "A Matter of Faith." Choose an option from the list below.

1. Write an article in the voice of a social scientist, explaining why religion is considered one of the main characteristics of culture. Use your country and its religions as examples.

2. Develop a chart showing how religions in your country are related to region, ethnicity, geography, traditions, human migration, social status, or other categories you identify.

3. Compose a poem *or* write a story with a "One World" theme that describes beliefs or ideas from a religion practiced in your country.

4. Create a timeline that shows the history of religions in your country. What are the origins of the religions? When and how did the religions become part of the history of your country? Were different religions practiced during different time periods? Who were some famous religious leaders and when were they active during your country's history?

ASSESSMENT CHECKLIST

☐ Produced an original document that is clearly focused on religions.

☐ Included correct information.

☐ Presented information in a logical, understandable form.

☐ Followed the guidelines provided for the chosen option.

☐ Demonstrated a commitment to quality.

One World
Assignment Sheet, Topic 7: Current Problems

Name: _____ **Date:** _____ **Country:** _____

You have chosen three topics from the "One World" Topic Board and received an assignment sheet for each topic. To fulfill the requirements of this project, you will complete a different assignment level (I, II, or III) from each sheet. Put a check mark on this sheet next to the assignment you intend to complete. When you are finished, fill out the Assessment Checklist for the assignment.

___Assignment: Level I

Complete a "Did You Know?" Fact Organizer about a current problem faced by your country, such as conflict, disease, homelessness, or discrimination. Record a brief description of the problem in the center space of the fact organizer. In each of the remaining spaces, record a current or historical event that contributed to the problem. Because this fact organizer is intended for use in a public exhibit, you are expected to use complete sentences.

ASSESSMENT CHECKLIST

- ☐ Identified a current problem faced by the country.
- ☐ Identified historical origins of the problem.
- ☐ Recorded entries on the fact organizer clearly and correctly, using complete sentences.
- ☐ Demonstrated a commitment to quality.

___Assignment: Level II

Complete the "Analyze This" Compare/Contrast Chart to show the similarities and differences in how a current global problem affects your country and how it affects the United States. Examples of global problems include terrorism, AIDS, global warming, energy costs, and poverty. Make an oral presentation to explain what your chart shows. As part of your presentation, offer a recommendation about what the host city should be told about the problems faced by your country, based on these similarities and differences. Support your recommendation by referring to the data on your compare/contrast chart.

ASSESSMENT CHECKLIST

- ☐ Developed the chart to correctly show similarities and differences in how the problem affects the two countries.
- ☐ Presented information in a clear and understandable way.
- ☐ Made a recommendation that makes sense and is supported by data on the chart.
- ☐ Demonstrated a commitment to quality.

continues ☞

217

___ **Assignment: Level III**

Create an entry for the host city's *One World* book, which will be displayed at the upcoming Olympic Games. Title the entry "Here's the Problem." Choose an option from the list below.

1. Write an article in the voice of a social scientist, describing the historical origins of a problem faced by your country. Include some of the current proposed solutions to the problem.

2. Develop a chart or concept map showing how a problem faced by your country is connected to historical events. Show some of the current proposed solutions to the problem.

3. Compose a poem *or* write a story with a "One World" theme that describes or explains a problem that your country shares with other people around the world. Mention some of the current proposed solutions to the problem.

4. Create a timeline that shows the history of a problem faced by your country. What are the origins of the problem? What events led to the current situation in your country? What are some of the current proposed solutions to the problem?

ASSESSMENT CHECKLIST

☐ Produced an original document that is clearly focused on a specific current problem.

☐ Included correct information.

☐ Presented information in a logical, understandable form.

☐ Followed the guidelines provided for the chosen option.

☐ Demonstrated a commitment to quality.

One World
Assignment Sheet, Topic 8: Economy

Name: _____ **Date:** _____ **Country:** _____

You have chosen three topics from the "One World" Topic Board and received an assignment sheet for each topic. To fulfill the requirements of this project, you will complete a different assignment level (I, II, or III) from each sheet. Put a check mark on this sheet next to the assignment you intend to complete. When you are finished, fill out the Assessment Checklist for the assignment.

____ Assignment: Level I

Complete a "Did You Know?" Fact Organizer about the various measurements of your country's economy. In the center space, record your country's GDP (gross domestic product). Choose four additional forms of economic measurement from the following list, and record the information in the remaining spaces on the fact organizer:

- ☐ GDP per capita
- ☐ Population below the poverty line
- ☐ Inflation rate
- ☐ Unemployment rate
- ☐ Industrial production rate
- ☐ Exports
- ☐ Imports
- ☐ External debt

In each space, briefly explain what the economic measurement you have chosen means in general. Because this fact organizer is intended for use in a public exhibit, you are expected to use complete sentences.

ASSESSMENT CHECKLIST

- ☐ Identified the country's current GDP.
- ☐ Identified four additional forms of economic measurement for the country.
- ☐ Explained what each form of measurement means in general.
- ☐ Explained what each specific measurement says about the country.
- ☐ Recorded entries on the fact organizer clearly and correctly, using complete sentences.
- ☐ Demonstrated a commitment to quality.

continues ☞

___ Assignment: Level II

Complete the "Analyze This" Compare/Contrast Chart to show similarities and differences between your country and the United States with regard to economic measurement. Focus on at least three forms of measurement from the list provided in Level I. Make an oral presentation to explain what your chart shows about the two countries. As part of your presentation, offer a recommendation about what the U.S. host city should understand about your country, based on these similarities and differences in economic measurement. Support your recommendation by referring to the data on your compare/contrast chart.

ASSESSMENT CHECKLIST

☐ Developed the chart to correctly show similarities and differences in economic measurement.

☐ Presented information in a clear and understandable way.

☐ Made a recommendation that makes sense and is supported by data on the chart.

☐ Demonstrated a commitment to quality.

___ Assignment: Level III

Create an entry for the host city's *One World* book, which will be displayed at the upcoming Olympic Games. Title the entry "How Are We Doing?" Choose an option from the list below.

1. Write an article in the voice of a social scientist, explaining the different ways to measure a nation's economy. Use your country and its economic measurement data as examples.

2. Develop a chart that compiles and presents economic measurement data for your country.

3. Compose a poem *or* write a story with a "One World" theme that includes economic data. Use this option to examine what the numbers tell us about the lives of real people in the country.

4. Create a timeline or graph that shows how economic data have changed over time. For example, construct a graph of your country's GDP for the past 20 years. Or, produce a timeline that provides information about your country's industrial growth or decline over time.

ASSESSMENT CHECKLIST

☐ Produced an original document that is clearly focused on economic measurement.

☐ Included correct information.

☐ Presented information in a logical, understandable form.

☐ Followed the guidelines provided for the chosen option.

☐ Demonstrated a commitment to quality.

One World

Assignment Sheet, Topic 9: Government

Name: _____ **Date:** _____ **Country:** _____

You have chosen three topics from the "One World" Topic Board and received an assignment sheet for each topic. To fulfill the requirements of this project, you will complete a different assignment level (I, II, or III) from each sheet. Put a check mark on this sheet next to the assignment you intend to complete. When you are finished, fill out the Assessment Checklist for the assignment.

___ Assignment: Level I

Complete a "Did You Know?" Fact Organizer about your country's government. Record your country's government system in the center space of the fact organizer. In three of the remaining spaces, briefly describe the executive, legislative, and judicial branches of government. In the final space, identify the country's main political parties. Because this fact organizer is intended for use in a public exhibit, you are expected to use complete sentences.

ASSESSMENT CHECKLIST

☐ Identified the country's government system.

☐ Described the executive, legislative, and judicial branches of government.

☐ Identified the country's main political parties.

☐ Recorded entries on the fact organizer clearly and correctly, using complete sentences.

☐ Demonstrated a commitment to quality.

___ Assignment: Level II

Complete the "Analyze This" Compare/Contrast Chart to show the similarities and differences between your country's form of government and the representative democracy of the United States. Make an oral presentation to explain what your chart shows about the governments of the two countries. As part of your presentation, offer a suggestion about what people from your country might need to understand more clearly the representative democracy in the United States. Support your suggestion by referring to the data on your compare/contrast chart.

ASSESSMENT CHECKLIST

☐ Developed the chart to correctly show similarities and differences between governments.

☐ Presented information in a clear and understandable way.

☐ Made a suggestion that makes sense and is supported by data on the chart.

☐ Demonstrated a commitment to quality.

continues ☞

___ Assignment: Level III

Create an entry for the host city's *One World* book, which will be displayed at the upcoming Olympic Games. Title the entry "Who Put You in Charge?" Choose an option from the list below:

1. Write an article in the voice of a social scientist, explaining what the purpose of a government is and how a specific form of government functions. Use your country's government as an example.

2. Develop a chart or concept map showing how your country's government is organized.

3. Compose a poem *or* write a story with a "One World" theme that describes how the government of your country gets along with other countries in the region, or about how the government gets along with its own people.

4. Create a timeline that shows the history of government in your country. What are the origins of the government? When and how did the current government gain power? Were different forms of government in place during different time periods? Who were some famous government leaders and when were they active during your country's history?

ASSESSMENT CHECKLIST

☐ Produced an original document that is clearly focused on government.

☐ Included correct information.

☐ Presented information in a logical, understandable form.

☐ Followed the guidelines provided for the chosen option.

☐ Demonstrated a commitment to quality.

"Did You Know?" Fact Organizer

Name: _____ Country: _____ Topic #: _____

Did You Know . . .

Underline the fact you find most interesting.

"Analyze This" Compare/Contrast Chart

Name: _____ Country: _____ Topic #: _____

Analyze This

Your Country	Both	United States

Teacher Form: Differentiation Planner

Fill out this form for each part of your curriculum that you plan to differentiate at some point during the year.

Title of Lesson/Unit: _____

Month(s) Covered: _____

Critical Standard(s): _____

_____

_____

You can differentiate by classroom instruction area, student characteristics, or any combination of the two. Start simple. (See pages 8–12 for more information.)

What will you differentiate?

Classroom Instruction:

☐ Content

☐ Process

☐ Product

How will you differentiate?

Student Characteristics:

☐ Readiness

☐ Interest

☐ Learner profile

How would you structure the lessons and materials to differentiate the area(s) you have chosen? (Brainstorm.)

What things do you need to do to make this happen?

Teacher Form: Project Organizer

Fill out this form for each model project you plan to use at some point during the year.

Subject:	Grade:

Project Title:

What topics or content standards could I cover with this project?

1	
2	
3	
4	

Project Component	Yes	Modify	No	Notes
Scenario				
Standards				
Assignment				

continues ☛

Project Component	Yes	Modify	No	Notes
Format/Process				
Differentiation Strategy/Strategies				
Student Forms				
Assessment Sheet/Checklist				
Final Product				
Extension or Modification Idea				

Teacher Form: Technology Planner

Fill out this form for each model project you plan to use at some point during the year. List Web sites you plan to reference, and include ways your class might use technology in the project, such as creating a PowerPoint presentation, Web page, or audio or video podcast.

Name of Project:

Web Site	URL	Content or Topic Area

Technology Integration Ideas:

Recommended Resources

The Differentiation Strategies

Jigsaw Grouping

The Jigsaw Classroom (www.jigsaw.org). The official Web site of the jigsaw classroom, published by Elliot Aronson and the Social Psychology Network. Provides a history, an overview, and instructions for implementing jigsaw grouping, as well as links to related topics.

Multiple Intelligences

Howard Gardner, Multiple Intelligences and Education (www.infed.org/thinkers/gardner.htm). An article providing detailed information about multiple intelligences, including other possible intelligences being considered.

The Model Projects

Project-Based Learning

The George Lucas Educational Foundation's Professional Development Modules Home Page (www.edutopia.org/teachingmodules/PBL/index.php). Among many other things, you will find in-depth, carefully organized coverage of these essential questions:

- What is project-based learning?
- Why is project-based learning important?
- How does project-based learning work?
- How does one teach others about project-based learning?

You will find a wealth of ideas, resources, and supporting research at this site. Emphasis is placed on the use of technology, but you don't need to be a technology wizard to make good use of the information provided. The only requirement is that you recognize the value of projects and be an advocate for kids and their learning needs.

Assessment Rubrics

Kathy Schrock's Guide for Educators (http://school.discovery.com/schrockguide/assess.html). Provides links to information about rubrics.

Assessing Learning in the Classroom by Jay McTighe and Steven Ferrara (Washington, DC: National Education Association, 2000). A handy little book that gives the reader a useful introduction to assessment and rubrics.

Assessing Student Outcomes by Robert J. Marzano, Debra Pickering, and Jay McTighe (Alexandria, VA: Association for Supervision and Curriculum Development, 1993). This book provides page after page of detailed criteria, using the 4-3-2-1 format, for task-specific rubrics. A valuable companion for creating rubrics.

The Candidates' Debate

CITING SOURCES ON INTERNET

Answers.com (www.answers.com). This site has a free poster (available via download or regular mail) that provides information about this citation process. On their home page, select "Teachers" at the bottom of the page, then "Poster Center." This site also has information about millions of topics, including global warming.

November Learning (www.novemberlearning.com). The Web site of renowned educator Alan

November and his team. Review the "Information Literacy Materials" section or click "Resources" to access additional information about using the Internet.

The American Library Association (www.ala. org). For information about doing Web searches, type "evaluating Web sites" in the search box at the top of the page (be sure to use quotation marks). The resulting PDF is a good, brief presentation on how to assess a Web site.

GLOBAL WARMING

Visit any of the following Web sites and type "global warming" into the search box to find information for this project's sample resolution.

U.S. Environmental Protection Agency (www. epa.gov/climatechange)

National Wildlife Federation (www.nwf.org)

U.S. Government (www.usa.gov)

National Climatic Data Center (http://lwf.ncdc. noaa.gov/oa/climate/globalwarming.html)

National Geographic (www.nationalgeographic. com)

National Aeronautics and Space Administration (www.nasa.gov)

World Wildlife Fund (www.worldwildlife.org)

Continental Cubing Competition

Read-Write-Think (www.readwritethink.org). This NCTE-affiliated Web site provides many lessons and resources for analyzing literature.

The Mathematute, Math Investment Plan, and You Gotta Have an Angle*

The Math Forum at Drexel University (www. mathforum.org/pow). The Math Forum's Problems of the Week (PoWs) are designed to provide creative, nonroutine challenges for students working with basic operations through geometry and algebra. Problem-solving and mathematical communication are key elements of every problem. For a minimal fee, you can become a registered

member and gain access to hundreds of PoWs and their solutions.

Express Yourself*

Small Planet Communications: Create Your Own Web Page (www.smplanet.com/webpage/ webpage.html). Follow these very basic steps to create an original Web page.

Building a School Web Site by Wanda Wigglebits (www.wigglebits.com). A learn-as-you-go, hands-on Web project that teachers and kids can do together.

Life on Planet X

Kathy Schrock's Guide for Educators (http:// school.discovery.com/schrockguide/sci-tech/ scibs.html). Lists various Web sites about biology.

BBC Science and Nature: Animals (www.bbc. co.uk/nature/animals). Extensive resource with information about animals.

American Institute of Biological Sciences (www.aibs.org/careers). Provides a lot of information about careers in biology.

Message in a Capsule

BBC Science and Nature: Space (www.bbc. co.uk/science/space). An extensive resource with information about astronomy and specialized topics of interest.

Fact Monster: Science: Astronomy and Space Exploration (www.factmonster.com/ipka/ A0769132.html). Fact Monster is a kid-friendly Web site with basic information about lots of topics, including astronomy.

NASA Planetary Photojournal (http://photo journal.jpl.nasa.gov/index.html). Includes information and photos of planets, our solar system, and space exploration.

NASA Solar System Exploration (http://sse. jpl.nasa.gov/index.cfm). Colorful and animated resource covering many space-related topics. Click on "People" to read about the astronomy careers of people who work for NASA.

American Astronomical Society (www.aas.org/ education/students.htm). Provides answers to lots

---

of questions that students may have about being an astronomer.

Hear Ye! Hear Ye!*

Visit these Web sites for topics in American history:

Smithsonian National Museum of American History (http://americanhistory.si.edu)

America's Library (www.americaslibrary.gov)

Library of Congress (www.loc.gov)

One World

Country Reports (www.countryreports.org). Cultural, historical, and statistical country information. Fee-based subscriptions for a school, district, library, or individual.

Discover Languages . . . Discover the World! (www.discoverlanguages.org). Under "Classroom

---

* denotes projects included on the CD-ROM only.

Resources," click on "Talkin' About Talk" to hear audio essays on language.

Languages of the World (www.nvtc.gov/lotw). Click on "World Languages" to learn about many different languages.

National Geographic (www.nationalgeographic.com). Click on "People and Places" for extensive information about countries and cultures of the world.

The CIA World Factbook (https://www.cia.gov/library/publications/the-world-factbook/index.html). Offers a lot of detailed facts about virtually every country in the world.

Official Web site of the Olympic Movement (www.olympic.org)

Moments in Time

Create a timeline using Microsoft Office Excel (www.microsoft.com/education/createtimeline.mspx).

Bibliography

Anderson, L.W., and Krathwohl, D., editors (2001). *A Taxonomy for Learning, Teaching, and Assessing: A Revision of Bloom's Taxonomy of Educational Objectives.* New York: Longman.

Aronson, E. (1978). *The Jigsaw Classroom.* Beverly Hills, CA: Sage Publications.

Bloom, B., editor (1956). *Taxonomy of Educational Objectives, Handbook 1: Cognitive Domain.* Reading, MA: Addison Wesley.

Gardner, H. (1983). *Frames of Mind: The Theory of the Multiple Intelligences.* New York: Basic Books.

Gardner, H. (2000). *Intelligence Reframed: Multiple Intelligences for the 21st Century.* New York: Basic Books.

Gregory, G., and Chapman, C. (2002). *Differentiated Instruction Strategies: One Size Doesn't Fit All.* Thousand Oaks, CA: Corwin Press.

Heacox, D. (2002). *Differentiating Instruction in the Regular Classroom.* Minneapolis: Free Spirit Publishing.

International Reading Association and the National Council of Teachers of English (1996). *Standards for the English Language Arts.* Newark, DE: International Reading Association; Urbana, IL: National Council of Teachers of English.

Kingore, B. (2004). *Differentiation: Simplified, Realistic, and Effective: How to Challenge Advanced Potentials in Mixed-Ability Classrooms.* Austin, TX: Professional Associates Publishing.

Lenz, B.K., Deshler, D.D., with Kissam, B.R., editors (2004). *Teaching Content to All: Evidence-Based Inclusive Practices in Middle and Secondary Schools.* Boston, MA: Pearson/Allyn and Bacon.

National Council for the Social Studies (1994). *Expectations of Excellence: Curriculum Standards for Social Studies.* Silver Spring, MD: NCSS Publications.

National Council of Teachers of Mathematics (2000). *Principles and Standards for School Mathematics.* Reston, VA: National Council of Teachers of Mathematics, Inc.

National Research Council (1996). *National Science Education Standards.* Washington, DC: National Academy Press.

Neeld, E.C., and Cowan, G. (1986). *Writing,* 2nd ed. Glenview, IL: Scott, Foresman.

Northey, S.S. (2005). *Handbook on Differentiated Instruction for Middle and High Schools.* Larchmont, NY: Eye on Education.

O'Dell, S. (1987). *Island of the Blue Dolphins* (Reissue edition). New York: Yearling.

Paulsen, G. (2006). *Hatchet* (Reprint edition). New York: Aladdin.

Renzulli, J., and Smith, L. (1978). *The Compactor.* Mansfield Center, CT: Creative Learning Press.

Schlemmer, P. (1987). *Learning on Your Own* (A five-volume series). West Nyack, NY: Center for Applied Research in Education.

Sousa, D.A. (2005). *How the Brain Learns,* 2nd ed. Thousand Oaks, CA: Corwin Press.

Tomlinson, C.A. (2001). *How to Differentiate Instruction in Mixed-Ability Classrooms.* Alexandria, VA: Association for Supervision and Curriculum Development.

Wiggins, G., and McTighe, J. (2005). *Understanding by Design* (Expanded 2nd ed.) Alexandria, VA: Association for Supervision and Curriculum Development.

Winebrenner, S. (2001). *Teaching Gifted Kids in the Regular Classroom: Strategies and Techniques Every Teacher Can Use to Meet the Academic Needs of the Gifted and Talented* (Revised edition). Minneapolis: Free Spirit Publishing.

Index

Note: Italicized page numbers indicate figures or reproducible pages.

About the Authors

 **Phil Schlemmer** is currently curriculum director for Holland Public Schools in Holland, Michigan. He has been a teacher, administrator, writer, consultant, and curriculum designer since 1973, and during that time has written nine books. His main areas of expertise are project-based learning and differentiated instruction. Throughout his career he has focused his efforts on helping students become self-directed, lifelong learners.

Dori Schlemmer designs and develops specialized resource materials for students and staff. She has coauthored four books with Phil and currently works as a high school career resource technician for Kentwood Public Schools.

Phil and Dori live in Kentwood, Michigan.

Other Great Books from Free Spirit

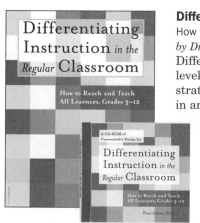

Differentiating Instruction in the Regular Classroom
How to Reach and Teach All Learners, Grades 3–12
by Diane Heacox, Ed.D.

Differentiation—one of the hottest topics in education today—means changing the pace, level, or kind of instruction to fit the learner. This timely, practical guide is a menu of strategies, examples, templates, and tools teachers can use to differentiate instruction in any curriculum, even a standard or mandated curriculum, and ensure that every child has opportunities to learn and develop his or her talents. Includes dozens of reproducible handout masters.
$29.95; 176 pp.; softcover; 8½" x 11"

Differentiating Instruction in the Regular Classroom CD-ROM
All of the forms from the book, plus additional materials and more examples of curriculum maps and matrix plans, ready to customize and print out.
$17.95; Macintosh and PC compatible, 5" CD-ROM.

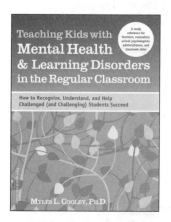

Teaching Kids with Mental Health & Learning Disorders in the Regular Classroom
How to Recognize, Understand, and Help Challenged (and Challenging) Students Succeed
by Myles L. Cooley, Ph.D.

Generalized Anxiety Disorder (GAD). Nonverbal Learning Disability (NVLD). Asperger's Syndrome. Depression. ADHD. How can educators recognize the symptoms, respond appropriately, and meet students' learning needs while preventing or addressing disruptive behaviors? Written by a clinical psychologist, this user-friendly, jargon-free guide describes mental health and learning disorders often observed in school children, explains how each might be exhibited in the classroom, and offers expert suggestions on what to do (and sometimes what not to do). An essential tool for teachers, special education professionals, school counselors and psychologists, administrators, and teacher aides.
$34.95; 224 pp.; softcover; 8½" x 11"

Teaching Kids with Learning Difficulties in the Regular Classroom
Ways to Challenge & Motivate Struggling Students to Achieve Proficiency with Required Standards
by Susan Winebrenner

A gold mine of practical, easy-to-use teaching methods, strategies, and tips, it helps teachers differentiate the curriculum in all subject areas to meet the needs of all learners—including those labeled "slow," "remedial," or "LD," students of poverty, English Language Learners, and others who struggle to learn. An essential resource for every educator. Includes reproducibles.
$34.95; 256 pp.; softcover; 8½" x 11"

Teaching Kids with Learning Difficulties in the Regular Classroom CD-ROM
All of the forms from the book, plus many additional extensions menus in several subject areas.
$17.95; Macintosh and PC compatible, 5" CD-ROM.

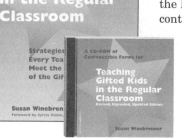

Teaching Gifted Kids in the Regular Classroom
Strategies and Techniques Every Teacher Can Use to Meet the Academic Needs of the Gifted and Talented
by Susan Winebrenner, foreword by Sylvia Rimm, Ph.D.

Teachers call it "the orange bible." Since 1992, it's been the definitive guide to meeting the learning needs of gifted students in the mixed-abilities classroom—without losing control, causing resentment, or spending hours preparing extra materials. It's full of proven, practical, classroom-tested strategies teachers love, plus many reproducibles: learning contracts, study guides, extensions menus, and more.
$34.95; 256 pp.; softcover; 8½" x 11"

Teaching Gifted Kids in the Regular Classroom CD-ROM
All of the forms from the book, plus many additional extensions menus in several subject areas. Macintosh and Windows compatible. All grades.
$17.95; Macintosh and PC compatible, 5" CD-ROM

The Complete Guide to Service Learning
Proven, Practical Ways to Engage Students in Civic Responsibility, Academic Curriculum, & Social Action
by Cathryn Berger Kaye, M.A.
Activities, quotes, reflections, resources, hundreds of annotated "Bookshelf" recommendations, and author interviews are presented within a curricular context and organized by theme to help teachers and youth workers engage young hearts and minds in reaching out and giving back. For teachers, grades K–12.
$29.95; 240 pp.; softcover; illust.; 8½" x 11"

The Complete Guide to Service Learning CD-ROM
All of the forms from the book, plus an additional section on how to create a culture of service, 11 more author interviews, and 45 more "Bookshelf" entries.
$17.95; Macintosh and PC compatible, 5" CD-ROM

The Free Spirit Service Learning for Kids Series
by Cathryn Berger Kaye, M.A.
Put service learning into students' hands with these inspiring workbooks. Each focuses on a specific topic kids care about and overflows with ideas, facts, stories about real people helping others, resources, tips, and activities to motivate young people to take action in their own communities. The goal of each book is to help kids develop their skills, knowledge, and abilities while having a successful service-learning experience. Use with *The Complete Guide to Service Learning*, or use independently in a classroom or youth-serving organization. For grades 6 and up.

A Kids' Guide to Hunger & Homelessness
A Kids' Guide to Helping Others Read & Succeed
Each Book: $6.95; 48 pp.; softcover; illust.; 8½" x 11"

Building Everyday Leadership in All Teens
Promoting Attitudes and Actions for Respect and Success
by Mariam G. MacGregor, M.S., foreword by Barry Z. Posner
Every teen can be a leader. That's because leadership is not just about taking the lead in big ways, but in everyday small things, too. The 21 sessions in this book help teens build leadership skills including decision-making, risk taking, team building, communication, creative thinking, and more. Choose specific sessions for your class or group, or explore leadership through an entire school year. Requires use of the student book, *Everyday Leadership*. Reproducibles include assessment tools and exams.
$29.95; 208 pp.; softcover; illust.; 8½" x 11"

Everyday Leadership
Attitudes and Actions for Respect and Success
by Mariam G. MacGregor, M.S., foreword by Barry Z. Posner, Ph.D.
Written and experiential activities help teens develop a leadership attitude, discover their leadership potential, and build leadership skills. Teens gain a greater understanding of who they are, what matters to them, how that translates into leadership, and how leadership relates to everyday life. Created for use with *Building Everyday Leadership in All Teens*, this consumable guide also functions as a stand-alone resource for personal growth.
$9.95; 144 pp.; spiral-bound, pockets, 7" x 9"

To place an order or to request a free catalog of SELF-HELP FOR KIDS®
and SELF-HELP FOR TEENS® materials, please write, call, email, or visit our Web site:

Free Spirit Publishing Inc.
217 Fifth Avenue North • Suite 200 • Minneapolis, MN 55401-1299
toll-free 800.735.7323 • local 612.338.2068 • fax 612.337.5050
help4kids@freespirit.com • www.freespirit.com